Exploring Ireland's
Wild Atlantic Way

Third Edition

DISCLAIMER
The activities described in this book carry risks and can be dangerous, and many of the sites featured are in remote locations. The authors and publishers have gone to great lengths to ensure the accuracy of the information herein, but they cannot be held legally or financially responsible for any accident, injury, loss or inconvenience sustained as a result of the information or advice contained in this book. Swimming, jumping, diving, cycling, climbing, walking, sleeping outdoors or any other activities at any of these locations are entirely at your own risk. The inclusion of an area in this guidebook does not mean you have a right of access.

All rights reserved. No part of this work may be reproduced by any means - graphic, electronic or mechanised including photocopying, recording, scanning, taping, web distribution, or information storage retrieval systems - without the written permission of the authors.

Copyright © 2024 David Flanagan, Richard Creagh
Published by Three Rock Books threerockbooks.com
Contact: info@threerockbooks.com

Printed in Ireland

ISBN 978-1-0685912-0-4

Mapping contains OpenStreetMap 2024 ©OpenStreetMap contributors available under the Open Database Licence from openstreetmap.org/copyright

Cover: Slea Head Drive, Dingle, Kerry (page 95) | Richard Creagh
This spread: Malin Head, Donegal (page 265) | Kent Wang

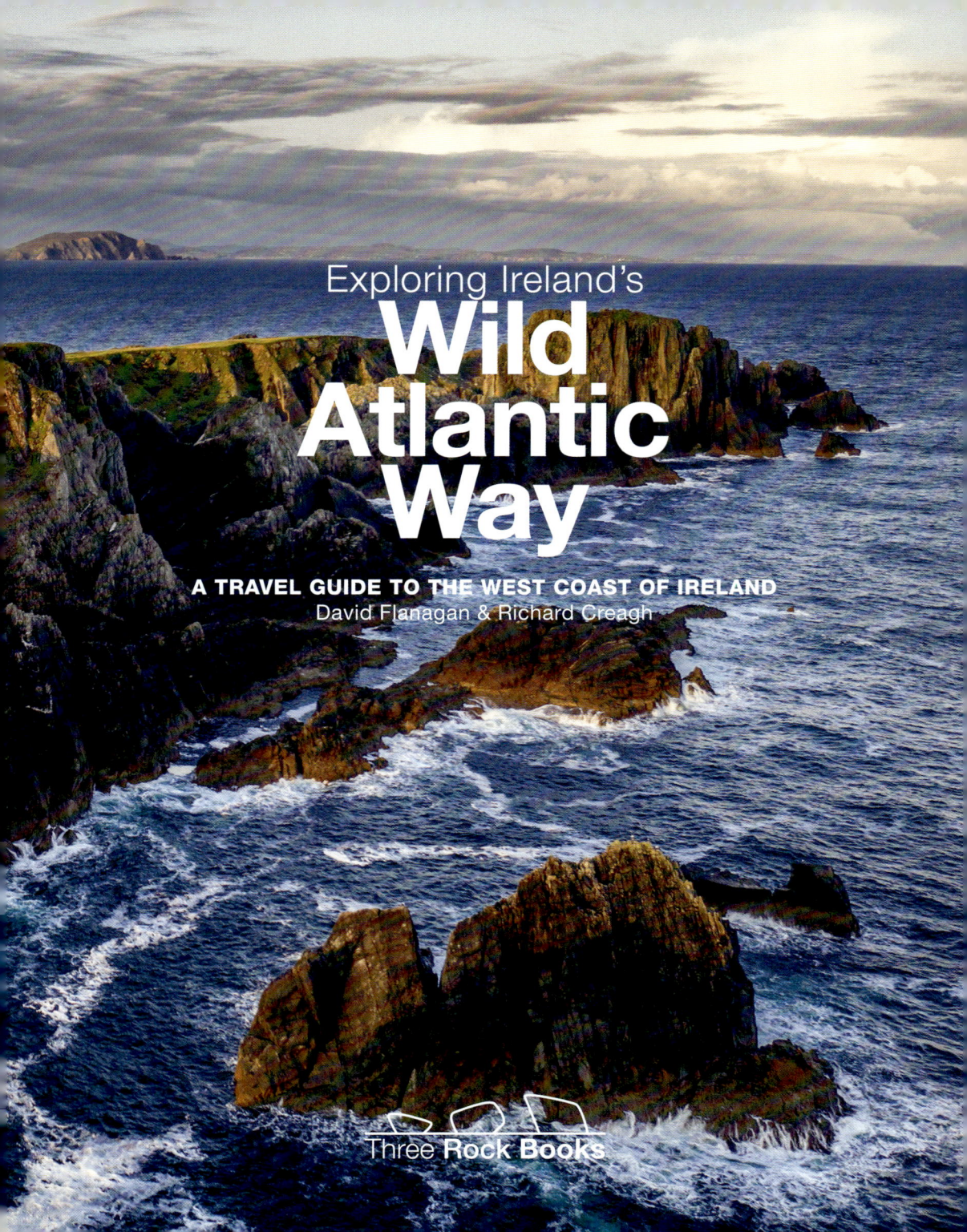

Ailladie cliffs, Clare (page 140) | RC

CONTENTS

Introduction 7
Information for Visitors 11
Accommodation 17
Food and Drink 17
Five Essential Experiences 19
Activities 21
Wild Food 35
Wild Atlantic Wildlife 37

CORK   43
Kinsale to Skibbereen 44
Baltimore to Mizen 54
Sheep's Head and Bantry 62
Beara 68

KERRY   77
Iveragh 78
The Dingle Peninsula 94
North Kerry and Limerick 108

THE SHANNON ESTUARY WAY   114

CLARE   121
Loop Head 122
Doonbeg to Lahinch 132
The Burren 136

GALWAY   149
Aran Islands 150
South Galway 160
Mid Connemara 168
North Connemara 176

MAYO   187
Killary and Clew Bay 188
Achill Island 200
North Mayo 208

SLIGO AND LEITRIM   221
Sligo and Leitrim 222

DONEGAL   235
Donegal Bay 236
North West Donegal 246
Fanad and Inishowen 258

INTRODUCTION

The Atlantic coast of Ireland is an amazing place, a land full of contrasts. Beaming sunshine one minute, thick cloud and rain the next. Deserted islands and packed pubs. Calm bays and raging open sea. Barren moorland and fertile fields.

Until recently most tourists were drawn to a few world-famous areas that have had the benefit of strong marketing to back their natural beauty. But the west coast of Ireland has always had more going for it than just a handful of well-publicised destinations. You could spend your whole life in this part of the world and you wouldn't see everything it has to offer. Between the scenery, the people, the heritage, the food, the music and the wildlife, there is something for everybody.

In 2014 Fáilte Ireland, the Irish tourist board, launched the Wild Atlantic Way, the 2,500km touring route that runs the length of Ireland's western seaboard. The concept has been a great success, encouraging visitors to explore every corner of the coast, including many areas that were often overlooked in the past.

This book, which documents hundreds of points of interest along the coast, from Ireland's most famous attractions to its hidden gems, will be of great interest to

Cnoc na dTobar, Kerry (page 89) | Denis Dineen

anyone planning to visit the Atlantic coast of Ireland. Whether you are travelling from abroad or living in Ireland and are looking for ideas for weekends away, you will find plenty of useful information between its covers.

The book's focus is on the outdoors, on getting out into the fresh air and discovering Ireland's greatest asset - its natural beauty. And it's while walking, cycling, swimming, climbing, fishing and paddling that you will encounter Ireland's second greatest asset, its people.

In our opinion the best way to experience the Wild Atlantic Way is to choose an area and linger there rather than rushing from one destination to the next. Like a lot in life, the more you put into getting to know a place - its locals, its wildlife, its weather and its seasons - the more you will get out of it.

Hopefully this book will encourage you to get outside, stretch your legs, arms and mind, and visit the wilder parts of Ireland that most people never get to see.

The signs that mark the route of the Wild Atlantic Way | RC

FINDING YOUR WAY
This book is organised by county (with two exceptions - Sligo and Leitrim share one chapter, as do Kerry and Limerick) and most counties are also further divided into sections. At the start of each section there is an overview map. Accurate and to scale, these maps are designed to give a sense of how places are positioned relative to each other. If you plan on exploring the back roads you will need a digital or paper map.

As the Wild Atlantic Way is a linear route it makes sense to follow it continuously in one direction. There isn't a 'best' direction as such, so decide your approach based on your plans and interests. For this book we had to choose a direction so we opted for south to north for the sole reason that when travelling north you will have a better view of the coast, being on the left-hand side of the road.

THE WILD ATLANTIC WAY
The Wild Atlantic Way has over 188 official discovery points, of which 15 have been designated as signature discovery points. They represent some of the best known and most popular sights along the Way but they are by no means the only things worth seeing. They are:

- Old Head of Kinsale, Cork (page 45).
- Mizen Head, Cork (page 58).
- Dursey Island, Cork (page 71).
- Skellig Michael, Kerry (page 84).
- Blasket Islands, Kerry (page 96).
- Loop Head, Clare (page 124).
- Cliffs of Moher, Clare (page 136).
- Derrigimlagh Bog, Galway (page 173).
- Killary Harbour (south), Galway (page 182).
- Keem Bay, Mayo (page 200).
- Downpatrick Head, Mayo (page 214).
- Mullaghmore Head, Sligo (page 230).
- Sliabh Liag, Donegal (page 239).
- Fanad Head, Donegal (page 258).
- Malin Head, Donegal (page 265).

PASSPORT
Fáilte Ireland have produced a Wild Atlantic Way passport which is a small booklet that has a space for each of the 188 discovery points that can be stamped at a designated post office or tourist information office nearby. They serve as a nice memento and are available (for €10) from selected post offices, tourist information offices, national parks, airports and Bus Éireann offices along the Wild Atlantic Way.

NAVIGATING
The route taken by the Wild Atlantic Way is well signposted and straightforward to follow. However if you want to explore off the main route then you will need a means to navigate.

The traditional option is a road map, which can be bought in most petrol stations, but the more modern alternative is a satnav or smartphone. Generally mobile phone coverage is good but there are some remote areas where there is no coverage, typically where you will need it most. One option is to install OsmAnd (osmand.net) on your phone as a backup. This map app works offline, so that once you have downloaded the map of Ireland in advance, you will always be able to find your way.

Throughout the book you will see pairs of numbers in *italics*, these are latitude and longitude coordinates in decimal degrees. If you enter them into any satnav, map website or app (such as Google Maps or Bing Maps) they will pinpoint the relevant location. A digital file, which can be loaded onto your smartphone or satnav device, containing all the locations in this book is available from threerockbooks.com.

Cruit Island, Donegal (page 248) | DF

INFORMATION FOR VISITORS

GETTING HERE
The three main airports in Ireland are Dublin, Cork and Shannon. While Dublin is the busiest, Cork and Shannon are more convenient if you want to travel directly to the west coast. Cork Airport is only a 30 minute drive from the start/finish of the Wild Atlantic Way and Shannon Airport in Clare is a good option if you want to head straight for the mid-west.

There are various other smaller airports that it may be possible to fly to, depending on where you're coming from. These include Knock in Mayo, Farranfore in Kerry and Carrickfinn in Donegal.

It's also possible to travel to Ireland by ferry. There are regular sailings into Dublin from Holyhead (Wales) and Liverpool (England), and into Rosslare (in the southeast corner of Ireland) from various ports in South Wales. Car ferries also run from Roscoff and Cherbourg in the north of France to Cork and Dublin.

GETTING AROUND
Public transport in rural areas of Ireland is limited. Buses and trains can be expensive and unless you're moving between cities, journeys will involve multiple transfers. Getting to some of the more remote towns and villages is impossible by public transport.

Car hire offers the flexibility to explore at will and can be good value. But be warned, many first time drivers in Ireland are initially taken aback by the narrow, winding roads. So take it slowly, remember to

Mullaghmore Head, Sligo (page 230) | DF

Bunowen Beach (page 172) | DF

stay on the left and if you're unsure just pull in to allow traffic pass, provided there's room to do so.

Hitch-hiking is still relatively easy in rural areas, where the roads are small and people are generally more open to helping out. The potential dangers are obvious but if you're stuck for a lift, it might be worth sticking out your thumb.

WHAT TO BRING

The most important item to bring is a good set of waterproofs, a hooded jacket and trousers will probably see plenty of use, especially if you plan on spending time outdoors.

A pair of sturdy, waterproof walking boots or shoes will also serve you well. Though most of the walks described in this book follow paths and tracks, you will still encounter mud, puddles and uneven ground. Bring warm clothes and long sleeves, even in summer. A nice summer day can still be chilly, especially if there is a sea breeze.

And while the sun is never that strong it's easy, particularly on windy days, to underestimate its strength. So use sunscreen.

MONEY

Ireland uses the Euro, meaning that if you're coming from most countries in Europe you won't need to change currency. Generally speaking larger business accept credit and debit cards, but many smaller business won't so it's wise to carry some cash. Most towns have ATMs where you can withdraw money.

WEATHER

Nobody comes to Ireland for a sun holiday. The weather is famously damp but it's rarely as bad as it's made out to be. Thanks to the influence of the Gulf Stream the Irish climate isn't particularly extreme (heavy snowfall or extended dry spells are rare) but it is unpredictable. We have seasons but the weather doesn't pay a massive amount of attention to them. Of course the winter is generally colder than the summer but that's about all that you can say with any certainty.

Suitable clothing and a sense of humour are your best defence against inclement weather. Don't let the weather dictate your plans, the hardest part is setting off but once you are out there you will often find it isn't nearly as bad as you expected.

WHEN TO VISIT?

SUMMER

The weather during an Irish summer can be glorious and miserable and everything in between, and all on the same day. By the middle of June there is over 17 hours of daylight, giving both early birds and night owls a chance to see some sun, should it make an appearance.

When the weather is nice in the summer, the west coast of Ireland is an amazing place to be. The hedges are filled to bursting with wildflowers, the mountains turn green and even the sea can feel warm (on a good day). There are few finer pleasures than lying out on a sun-warmed rock after an invigorating swim in the Atlantic.

Anybody not familiar with higher latitudes will savour the sun as it hangs near the horizon, and dusk lingers long into the night.

While the main tourist hubs can be packed at this time of year it's not that hard to escape the hordes. The islands are best in summer; away from it all but still lively.

WINTER

While summer is the most popular time with tourists that doesn't mean it's not worth visiting at other times of the year. Though the winter tends to be cold, wet and windy, the same conditions can be had at any time of year, and at least in winter you will be expecting them. The days are quite short (about 8 hours of light in early December) but the rawness of a breezy hillside walk or a mind-numbing surf in mid-winter will appeal to some. And a warm fireside and quiet pint is all the sweeter after time outdoors in the cold, dark months.

Stargazing in rural Ireland is best during the long, dark nights of winter (if you're lucky enough to get clear weather). The sea can be particularly ferocious in winter, and is worth seeing in its own right (from a safe position). The low light and mixed weather of the darker months might appeal to photographers too.

Come in the winter if you want to avoid the crowds, but plan well as some accommodation and activity providers will be closed.

SPRING

March and April occasionally have some of the best weather in Ireland. The first high pressure system after the winter is sometimes the most stable of the year, giving weeks of settled weather. That said, there is no real predictability with the Irish climate and anything can happen at any time of year.

Spring visitors will avoid the summer crowds, and enjoy a time of year when the landscape is coming to life again after winter. This can also be a great time of year for the outdoor enthusiast; temperatures are pleasant for walking, the days aren't so long that the sun wakes you in your tent at 5 am, and the dreaded midges (tiny, infuriating biting insects) haven't come out yet.

In May the woods come alive with wild garlic and bluebells, making for pretty scenes. The sea thrift that thrives along most of Ireland's coast is at its best in the early days of summer, adding colour to the sea cliffs. Seabird colonies are well and truly established

A quiet boreen on Lettermore Island, Galway (page 163) | DF

by the middle of spring, giving birdwatchers plenty to look at.

AUTUMN
Autumn is a good time of year for fishing and foraging. Nearly every ditch and hedge on the west coast is laden with blackberries in September, making a great addition to porridge or an evening stroll. The inshore mackerel season lasts well into autumn, and experienced foragers will find fungi in the forests.

Many rural communities have harvest festivals in August, with all sorts of activities on offer. The sea is at its warmest in September, and the first swells of winter often produce stellar surf before the wind starts howling.

Autumn can be a good time to grab a bargain with accommodation providers keen to stretch out their season after the summer has finished. And because school starts in September many families are finished with their holidays, meaning less crowds, but still pleasant weather (if you're lucky).

PLACENAMES
The vast majority of Irish placenames are anglicised versions of old Irish names, translated phonetically from their original forms. This leads to a lot of similarities, as most of the original names describe generic features of the landscape. After centuries of the language evolving the origin of some placenames has been lost.

Toponymy, the study of the origins of placenames, is a fascinating subject that can reveal a huge amount about the history, culture and landscape of a place. If you are interested in this subject it's worth checking out Logainm (logainm.ie), a vast bilingual database of Ireland's placenames.

Some familiarity with the words that occur frequently in placenames will give an extra insight into a trip along the west coast. Below is a table of some of the most common placename elements that you may encounter.

Bally	From the Irish word baile, meaning town or place e.g. Ballyferriter - Ferriter's Town (Ferriter being a surname).
...beg	Usually seen at the end of a name, from the Irish word beag, meaning small e.g. Killybegs - The Small Cells (of a monastic settlement).
Bun	From the Irish word bun, meaning foot of or end of (usually a river) e.g. Bunbeg - The Small Mouth of the River.
Derry	From the Irish word doire, meaning oak wood e.g. Derrymore - The Big Oak Wood.
Gort	From the Irish word Gort, meaning field e.g. Gort na gCapall - Field of the Horses.
Inish	From the Irish word Inis, meaning island e.g. Inis Meáin - Middle Island.
Kill	From the Irish word cill, meaning church, or sometimes from coill, meaning a wood e.g. Killarney - Church of the Sloes (the sloe being the fruit of the blackthorn tree).
Knock	From the Irish word cnoc, meaning hill e.g. Knockmore - The Big Hill.
Lis	From the Irish word lios, meaning ring fort e.g. Listowel - Tuathal's Ringfort.
Rath	From the Irish word ráth, meaning circular fort e.g. Rathmore - The Big Ring Fort.
Roe	From the Irish word rua(dh), meaning red e.g. Carraroe - The Red Quarter.
Slieve	From the Irish word sliabh, meaning mountain e.g. Sliabh Liag - Mountain of the Flagstones.
Tra	From the Irish word trá, meaning beach. e.g. Tralee - Beach of the Lee (a river).

Wild Meadow Huts, Clare (page 146) | Wild Meadow Huts

ACCOMMODATION

For the most part there is plenty of accommodation available along the Wild Atlantic Way, with everything from basic campsites to five-star hotels.

For this edition of the book we have added some accommodation information to each section. The goal is to highlight a small number of the most interesting and quirky places to stay, with a focus on self-catering accommodation and glamping sites as well as other unusual places that we think might be of interest.

If you want to research B&Bs, guesthouses or hotels then TripAdvisor is an excellent starting point.

FOOD AND DRINK

The quality, variety and provenance of Irish food is improving at a vast rate, and there are plenty of excellent places to eat all over the country. From busy cafes to fancy restaurants there is a huge amount of choice. Even most pubs serve decent food nowadays.

Naturally, given the proximity of the ocean, fresh seafood is a popular item on menus along the Wild Atlantic Way. From humble fish and chips to more luxurious items like lobster and oysters, there is something for everyone.

BEER

If Ireland is famous for anything other than its scenery it's the pubs and the beer and spirits that it produces. In recent years Ireland's craft brewing industry has really taken off and many towns now have their own breweries.

Many of these breweries source their ingredients locally, sometimes from the fields surrounding them, giving these beers a unique taste, distinct to that time and place.

Check out the following list of breweries along or near the Wild Atlantic Way:

- Blacks Brewery, Kinsale, Cork
- Tom Crean Brewery, Kenmare, Kerry
- McGill's Brewery, Waterville, Kerry
- Killarney Brewing & Distilling Company, Kerry
- West Kerry Brewery Dingle, Kerry
- Western Herd Brewing Company, Kilmaley, Clare
- Galway Bay, Oranmore, Galway
- Connemara Brewing Company Carraroe, Galway
- Mescan Brewery, Kilsallagh, Mayo
- Reel Deel Brewing, Crossmolina, Mayo
- Lough Gill Brewery, Sligo
- Kinnegar Brewing Letterkenny, Donegal
- Otterbank Brewing and Blending, Muff, Donegal

Great Blasket, Kerry (page 96) | RC

A pub in Milltown Malbay, Clare (page 133) | RC

Croagh Patrick, Mayo (page 194) | Dale Simonson

Dunmore Head, Kerry (see page 96) | RC

Kayaking in Clare (page 145) | North Clare Sea Kayaking

FIVE ESSENTIAL EXPERIENCES

At over 2,500km in length the Wild Atlantic Way has a lifetime's worth of sights to see and things to do. It's impossible to see everything in just a week or two so to help people plan their trip we have compiled the following list, in no particular order, of essential experiences that can be found almost anywhere along the Wild Atlantic Way.

1 CLIMB A MOUNTAIN

A large portion of the Atlantic coast is mountainous, and while modest by international standards, many of the mountains rise directly from sea-level, offering a stern test for any hiker.

A number of these hills and mountains have been places of pilgrimage for millennia, and while the motives for going to these sacred summits may be different in this day and age, there are plenty of reasons to keep the tradition alive. The views from these mountains are hard to beat, and the satisfaction of a challenging walk and being out in the elements can last for days.

Most of the Wild Atlantic Way's iconic peaks have well-worn paths to their summits meaning that they are within most people's ability. But there are also a number of more challenging mountains that don't have distinct paths, and these will be of great interest to more experienced hikers.

Here are some suggestions:

- Mount Brandon, Kerry (page 102)
- Diamond Hill, Galway (page 181)
- Croagh Patrick, Mayo (page 194).
- Knocknarea, Sligo (page 225).
- Sliabh Liag, Donegal (page 239).
- Errigal, Donegal (page 255).

2 VISIT AN ISLAND

A visit to one of Ireland's offshore islands is like a trip back in time. That's not to say that the islands are backward places, almost all enjoy the conveniences of the modern world, but they have held onto a relaxed pace of living that has vanished from most of the world.

Many of the islands are strongholds of the Irish language, and visitors are just as likely to hear people speaking Irish as they are English in places like Cape Clear (page 55), the Aran Islands (page 150) and Tory Island (page 250). They generally also have vibrant traditional music scenes, and folklore is treasured in these places.

No matter which island you visit be sure to spend the night. When the day-trippers have all left you'll get a real sense of life on these remote Atlantic outposts.

3 A NIGHT IN THE PUB

Ireland is rightly famous for its pubs. Even in the smallest communities you will often find two or three bars, so whether you want to experience the buzz of a crowded pub or enjoy a drink in a quiet corner you will have plenty of choice.

Pubs are the social hubs of every town or village and visitors often spend many an evening in the pub chatting to locals, listening to traditional Irish music or just sitting beside the fire enjoying a meal or a pint.

In recent years the standard of food in pubs has improved significantly so they aren't just for night time visits, they are also great places to retreat to on wild days to warm up with a hot drink or a hearty meal.

Many pubs host traditional music sessions, particularly during the summer months.

4 WALK THE COAST

In Ireland you are never far from the sea and the huge variety of coastline, ranging from towering cliffs to vast sandy beaches, is one of the country's major attractions.

The best way to experience the coast is on foot so that you can hear the crunch of pebbles under your feet, smell the sea salt and feel the wind on your face. And it's only when wandering the shore that you will find a hidden rocky cove, get eyeballed by a curious seal or find the perfect pebble on the sand.

In the summer you can take a gentle evening stroll as the sun sets into the sea. While in the winter you can battle the fierce winds and rain to watch the waves crash into exposed headlands.

See page 21 for more information about walking on the Wild Atlantic Way.

5 TRY SOMETHING NEW

Ireland's reputation as a destination for outdoor activities is growing fast. With a great diversity of terrain Ireland is the ideal place to try a new activity. Watersports such as surfing, kayaking and paddleboarding offer a unique perspective on the coastline, while land-based activities such as mountain biking, rock climbing and caving allow you to visit places you might never get to see otherwise.

Culdaff Beach, Donegal (page 267) David Ardron

ACTIVITIES

Ireland's Atlantic coast is a paradise for those who enjoy the outdoors and the following pages offer some general advice on the many outdoor activities that can be enjoyed along the Wild Atlantic Way.

WALKING

There is an endless variety of walks along the Atlantic seaboard, from leisurely strolls along sandy beaches to long days out on mountains that slope down to the sea. You can walk miles and miles of beaches in Cork and Kerry, explore the rocky shorelines of Clare, get lost on the empty boreens of Connemara, or range over the huge, rugged sea cliffs of Mayo and Donegal.

The rural nature of the west of Ireland means many of the roads are quiet, and ideal for walking. These small roads are often lined with grass down the middle and bordered by high, verdant hedges that bustle with wildlife in summer. Much of the coast in these quiet corners is left untended by farmers, leaving a wild and open border between land and sea that is ripe for exploration.

The majority of the walks described in this guide are signposted trails that are easy to follow and suitable for people of average fitness. Signposted routes are thankfully becoming more prevalent, and the Irish Trails website (irishtrails.ie) is a brilliant resource for walkers. As well as detailed maps and route descriptions, there is feedback from people who have walked the trails, offering first-hand information to others.

Good footwear is recommended for off-road walking in Ireland. The damp climate and soft ground mean paths are often wet and muddy, particularly during the winter months.

Almost all the land in Ireland, from the tops of the hills down to the high tide mark, is privately owned, and walkers must respect the rights of the landowners. Ignoring their requests could result in the loss of access, so please observe any signs you see while out walking, be they about trespassing, gates or dogs. Much of the west of Ireland is farming land and dogs can stress livestock, especially sheep. Please avoid bringing dogs where the signs say so. Park carefully, making sure not to obstruct gates, take all litter home and leave places as you would wish to find them.

LONG DISTANCE TRAILS

Ireland has a good network of long-distance walking trails, over a dozen of which are on or near the west coast. Of particular note are the four trails in the southwest (the Dingle Way, the Kerry Way, the Beara Way and the Sheep's Head Way), the Western Way, which runs through Connemara and Mayo to the Sligo border and the Slí Dhún na nGall in Donegal. For more information about Ireland's long-distance waymarked trails see irishtrails.ie.

TICKS

If you're walking off the beaten track in Ireland it's important to be aware of ticks. These tiny spider-like creatures feed on the blood of animals and occasionally humans. A small minority of them carry Lyme disease. Wearing long sleeves and tucking trousers into socks can help prevent them coming into contact with your skin. Check yourself for ticks after walking in long grass, woodlands, ferns or any other wild green places, or if you've been in contact with animals. See ticktalkireland.org for more information.

MIDGES

Midges are tiny flying insects that can be a nuisance on calm, humid days between May and September, especially near lakes, rivers and bogs. And while they don't carry disease, their bites are very annoying. As they are blown away by even a gentle breeze and the west of Ireland is generally windy you needn't worry about them too much. But it's no harm to have some insect repellant to hand, even though it often achieves little.

MOUNTAIN SAFETY

Ireland's mountains may be modest in height but the weather in the hills is particularly fickle and can deteriorate quickly. While most of the walks in this book follow signposted trails in low-lying areas where help is never far and conditions are unlikely to become life threatening, there are also some more serious walks that are only suitable for experienced, well-equipped hikers.

If you are venturing into the mountains be sure to plan your route (including possible escape options), wear suitable footwear, and carry a map and compass (and know how to use them), extra food and warm waterproof clothing.

Always let somebody know where you're going and what time to expect you back. In case of an emergency dial 112 or 999, but be warned that many mountainous areas have poor phone signal.

MAPS

Ireland is covered at a scale of 1:50,000 by the Discovery Series of maps published by Ordnance Survey Ireland (store.osi.ie). They are designed for hikers and have plenty of detail.

Beginish, Kerry (page 89) | RC

CAMPING

Camping is a great way to experience the great outdoors, and while the weather in Ireland may be unsettled don't let it put you off spending a night or two in a tent. There are few greater pleasures than waking up to the early summer sun on a quiet coastal headland or sitting around a driftwood fire before bedding down under the stars.

There are plenty of commercial campsites along the Wild Atlantic Way. Some are large sites with excellent facilities while others are little more than some flat grass and a toilet block. During the high summer they will be busy but most close during the colder months.

GLAMPING

In recent years a new category of camping has emerged, glamping, which offers reluctant campers the chance to experience the best aspects of sleeping outdoors without the perceived discomfort. Glamping accommodation can range from a night on the floor of a glorified garden shed to a five-star hotel experience in a beautiful, bespoke shelter.

Along the Wild Atlantic Way there are a number of high-end glampsites, catering for couples or families, where you can stay in unique custom-built lodgings. There are also an increasing number of conventional campsites that offer more modest accommodation ranging from canvas tents to wooden cabins.

Glamping can be good value and is an excellent way to immerse yourself in the great outdoors without having to rough it.

WILD CAMPING

In spite of the fact that virtually all land along the Irish coast is privately owned, wild camping is still an option once it's done discretely.

The trick is to walk some distance from the nearest road, this way you will be guaranteed peace and quiet. Remote beaches and upland areas are the best options. Don't be afraid to ask the locals for advice, most landowners, once approached with respect, will be happy to suggest a place to camp that won't be in anybody's way.

Discretion is essential when wild camping: pitch your tent late, take it down early and don't draw attention to yourself. If you are planning on lighting a fire choose suitable ground and minimise its effect on the landscape. And remember to take all your rubbish away with you.

Sunset at Garretstown, Cork (page 45) | RC

CAMPERVANS AND MOTORHOMES

Travelling the Wild Atlantic Way in a campervan allows you to stop and explore at your own pace. With no timetable to follow you can immerse yourself fully in your surroundings.

The number of campervans on the west coast has increased considerably since the creation of the Wild Atlantic Way and there are more companies than ever offering rentals. Even so, the west coast of Ireland doesn't get as crowded with vans as some places in continental Europe and it's generally not too difficult to find somewhere quiet to spend the night. Height barriers are rare and locals are generally quite accepting of overnighting vans, as long as you are discreet and tidy of course. Consider spending a little money locally if you're staying in a public carpark.

Those who enjoy 'wild' camping, (i.e. parking up outside of campsites) will get the most out of a van trip to Ireland. You should be prepared to be a bit more self-sufficient than you might have to be in other parts of Europe. Dedicated areas for motorhomes, with water, toilets and wastewater disposal (known as aires on the Continent) are rare, and paid campsites aren't as common as in mainland Europe. It's worth carrying plenty of fresh water and topping up if you stay in a campsite. Note that larger vehicles might be more stressful to navigate on some of Ireland's narrow and winding roads.

If you're parking on a beach be mindful of the tides. Getting bogged down in soft sand or caught by the rising tide won't do your van much good.

CYCLING

There is no better way to experience the Wild Atlantic Way than from the saddle of a bike. Faster than walking so you still get to cover a reasonable amount of ground, but not so fast that you can't take it all in. The quiet roads and tracks of the west coast lend themselves to leisurely cycles.

It's possible to rent a bike in many of the towns along the Wild Atlantic Way. Electric bikes are increasing in popularity meaning that those who aren't as fit as they might like can still enjoy a cycle.

And just like with the walking trails, signposted cycle routes are starting to become more common. Currently there are eight cycle hubs spread along the west coast in Skibbereen, Doolin, Clifden, Louisburgh, Westport, Achill Island, Belmullet and Ballyshannon.

However you aren't limited to these established routes - with the aid of a map and some imagination you will find miles of quiet roads to cycle all along the west coast. *Cycling in Ireland*, which is also published by Three Rock Books, offers details of over 80 routes all across the island of Ireland, including plenty that are on or near the Wild Atlantic Way.

Remember that traffic (including bikes) travels on the left side of the road in Ireland. Helmets are strongly recommended, as are lights (required by law)

Looking north from the top of the Healy Pass (page 69) | DF

and a high visibility vest. Many main roads in Ireland are quite narrow by international standards, so cycling on them is best avoided in summer, especially when tour buses and extra traffic is more likely.

CYCLE TOURING

Prior to the launch of the Wild Atlantic Way Ireland's west coast attracted cycle tourers with its spectacular scenery, unique culture and fascinating history. However the packaging of the most scenic parts of the country into a well-defined route has raised its profile significantly and the Wild Atlantic Way has been very popular with cyclists from its inception.

It's important to note that the Wild Atlantic Way wasn't created specifically for cyclists and that in a number of places the route follows busy national and regional roads, however, in most cases, it's possible to find better, safer alternatives.

Most people won't have the time or inclination to cycle the entire 2,500km route so the best approach is to pick a section of the route and take your time, exploring as you go, taking advantage of the freedom that cycling offers. A linear approach, using public transport to access the start and/or finish, is a sensible way to maximise your time and see as much of the route as possible. If you only have a weekend then there are plenty of excellent shorter loops, a circuit of any of the three Kerry peninsulas for instance.

The best direction to cycle the route is from south to north to take advantage of the prevailing southwesterly wind. This also means that you will be cycling on the side of the road closest to the coast and will have a better view.

MOUNTAIN BIKING

A number of signposted trails cross paths with the Wild Atlantic Way including (from south to north): the Sheep's Head Way, Beara Way, Kerry Way, Dingle Way, North Kerry Way, Burren Way, Croagh Patrick Heritage Trail, Western Way and Slí Dhún na nGall. These trails feature a mix of quiet roads, tracks and paths, many of which may be suitable for mountain biking. However they aren't designated for this purpose so tread carefully. See irishtrails.ie for details.

On the west coast there is one dedicated mountain bike trail at Derroura in Connemara (see page 165) and work is ongoing on a large network of trails in Coolaney in Sligo.

Glassillaun beach in Connemara (page 182) | RC

SWIMMING

There are thousands of quiet coves, open beaches, mountain lakes and sheltered harbours along the Wild Atlantic Way, and many would say that a visit to the coast isn't complete until you have swum in the sea.

Even though the water never quite reaches tropical temperatures it's far from freezing in the summer, and a dip in this corner of the Atlantic is always invigorating. Now that cheap wetsuits are widely available there is little excuse for not diving in. With Ireland's changeable weather, getting into the sea is a perfect wet-weather option, as being wet becomes something to do rather than avoid.

Many of the most popular beaches have lifeguards in the summer. In general they will be present at weekends in June and September, and daily in July and August, but this isn't always the case. The Irish Water Safety website (iws.ie) has plenty of information on lifeguards, water quality and beaches with Green Coast and Blue Flag awards.

SOAKING AND SAUNAS

Most people who visit the west coast don't venture into the sea (understandably, though we still feel you're missing out) but there are other ways of getting into the water along the Wild Atlantic Way while staying warm. There are long-established heated seaweed baths in Ballybunion and Enniscrone, at the time of writing there are over fifty newly established saunas along the Wild Atlantic Way. Most of these are within a stone's throw of the sea, which makes it easier for even the most cold prone people to consider taking a dip. The warm up afterwards is all the more enjoyable for having been in the sea.

WATER SAFETY

Ireland's Atlantic coast can be a dangerous place. It's prone to unsettled weather, with high winds and rough seas common even in the summer. If you plan on swimming be sure to check the sea conditions, the forecast and the tide. Heed warning signs and if you're unsure just stay on land. Things can go wrong very quickly when the sea is involved, so be vigilant.

Be especially careful near cliff edges. Some softer sections of the coast are badly eroded and the tops of some cliffs can be undercut at the edges, with little but air beneath a thin cover of soil.

Always be conscious of rogue waves near the sea. Whether you're fishing, taking photographs or just having a look, be sensible and don't stand with your back to the ocean.

In case of emergency dial 112 or 999 and raise the alarm as soon as possible.

Irish waters are home to about half a dozen species of jellyfish, the majority of which pose little problem to swimmers. However, there are two species that you should be very wary of, the lion's mane and the Portuguese man o'war. The former

Kayaking near Cahersiveen, Kerry | RC

can cause severely painful stings and contact with the latter can be potentially fatal. The chances of an encounter are very low so unless you've been specifically warned you shouldn't be deterred from getting into the water.

Another hazard to be aware of is the weever fish, which buries itself in the sand at the low tide mark leaving its dorsal fin exposed. If stood on it can cause considerable pain that can last for weeks. They are quite rare but it's a good idea to wear something on your feet in the water.

SNORKELLING

Being in the sea isn't all about working on your butterfly stroke. Snorkelling is a really interesting way to enjoy the water and Ireland's temperate seas are teeming with coastal marine life just beneath the surface.

There are five designated snorkelling spots, known as Blueways, along the Wild Atlantic Way: Mannin Bay (see page 173), Inishbofin (see page 179) and Glassillaun (see page 182) in Galway and Louisburgh (see page 193) and Achill Island (see page 201) in Mayo.

COASTEERING

Coasteering is another increasingly popular way to enjoy the shoreline. Combining swimming, cliff jumping and scrambling, it is an active and thrilling way to spend a few hours. More and more activity providers are offering coasteering as part of their lineup, and it's highly recommended for the adventurous traveller.

KAYAKING

What cycling is to walking, kayaking is to swimming; a great way to cover plenty of ground in an active, enjoyable manner. Once the realm of the experienced enthusiast, kayaking has now become a more family-friendly pastime as boats have become cheaper and people's interest in the outdoors increases. Of course that's not to say that anybody can just pick up a boat and start paddling to a distant offshore island. Any activity on the water must be undertaken with the utmost respect for the sea. But with common sense and some basic knowledge there are hundreds of sheltered beaches and bays on Ireland's west coast where kayaking can be enjoyed safely.

Most people don't own a boat, but there are plenty of activity providers offering rentals and guided kayaking trips up and down the west coast, many are mentioned in the main text.

Another welcome development is the Blueways, the aquatic equivalent of the Greenway walking and cycling routes. While there aren't a huge number of these yet, hopefully in time they will be more common along the Irish coast.

Surfing at Long Strand, Cork (page 48) | RC

For the experienced sea kayaker Ireland is a world-class place to paddle. A full circumnavigation of the island is a feat sought after by kayakers from all over the world, and the hundreds of offshore islands make for excellent shorter trips. While most of these adventures are beyond the scope of this book it doesn't take too much imagination to plan a good kayaking excursion in the west of Ireland.

David Walsh's excellent website oileain.org is an invaluable resource for paddlers looking for information on Ireland's islands. Needless to say, no matter what your level of experience, always be prepared: a detailed weather forecast, knowledge of the tides and the know-how to keep yourself safe are essential requirements for any kayak trip.

SURFING

The Wild Atlantic Way faces over 4,000km of open ocean, and sits in the way of the prevailing southwest wind of the North Atlantic, and the swell that it creates. These conditions make Ireland a great spot for surfing.

From gentle beach breaks to world-famous big waves, Ireland has surfing for everybody. In the past thirty years it has gone from being a fringe activity to a sport that's reinvigorated many coastal towns. There are multiple surf schools in every county of the Wild Atlantic Way, even Leitrim, which has the shortest length of coast in Ireland.

While some of the more popular surf spots - such as Inch in Kerry, Lahinch in Clare and Bundoran in Donegal - get busy on the best days, there are hundreds of other empty breaks.

The recent advances in weather forecasting and up-to-date online information have made finding good surf much easier, so there is little stopping those with enough motivation.

While the winter may be the best season for dedicated surfers, there are plenty of opportunities to catch waves throughout the year. And if you've never surfed before then it doesn't really matter if the waves aren't perfect, once there's enough whitewater to stand up then anybody can experience the feeling of being propelled along by a wave that has travelled hundreds or thousands of kilometres to wash up on the shores of Ireland.

SUP

As well as surfing, Ireland is becoming increasingly popular for SUP (Stand Up Paddleboarding), kite surfing and some of the more esoteric activities like kite buggying. Paddleboarding in particular is very popular and very accessible for people of all abilities.

WILD FOOD

Throughout the year there is an abundance of wild food growing in Irish waters, shores, fields, hills and hedges. And you don't need to have military survival training to find some of the more common edible foods - with a little research and a bare minimum of equipment it's quite possible to get outside and grab a free lunch.

Even though it was first published in 1972, *Food for Free* by Richard Mabey is still one of the best foraging guides. As there are numerous toxic berries and many mushrooms it's vitally important to know what you're doing when foraging for wild food, but don't let the risk put you off. Armed with common sense and help from a book or a knowledgeable guide, foraging can be an enjoyable way of satisfying your hunger.

FISH

In spite of the fact that Ireland is surrounded entirely by sea it's only in relatively recent times that the Irish have really embraced the wonderful fish and seafood that are found in our island's waters.

It doesn't take much effort to head down to the coast and catch some for yourself. The late summer months are best suited to fishing, and mackerel and pollock are the fish that are most commonly caught and eaten. Many coastal towns have shops selling fishing gear and they will be happy to share some local knowledge about the best fishing spots in the area. You will also find boats offering angling trips all along the coast.

River and lake fishing is also possible along much of the west coast. However, licenses are required for most species and there are strict seasons. See fishinginireland.info for more information.

If you are going fishing, only catch what you will eat and please take all your rubbish home with you.

SHELLFISH

Though more of an acquired taste it can be easier to gather some types of shellfish than to catch fish. Common shore species like mussels, limpets and periwinkles are straightforward to identify and they provide an easy meal for the modern day hunter-gatherer. Razor clams require a bit more work but can be found on many Irish beaches. Delicacies like scallops and oysters can sometimes be found at the very lowest reaches of the shore on a low tide.

Shellfish poisoning can be an issue but with care it is easily avoided. Don't collect shellfish near towns or cities where raw sewage could be discharged into the sea. Always wash what you find very well – both inside and out. Don't cook dead shellfish – check before cooking that it is still alive by gently forcing the shell open. Any animal that is still alive will quickly shut its shell again.

SEAWEED

Freely available on most stretches of the coast, seaweed is an intriguing food full of minerals. Though many people aren't that keen on the idea of eating it, seaweed is an extremely healthy and useful food, and seaweed extracts are used in many common household products and foods. Not all seaweeds are palatable but many can be eaten raw as a tasty snack.

As for shellfish, avoid picking seaweed close to towns or villages or anywhere where there might be harmful run-off from land. Most seaweeds are best harvested in early summer, and it's best not to cut them too close to the 'root' so as to give them the best chance of re-sprouting.

BERRIES

In late summer most Irish rural roads are bordered by brambles weighed down with plump, juicy berries. Blackberry picking is a rite of passage for most children in the countryside, and they are delicious on their own or as an addition to porridge or ice cream.

Wild strawberries are far less common but don't pass one by if you see them. Though small, they are incredibly tasty.

More common than wild strawberries are bilberries, or fraughans as they are known in much of Ireland. A relative of the blueberry, fraughans are smaller but far tastier. The shrub mostly grows in thick heather, making it hard to find sometimes, but a good haul in late July is a just reward for the effort.

FUNGI

Most people are very reluctant to gather wild mushrooms as there is a real danger of serious or potentially fatal poisoning if you make a mistake. However plenty of mushrooms are safe to eat, and the better tasting ones are vastly superior to anything from the shops.

Autumn is generally the best time for mushroom picking, and Ireland's mild and wet climate is ideal for many types of fungi. If you don't know what you're looking for then you'd better get help, and there are guides and workshops available that will help you get the most from your foraging trip.

The photos on facing page are by Richard Creagh, David Flanagan, Yoko Nekonomania, Chris Cant, Féron Benjamin, Conor Ryan.

Gannets

WILD ATLANTIC WILDLIFE

The west coast of Ireland is the border between two worlds, the edge of Europe and the northeast Atlantic. As a consequence the Wild Atlantic Way is a haven of biodiversity, with a huge number of land and sea species, from the tiniest barnacles to the largest whales.

IN THE COUNTRYSIDE

In the past Ireland was home to a number of large land mammals including wolves and wild boar, but nowadays only deer remain. The mountains of Kerry and Donegal hold most of the deer on the west coast, though they can also be found in some lowland areas.

Wild goats aren't uncommon, and like the deer, they were brought to Ireland by humans as a domestic animal. Herds of feral goats can be found on the Beara Peninsula in Cork, in parts of the Burren in Clare and many other wild pockets in between.

While the agricultural landscape that forms much of the country isn't suited to large wild mammals there are plenty of smaller ones, including foxes, badgers, stoats, red squirrels, hares and rabbits. In the past, when most of the population lived in the countryside, people were more familiar with these elusive creatures, but now unfortunately most sightings of Irish mammals are as roadkill.

Hares are relatively common in the uplands, and if you're very lucky you may see a stoat on a quiet country lane. These charming animals can be quite ferocious, and will often catch rabbits far larger than themselves. They will even stand and stare down an approaching human before darting away.

Otters can be seen near rivers and low-lying coast, and a sighting is a welcome bonus to any walk. You are most likely to glimpse a fox or a badger at dawn or dusk in summer, when they're heading out to hunt.

HEDGE LIFE

In a country with only a small amount of woodland, the hedgerows that line many of our country roads are important refuges and corridors for birds, wildflowers and thousands of invertebrate species. A walk between healthy hedges in summer will reveal countless butterflies, hoverflies, bees and bugs as well as songbirds and a huge range of wildflowers. Those with a keen eye could easily while away an hour along a 100m stretch of roadside just watching the life in the verges.

Small copper butterfly

Emerald damselfly

Blue-rayed limpets

Dahlia anemone

Humpback whale

Common dolphin mother and calf

Grey seal

Curlew

Puffins

BOGLAND

The bogland of Ireland's west coast may appear empty but there's a lot more going on than first impressions suggest. There is a range of species that are well adapted to the waterlogged, acidic conditions of blanket bog.

Many species of orchids are found as well as plants like lousewort, bog asphodel and great swathes of bog cotton. Some plants have adapted to the low nutrient habitat by becoming insectivores. Sundew and butterwort are both common insect-eating bog plants.

Many birds also favour open moorland. Red grouse are a relatively common sight in the blanket bogs of Mayo and geese and plover, among others, depend on the bogs for feeding and breeding.

ON THE COAST

As an island, perched at the fringe of an enormous ocean, the seas around Ireland are home to many times more species than its dry land. Though most of us never see it, the wildlife in the sea is rich and varied and Ireland's position at the edge of Europe makes it a major stopping ground for migrating animals that feed in our coastal waters.

There are huge colonies of seabirds making use of the cliffs and remote islands. Many of these outposts host internationally important numbers of certain species, like gannets on Little Skellig and storm petrels on the Blaskets. While most of us are familiar with gulls, who often venture inland, the majority of ocean-going birds only visit the shore to breed. Once breeding is complete most of these birds head to sea. Manx shearwaters spend the winter off the coast of South America and the summer in Ireland. For a bird that can live over 60 years that's a lot of mileage.

OPEN SEA

The water off Ireland's coast is an important habitat for whales, dolphins, sharks and seals. The Blasket Islands off Kerry and the Inishkea Islands off Mayo host plenty of grey seals, an animal whose life has long been interwoven with coastal people.

Recently the whales and dolphins off the Irish coast have been attracting more attention, and it's clear that the south and west coasts in particular are important feeding grounds for some of the largest animals in the world. Fin whales (the second biggest whale) can be seen close to land every year and humpback whales have been seen off both the southwest and northwest coasts in numbers over the past few years.

Added to this is Europe's largest group of resident bottlenose dolphins at the mouth of the Shannon Estuary and annual sightings of basking sharks (the second biggest shark in the world) all along the coast.

Most people probably aren't aware that Ireland has about 30 species of shark but don't let that stop you from getting into the water. The chances of a shark attack are practically zero.

THE SHORELINE

While the well-known megafauna are undoubtedly impressive, there are many equally interesting species to be found almost everywhere along the coast. Rock pooling is a fantastic seashore activity, especially for kids. There are hermit crabs, fish, urchins, seaweeds and a range of alien-like anemones to be seen.

Snorkelling is another superb way to inspect this underwater world, and there is no shortage of suitable spots along the Wild Atlantic Way (see page 31). Even the humble barnacle becomes a fascinating creature when viewed under water; if you look closely you'll see thousands of minute, feathered 'arms' reaching out to filter food from the sea.

So while you may not have travelled to the west of Ireland specifically for its wildlife it's worth keeping an eye out - you never know what you might see.

All photos on this and the previous spread are by Richard Creagh.

The Wild Atlantic Way

Glengarriff Harbour (see page 68) | RC

CORK

From its starting (or finishing) point in the town of Kinsale the Wild Atlantic Way travels west along the coast of County Cork. Initially the terrain is gentle with grassy green fields, but gradually it becomes wilder and more rugged. The steady change exposes the traveller to an ever-evolving landscape, from the lively market towns and lengthy beaches in the east, to the lonelier villages and exposed, open coasts further west.

The quiet country lanes west of Kinsale are ideal for cyclists and the beaches around Clonakilty are golden. The seas between Galley Head and Baltimore welcome some of the planet's largest animals each year. The islands of Roaringwater Bay are a world away from the mainland. Sheep's Head is a walker's paradise and Beara is rugged and remote.

West Cork is generally somewhat tamer than the rough-edged landscapes along the rest of the Wild Atlantic Way. The climate is also more forgiving, though nobody in Ireland can make any guarantees about the weather. Nonetheless, the coast of Cork is a pleasant one, with enough variety to keep all lovers of the seashore happy.

KINSALE TO SKIBBEREEN

This, the first, or last, stretch of the Wild Atlantic Way serves as a gentle introduction or wind down. The terrain is, in contrast with counties further west and north, less wild, with abundant green fields and thick hedges.

And while it may not have the drama of the Kerry mountains or the wide open spaces of County Mayo, this is an incredibly attractive length of coastline. There are countless small bays, classically beautiful beaches and peaceful coastal walks where you're unlikely to meet another soul. Pockets of woodland reach down to the sea in many of the sheltered coves, an unusual feature in most of Ireland.

There are plenty of options for watersports enthusiasts, and both surfing and sea kayaking are popular in these parts. As is wildlife watching; this section of the West Cork coast is a haven for all sorts of migrants, from the smallest birds to the largest whales.

KINSALE
This pretty seaside village is a very popular tourist hub. It has a number of excellent restaurants and is considered by many to be the gourmet capital of Ireland.

CHARLES FORT
A pleasant walk east of town takes you out to the historic ruins of Charles Fort where there is a great view of Kinsale Harbour (*51.6979, -8.4988*). From the main carpark (*51.7055, -8.5215*) follow the road east along the water's edge (signposted Scilly Walk and Charles Fort). Leave the road and follow the wooded path that emerges at Summer Cove, and shortly after that at Charles Fort.

JARLEY'S COVE
If you fancy a swim, head west from the town and cross the bridge over the Bandon River. Turn left and follow the road down to a small sheltered beach known as Jarley's Cove (*51.6964, -8.5144*). Call in to The Dock for a pint afterwards, or take a look around the lesser-known James Fort.

SANDY COVE
About 3km south of Kinsale is an attractive little bay, known as Sandy Cove. It's sheltered from the worst of the weather by the island lying just offshore. Swimming around this island, a distance of about 1.8km, is a rite of passage for local swimmers, but be wary of tides and sea conditions if planning a

Kayaking through the Old Head of Kinsale | RC

Garrylucas Cliff Path | RC

circumnavigation. The beach at the cove and the sandy shores on the island opposite are lovely, and make for a pleasant few seaside hours close to Kinsale. The sand is covered at high tide but there is a nice stroll along the clifftop path that starts beside the whitewashed cottage near the carpark.

Heading west from Kinsale look out for the signs for 'Sandycove' after the bridge. Follow the coast road to the carpark (51.6771, -8.5240).

THE OLD HEAD OF KINSALE

The Old Head is one of the finest headlands along the Irish coast, sticking nearly 5km out to sea and almost cut off from the mainland in the middle. Unfortunately a private golf course occupies the southern half of the headland, so you must end your journey at the entrance to the course (51.6178, -8.5415). Nonetheless, the views to the east and west are excellent.

There are a number of natural tunnels that pass through the Old Head, carved out by countless tides. It's possible to kayak through the headland, or at least part of the way through it if the tides aren't right. Boats can be launched from Bullens Bay (51.6414, -8.5497) leaving a 4km paddle south to the tunnels. It hardly needs to be said that this trip is only suitable for those with experience and in good conditions.

GARRYLUCAS

The Blue Flag beach at Garrylucas is a pleasant one, and popular with Cork holidaymakers (51.6387, -8.5606). There is a lifeguard on duty every day in July and August and at weekends in June and September.

At the east end of the beach there is a path along the cliffs that leads to a series of smaller, scenic sandy bays. While the walk to the end isn't very long there is a spectacular sea cave worth seeking out. Only accessible at low water, it's a dark, deep and damp cavern, hidden until you're at the mouth. We'll leave you to explore and find it yourself.

The Sauna Snugg operates at the beach and can take up to ten people (thesaunasnugg.com).

GARRETSTOWN

Just west of Garrylucas is another Blue Flag beach, Garretstown (51.6438, -8.5787). It's possible to walk between the two beaches at low tide. There is a lifeguard on duty at the beach every day in July and August and at weekends in June and September.

If the sauna at Garrylucas is booked up there's a second option here, which can take up to six people (wildwellness.ie).

Garretstown is popular with beginner surfers in both summer and winter. If you plan on taking to the water, be wary of the wooden posts in the sand, which are submerged at high tide. G Town Surf School (surfgtown.com) rents boards, offers lessons and

Cliff jumping, Seven Heads | RC

Courtmacsherry Woods | RC

runs coasteering trips during the summer. Manning's Caravan Park (fb.com/ManningsCaravanPark) is located between the two beaches and is open during the summer. Garretstown House Holiday Park (garrettstownhouse.com) is another campsite based around an 18th century mansion, just 1km north of the beach (51.6532, -8.5909).

COOLMAIN STRAND
The fine sandy shoreline, also known as Harbour View Beach, makes for a decent walk, with plenty of opportunities for birdwatching. There is a carpark on the western end of the beach (51.6486, -8.6794).

TIMOLEAGUE
Timoleague is a quiet town with pubs, restaurants and a few B&Bs. Dominating the village is the 13th century Franciscan abbey. The mudflats between Timoleague and Courtmacsherry are a good place for birdwatching, particularly during the winter when thousands of shorebirds feed in the estuary at low tide.

There is a pleasant 5km stroll along the path of the old railway line that used to link Timoleague to Courtmacsherry.

SEVEN HEADS PENINSULA
West of Timoleague the Wild Atlantic Way stays inland, heading directly to Clonakilty, bypassing the Seven Heads Peninsula. This is a pity as the peninsula is a compact area of quiet, rural countryside with a beautiful coast. It's a wonderful place to walk or cycle, and there are sheltered bays for swimming, rock-pooling, snorkelling and kayaking.

COURTMACSHERRY
A leg of the Wild Atlantic Way runs out to the attractive village of Courtmacsherry which has a few pubs, a safe beach and hosts a family festival every August.

FUCHSIA WALK
A very pleasant trail taking in woodland, coastal paths, farmland and rural roads. Do it during mid-May to see the bluebells and wild garlic carpeting Courtmacsherry Woods.

Start in the carpark at the beach (51.6359, -8.6974). There is a track running parallel to the shore just above the carpark. Follow this to the woods and keep on the path until you come out into the open again at Wood Point. The path contours along the shore with great views over to the Old Head of Kinsale. Pass through a number of fields and a small conifer wood until you reach a pleasant, narrow lane with high hedges on each side that almost join at the top. Follow this tunnel to the road and take a left. At the next crossroads (51.6285, -8.7030) a right brings you back to the main road into Courtmacsherry and onwards to the carpark.

Inchydoney | RC

WEST CORK MARKETS
Most of the bigger towns hold weekly markets, some of which are listed below.

KINSALE
Wednesday, 09:30-14:30, The Temperance Hall.

CLONAKILTY
Friday, 09:00-14:00, Recorder's Alley.

SKIBBEREEN
Saturday, 09:30-14:00 at The Fairfield.

SCHULL
Sunday, 09:30-14:00 (Easter to the end of September and Christmas), Pier Road carpark.

KILCROHANE (SHEEP'S HEAD)
Sunday, 11:00-14:00 (Easter to the end of September), Village Square.

BANTRY
Friday, 09:30-13:00, Town Square.

CASTLETOWNBERE
First Thursday of each month and every Thursday in summer, 09:00-14:30, Town Square.

For a longer option take a left at the crossroads, down to Broadstrand and walk the beach.

BROADSTRAND
A nice beach and a sheltered place for kayaking. For those who want a longer paddle there are a few smaller bays to the north and another beach (Blind Strand) around the headland to the south. From Courtmacsherry take the road south towards Barryroe. After a tight bend in the woods take the second left and follow the road to a small carpark (51.6214, -8.7016).

SEVEN HEADS WAY
The 42km Seven Heads Way follows the coast from Timoleague, through Courtmacsherry and around to Dunworly. Follow the trail over a couple of days or incorporate a section of it into a shorter loop. More information is available on sevenheadspeninsula.ie.

SEVEN HEADS BAY
On calm days this bay is a great spot for rock pooling, swimming and to launch a kayak and explore the coast (51.5913, -8.7057). There are caves and gullies at the southern end while the north coast of the bay has a sandy beach when the tide is out, and more caves. The Coolim Cliffs are just a bit further north and are also worth a look. The beach below the huge cliffs is only accessible by boat.

DUNWORLY
There are two beaches in Dunworly Bay, both signposted from Barryroe. The first is near the castle ruin set back from the road (51.5931, -8.7591). At low tide there is plenty of sand, however it's usually a little too shallow for swimming.

The second is a little further south and has plenty of parking (51.5836, -8.7514). It's covered at high tide but low water leaves a brilliant sandy beach. There are plenty of caves and rock pools and it's a good swimming spot, although the waves can be powerful.

Element Wellness (elementwellness.ie) operate a mobile sauna in the area.

CLONAKILTY
The town of Clonakilty is world famous for its black pudding but it's also home to DeBarra's Bar. This legendary pub is one of the best live music venues in Ireland.

INCHYDONEY
Inchydoney is renowned for its luxury hotel and the its pair of Blue Flag beaches (51.5970, -8.8625). It's a good surfing spot, with beginner friendly waves for the most part, though watch out for rip tides. There is a surf school (inchydoneysurfschool.com) renting boards and offering lessons, and the Recovery Pod Sauna is a great place to warm up after a surf or a swim (therecoverypods.com). A lifeguard is on duty

Winter at Long Strand | RC

every day in July and August and at weekends in June and September. There is plenty of parking just below the hotel.

CLONAKILTY TO ROSSCARBERY

The next section of the Wild Atlantic Way takes you close to the iconic lighthouse at Galley Head and has some nice beaches.

BEACHES

As you travel west from Clonakilty on the Wild Atlantic Way the coast becomes indented with small bays. For the most part these are sheltered, safe and secluded coves, ideal for anyone looking for some peace and quiet. Look out for Duneen Bay just beside the road (*51.5794, -8.8734*). Further along the road Dunnycove Bay (*51.5589, -8.8932*) and Sands Cove (*51.5527, -8.8985*) are signposted to the left.

The first large beach is Red Strand, a great place for a swim with a lifeguard in the summer (*51.5482, -8.9270*). It has a Green Coast award.

Galley Head is the prominent lighthouse in the distance. The first light was built there in 1875. It's only possible to go as far as the main gates, where there is a good view (*51.5350, -8.9517*). The lighthouse itself is available as self-catering accommodation (greatlighthouses.com).

LONG STRAND

Long Strand is a superb stretch of beach with high dunes behind and often wild surf eating into the soft shoreline. Swimming is not recommended but surfers sometimes take to the waves here (see the photo on page 32).

The Fish Basket Restaurant opens seasonally at the west end of the beach (thefishbasket.ie).

There is also a very enjoyable 5km loop walk to be had from the carpark at the western end (*51.5607, -8.9764*). Start by walking east along the beach. At the river turn left and follow the road to an attractive stone cottage. Take the rougher road past this house, along a pleasant track that hugs the shore of Kilkeran Lake. On meeting the road again head straight past another stone house and take a left into the woods at the sign for Castlefreke. The track eventually ends at a barrier, where you gain the main road again, until the next large layby on the left. Re-enter the woods for a short walk back to the carpark, not before a great vista of the beach where the track leaves the woods.

OWNAHINCHA AND ROSSCARBERY

Further west are two more beaches, Ownahincha (*51.5671, -9.0010*) which has a Blue Flag and Rosscarbery (*51.5659, -9.0143*). Both are worth a visit, though they can get busy. It's possible to walk the clifftop path that joins them.

Drombeg Stone Circle | RC

The estuary behind the beach at Rosscarbery is another good place for birdwatching. There is a lifeguard daily in July and August and at weekends in June and September at Rosscarbery.

Surf n SUP (surfnsup.ie) offer surf camps, lessons and rentals here, and the Better Dayz Sauna (betterdayzsauna.as.me) is here also.

DROMBEG STONE CIRCLE
West of Rosscarbery is Drombeg Stone Circle (*51.5659, -9.0864*). On the winter solstice the setting sun passes through the portal stones of this ancient monument before dipping below a notch in the hills.

GLANDORE HARBOUR
The Wild Atlantic Way bypasses the intricate coastline west of the villages of Glandore and Union Hall, but those with a wandering mind will find plenty of interest in this area. The OSI map (sheet 89) will guide you to little bays such as Carrigillihy, Squince Harbour (a good place to embark on the short kayaking trip to the beautiful Rabbit Island) and Blind Harbour. There are a half dozen walks described at unionhall.ie.

RINNEEN WOODS
This small woodland hugs the shores at The Narrows, a long inlet. A local artist has built fairy houses in the trees, giving the place a mystical feel. Wear boots as the trail can be muddy. From the church outside Union Hall follow the twisting hilly road to Skibbereen as far as the large layby on the left (*51.5518, -9.1704*).

CASTLETOWNSHEND
Built up around the 17th century castle, this attractive village retains an air of old England about it. Nearby are some small beaches (Tracarta Strand and Sandy Cove) and historic megalithic monuments including Gurranes Stone Row (*51.5308, -9.1905*) and Knockdrum Stone Fort (*51.5266, -9.1937*).

A local guide offers history walks and sunrise swim and breakfast tours nearby - see gormu.com.

TOE HEAD
Toe Head is the most prominent headland in the area, rising high above its surroundings. The view from the top is wide ranging and it's a good place to spot whales and dolphins when the sea is calm. Not far from the headland are two stony beaches which might not be the prettiest West Cork has to offer, but are pleasant and safe for bathing.

TRAGUMNA
A little west of Toe Head is the Blue Flag beach of Tragumna (*51.5029, -9.2652*). A safe and enjoyable swimming spot, there is a lifeguard every day in July and August and at weekends in June and September.

Gurranes Stone Row | RC

Humpback Whale | RC

Sea Kayaking, Castletownshend | RC

Castlefreke Castle | RC

WILDLIFE TOURS
Calvin Jones of Ireland's Wildlife (irelandswildlife.com) offers personalised, guided tours on the wildlife of West Cork. Covering animals and plants of all shapes and sizes there is plenty to be seen and even seemingly boring, common species can be full of interest once you learn about them and their habitats.

CYCLE WEST CORK
Cycle West Cork (cyclewestcork.com) offer guided bike tours of West Cork, from 3 to 7 nights, with accommodation and luggage transfer provided. Itineraries can be tailored to the group, but usually take in the major towns, as well as some of the more popular sights along the coast.

SEA KAYAKING
West Cork is full of sheltered bays and inlets, as well as more remote islands and headlands that are best seen from a boat, or even better, a kayak.
 Atlantic Sea Kayaking (atlanticseakayaking.com) offer trips to suit all tastes and abilities. From multi-day excursions taking in the best of West Cork, to half-day taster sessions there's something for everybody. The night trips are hugely popular; at the right time of year (usually spring and autumn) the water is full of bioluminescent plankton that sparkles with every paddle stroke. It is something that everyone should experience at some stage.
 H20 Sea Kayaking (h2oseakayaking.com) offer half and full day sea kayaking tours in the area surrounding Kinsale and beyond. They also teach paddling skills for those looking to improve.

WHALE AND DOLPHIN WATCHING
Unbeknownst to most people, the coast of Cork has some of the best whale watching in Europe. In the right season you can see fin whales (second in size only to the blue whale), humpback whales and minke whales, sometimes all on the same day. Various dolphin species, harbour porpoise, grey seals, and basking sharks are often seen too, as are many different species of seabird, and of course, the fantastic West Cork coastline.
 There are a number of whale watch operators based in West Cork. In Courtmacsherry try Atlantic Whale and Wildlife Tours (atlanticwhaleandwildlifetours.com), and a bit further west Cork Whale Watch (corkwhalewatch.com) sails from Reen Pier, near Union Hall (51.5320, -9.1656). Other operators are based out of Baltimore, see page 54 for details.

Toe Head | RC

SKIBBEREEN
Every year at the end of July this bustling town hosts the Skibbereen Arts Festival, which includes community based projects as well as national and international films, theatre, visual art and music.

The Skibbereen Heritage Centre has two excellent permanent exhibitions - on the history of the Famine and the ecology of nearby Lough Hyne. See skibbheritage.com for details including opening times.

ILEN RIVER BLUEWAY
The Ilen River connects Skibbereen to Baltimore and the recently developed blueway encourages people to paddle between the two towns on this historic route. The blueway is divided into three sections, each progressively more challenging than the last, though in good conditions and at the right tides it's a pleasant trip that almost everybody can enjoy. See skibbereen.ie for more information.

CYCLING
The town is the start and finish point for three signposted cycling routes through some of the nicest parts of the surrounding countryside. The routes are 24km, 35km and 46km, offering something for all fitness levels, see irishtrails.ie for detailed maps.

LISS ARD ESTATE
A little outside of town is the 80 hectare Liss Ard Estate (lissardestate.ie). While the accommodation may be a little upmarket for most travellers the gardens have become quite famous for the landscape installation by James Turrell known as The Crater. The centre of this giant crater has a 'Vault Purchase' where visitors can to lie on their back and gaze up at the sky. The gardens are free but The Crater is viewed by appointment only and there is a small fee.

From Skibbereen take the R569 towards Castletownshend. The estate is 1km down this road on the right (*51.5301, -9.2537*).

LOUGH HYNE
Lough Hyne is an unusual saltwater lake south of Skibbereen (*51.5061, -9.3036*). Its wildlife has attracted academics for over 100 years and in 1981 it was designated as Ireland's first marine sanctuary. It's impressively deep and a popular spot with divers (a permit is required). There is great snorkelling on the edges of the lake, where the steep walls are plastered with marine life.

Knockomagh Hill looms over the lake to the north and a pleasant woodland path leads to the summit, which has great views over the attractive West Cork coastline. From Skibbereen, head west along the Wild Atlantic Way towards Baltimore. There is a left turn for Lough Hyne 3km from the edge of town. ∎

Mountain Forge Escape | Mountain Forge Escape

KINSALE TO SKIBBEREEN
ACCOMMODATION

BALLINADEE BUS, KINSALE
51.7060, -8.6341
ballinadeebus.com
This 50 hectare family farm a short distance west of Kinsale is home to a pair of converted double-decker buses. Each bus sleeps six. The farm also has a number of rescue animals and a coffee truck that serves hot drinks and sweet treats.

NESBITT, BALLINSPITTLE
airbnb.ie/rooms/26257743
This 12m boat is enjoying a second life as cosy accommodation for two in a private garden, with donkeys for company. It is within walking distance of Ballinspittle village and a five minute drive from Garretstown beach.

SHEPHERD'S HUT, KILBRITTAIN
airbnb.ie/rooms/910646479580902286
This beautifully decorated wagon sleeps two. Set in a verdant garden with Coolmaine Bay a five minute walk away.

MOUNTAIN FORGE ESCAPE, ARDFIELD
51.5797, -8.9044
mountainescape.ie
This site near Ardfield village has pitches for tents, caravans and campers as well as a geodesic dome, a bell tent and a pod. On-site facilities include a playground, cafe and fire pit. Only a five minute drive from Duneen Bay beach.

THE LONG STRAND NESTS
airbnb.ie/rooms/1200431256842981080
This distinctive cedar-clad chalet is divided into two brightly decorated self-contained units (each sleeps 4). Right on the coast there are great views over the beach and Galley Head Lighthouse from the veranda. Just opposite is the Fish Basket (thefishbasket.ie) which serves locally sourced fish and chips.

HIDEAWAY, ROSSCARBERY
airbnb.ie/rooms/23022567
A peaceful private room near Rosscarbery, on a beautiful site. No kitchen facilities, but there is a gorgeous garden to enjoy with a stream running through. Sleeps up to three, and pets are welcome.

The Speckled Door | RC

KINSALE TO SKIBBEREEN
FOOD

KINSALE FOOD TRUCKS
51.6945, -8.5284
Kinsale has plenty of food options to suit all budgets, and this being a fishing village means there's lots of good seafood on offer. If you'd rather escape the crowds head a little west of town, where there are a number of roadside food trucks at the bridge over the Bandon River. From coffee to fish and chips there's plenty on offer, and it's a nice place to sit and eat by the water when the weather is fine.

THE SPECKLED DOOR, OLD HEAD
51.6397, -8.5506
This pub restaurant is well-loved by those who know it and for good reason. The food is great and the views from the back room and beer garden are hard to beat.

MONK'S LANE, TIMOLEAGUE
monkslane.ie
51.6437, -8.7658
One for the foodies. This higher-end restaurant draws crowds from far and wide to the quiet village of Timoleague. Even the seating and setting, both indoors and out, is charming.

CONNOLLY'S OF LEAP
51.5809, -9.1438
connollysofleap.com
A legendary pub and live music venue that reopened its doors in 2015, and nowadays serves superb pizza, alongside a range of craft beers. Definitely one to keep an eye on if you're into music, this being a standard venue for bands touring Ireland.

KALBO'S CAFE, SKIBBEREEN
51.5499, -9.2656
kalbos.ie
Beautiful lunches and sweet treats, with much of the produce coming directly from the owners' own organic farm.
There's also an online takeaway option for those who'd like to order ahead of arrival, and plenty of indoor seating for brunch and lunch. Just make sure to check opening hours ahead of time.

BALTIMORE TO MIZEN

Looking at a map of West Cork it's easy to imagine the peninsula that once struck southwest from Baltimore, now divided by the sea into the islands of Roaringwater Bay. These islands are havens from the rest of the world, some still inhabited and some long abandoned, but all are peaceful and ideal for those looking to get away from the busy pace of city life. The remotest of the islands, Fastnet Rock, lies over 10km from the closest point on the mainland.

To the north is the Mizen Peninsula, the southernmost of the five fingers of land that make up the southwest of Ireland. Indeed Mizen Head itself is the most southwesterly tip of the country. Here the landscape is wilder; more mountainous and craggier, and the coast is more exposed to the power of the Atlantic.

RINGAROGY ISLAND

Though connected to the mainland by a bridge this small island feels as remote as many of the true offshore islands around the Irish coast. There is little to do here but walk, but what walking there is to do! The roads are quiet and the hedges luxuriant in the summer months, making it a fine place for an easy evening stroll or a short cycle from Baltimore.

Coming from Skibbereen along the Wild Atlantic Way turn right at the sign (*51.5063, -9.3507*) for Beacon Designs.

BALTIMORE AND THE ISLANDS

In the summer Baltimore is a busy seaside hub, with ferries to Sherkin and Cape Clear coming and going amongst the many yachts, fishing charters and sailing dinghies. Every May the village hosts a world famous Fiddle Fair (fiddlefair.com).

There are also plenty of water-based activities on offer, a few of which are listed below:

- Snorkelling, diving aquaventures.ie
- Diving baltimorediving.com
- Whale watching whalewatchwestcork.com and baltimoreseasafari.ie

There is a nice, short walk out to the Baltimore Beacon on the western end of town (*51.4746, -9.3864*). This unusual structure was built in 1849 to act as a marker for Baltimore Harbour to passing ships. The view out to Sherkin and Cape Clear is one of the classic vistas of West Cork.

Baltimore Beacon | Denis Dineen

SHERKIN ISLAND
This beautiful island is only 15 minutes by ferry from Baltimore. Upon arrival you can't miss the impressive Abbey, built all the way back in 1460. It's possible to traverse all the roads in a day and visit the two biggest beaches, Silver Strand (*51.4740, -9.4235*), which has a Green Coast award, and Trabawn (*51.4654, -9.4258*). Both beaches rank among the nicest in West Cork, offering safe swimming and good snorkelling in fine weather.

There isn't a shop on the island, but you can get food and drink at The Jolly Roger (the local pub) or Sherkin House (the hotel) while you wait for the ferry back to reality.

There is a hostel on the island, Sherkin North Shore (sherkinnorthshore.com), which provides accommodation in a relaxing setting (*51.4778, -9.4253*). The ferry runs all year round, but is more frequent in the summer (sherkinisland.ie).

CAPE CLEAR
Cape Clear (or Clear Island on some maps) is one of only two Gaeltacht areas (an area where Irish is the main language) in County Cork. The rugged island is well worth a few days of exploration. The Bird Observatory (*51.4413, -9.5059*) is world famous and provides accommodation for nature lovers.

The coastal walking is superb, with the high cliffs either side of the South Harbour providing great sea views. There are two impressive sea arches, one east of the harbour at Pointanbullig, the other to the west at Blananarragaun.

There are two signposted walks on the island which start from the shop: the 4km Cnoicín's Loop (green arrows) and the 7km Gleann Loop (red arrows).

Also worth visiting are the Cape Clear and Fastnet Rock Heritage Centre, the goat farm which produces ice cream, and the disused lighthouse that was built too high up and is often obscured by fog. There are plenty of historic monuments and two pubs, a generous number for a relatively small community.

The ferry runs daily from Baltimore and seasonally from Schull. See capeclearferries.com and schullferry.com for timetables.

FASTNET ROCK
Fastnet Rock is the most southerly point of land in Ireland and sees few visitors. The lonely outcrop was known locally as the Teardrop of Ireland, as the lighthouse was often the last bit of Ireland emigrants would see on the long boat trip to America. The current lighthouse is one of the best designed in the world.

The first lighthouse was built in the 1850s, but it wasn't considered sound enough. The current tower is built of Cornish granite and was an incredible feat of engineering. Construction began in 1899 in England. The 2,074 numbered blocks (weighing up

Sherkin Island | RC

to 3 tons each) were assembled, then disassembled and brought to Ireland. Satisfied that the feat could be repeated, the tower was reconstructed on Fastnet Rock. The whole project took five years and, surprisingly, nobody died in the process.

It's possible to take a boat out to get a close look at Fastnet, and marvel at what a feat of engineering it was to build a lighthouse in such an exposed place. See fastnettour.com for more information on trips from Baltimore and schullferry.com for trips from Schull.

HEIR ISLAND

Tucked into the eastern end of Roaringwater Bay is Heir Island, a small, pleasing little world of its own. It's worth a trip over in the summer to see the hedges in full bloom and to explore the little beaches and bays. There is plenty of accommodation and even a very well regarded restaurant (islandcottage.com), which offers cookery classes as well as excellent food.

The ferry runs from Cunnamore (51.5041, -9.4249) which is signposted off the Wild Atlantic Way at Church Cross, between Skibbereen and Ballydehob. For a timetable see heirislandferries.com.

BALLYDEHOB

At the gateway to the Mizen Peninsula stands this village, notable for its twelve arch railway bridge. Three signposted walks along quiet back roads start and finish at the eastern end of town beside the river (51.5622, -9.4580). As most of the trails follow roads it's also possible to cycle them.

SCHULL

With the imposing bulk of Mount Gabriel looming above the town it might seem as though Schull was named after the cranial appearance of the hill behind it. The Irish name, An Scoil (The School) or Scoil Mhuire (Mary's School) gives a better hint at the source of the name; the town was built on the site of a medieval monastic school, of which no trace remains.

Five signposted walking trails explore the town's surroundings, all starting from the main carpark (51.5269, -9.5441).

The town has an upmarket vibe, and there is a gourmet food market held every Sunday, and numerous sailing schools.

Just east of the town is a small Green Coast beach, known as Cadogan's Strand (51.5302, -9.5343).

South of the harbour are many pleasant islands. On a calm day a competent kayaker could easily visit some of these, where they will find solitude, shoreline exploration and pleasant camping. Castle Island and East Skeam are particularly attractive, as are the Calf Islands, though they are further out in the bay.

MOUNT GABRIEL

Copper was mined extensively on this hill behind Schull as far back as the Bronze Age. These days, the

Crookhaven | RC

Cape Clear | RC

Ballyrisode | RC

Toormore Wedge Tomb | RC

main industrial action on the mountain is the collection of air traffic information in the two massive radar domes on the summit.

A pleasant cycle does a circuit around Mount Gabriel, and masochists will enjoy the tough climb to the top (the lazier among us can drive to the summit) where there are unrivalled views of Ireland's southwest.

Heading west from Schull take the second right opposite a blue farmhouse (*51.5279, -9.5795*) and follow this road around the north slopes of the mountain. Another right past the road to the summit will take you back to Schull through Barnancleeve, a tight gap between hills that frames a great view of Roaringwater Bay.

TOORMORE

A little west of Schull is the Toormore Altar Wedge Tomb, built over two thousand years ago (*51.5138, -9.6437*). It is well signposted just off the road, with nice views to the distant hills of Mizen.

On the other side of Toormore Bay is Ballyrisode Beach, a gorgeous strand with woodland behind and clear water before you (*51.5111, -9.6622*). The Green Coast beach is signposted off the Wild Atlantic Way between Schull and Goleen. The carpark is at the second of the two beaches. The road is quite narrow, so please park considerately if the carpark is full.

CROOKHAVEN

The protected harbour at Crookhaven has been used by ships seeking shelter for a long time. White Strand is a pleasant beach at the back of the harbour, and is a good place to launch a kayak to get a sea level perspective of the area (*51.4632, -9.7512*).

Just a stone's throw to the south is the Green Coast beach at Galley Cove (*51.4616, -9.7443*). It is a pleasant walk from the Cove to Brow Head, the most southerly point of mainland Ireland, where there are great views of the West Cork coast. At the summit is a Napoleonic watchtower from the early 19th century and the remains of a telegraph station from the early 20th century.

CORK

Barleycove | RC

BARLEYCOVE
A favourite among West Cork visitors and locals, Barleycove's popularity is easy to understand (*51.4685, -9.7790*). Its gorgeous Blue Flag beach is surrounded by gentle hills on three sides, offering shelter on nice summer's days and funnelling the southwesterly wind during storms.

During the summer a floating pontoon stretches across the channel that connects Lissagriffin Lake with the sea, allowing easy access to the beach from the public carpark (*51.4732, -9.7678*).

There are lifeguards and a surf school during the summer months (barleycovesurfcamp.com).

MIZEN HEAD
Mizen Head is the southwestern tip of Ireland, and well worth a trip to experience its 'edge of the world' setting. There is a visitor centre (*51.4515, -9.8110*) with a cafe, and a footbridge leads across the impressive steep-sided chasm to the lighthouse. In the summer the centre is open daily and between November and mid-March it only opens at weekends. The small entry fee is well worth it for the views of the outrageous cliffs from the footbridge and the very informative local history exhibits. During winter storms the carpark is a good place to watch the heaving sea.

DUNLOUGH
A little north of Mizen Head is Dunlough Bay and Three Castle Head. There is a car park just above the small pier (*51.4790, -9.8151*) and it's possible to walk across the private land to admire the coastline and castle at Dunlough. The cliffs are over 100m high in places and this must have been a dizzying place to live back in the 15th century when the castle was built.

MIZEN NORTH SHORE
The north coast of Mizen is much quieter than the southern one. Following the signposted coast road from Barleycove (*51.4804, -9.7627*) will take you along a beautiful, open road with the sea to the left and the hills to your right. Though hilly, it's ideal for the cyclist. Equipped with a map, it is quite easy to concoct a loop linking the north and south shores.

There are two small piers along this stretch of coast that are worth a visit for a quick swim or a quiet picnic; Toor Pier (*51.4938, -9.8020*) and Gortdubh Pier (*51.5251, -9.7302*). Both are at the ends of narrow, hilly, winding roads, and so are better suited to smaller vehicles. ■

Mizen Head Cliffs | Seán Murray

Cape Clear Yurts | RC

BALTIMORE TO MIZEN
ACCOMMODATION

CAPE CLEAR YURTS
51.4347, -9.4995
chleire-haven.com
Cape Clear's campsite caters for those carrying their own gear, but also has a number of beautiful yurts available. The location is stunning too, overlooking the South Harbour.

THE BARN, BALLYDEHOB
airbnb.ie/rooms/43502442
This converted barn is a 15 minute walk outside the village of Ballydehob. The barn, with its distinctive rusty corrugated roof, has a double bed and sleeping loft with room for five in total. There are also two handmade teardrop trailers that each sleep two.

GOLEEN GLAMPING
51.4964, -9.7037
goleenharbour.ie
A campsite with a lot to offer. Pitch your own tent or stay in one their fancy bell tents, cabins or geodesic domes. The site has a hot tub and work is underway on a sauna. The associated organic farm supplies local eateries with fresh vegetables, apples and honey, with the option for guests to buy direct too. A variety of land and sea based experiences are also available.

THE CABIN, SCHULL
airbnb.ie/rooms/52714535
An instantly Instragrammable cabin for two, with double bed, kitchen and bathroom.

COWSHED, GOLEEN
airbnb.ie/rooms/1174570348640224586
These tastefully restored 19th century cowsheds sleep six across three bedrooms and have full kitchen facilities, living room and a nice outdoor eating area. Minimum seven night stays, makes an ideal base for the Mizen area.

DUNBEACON CAMPING AND GLAMPING
51.5966, -9.5707
dunbeaconcampsite.ie
A traditional campsite for tents and vans on the northern coast of the Mizen. There are also the fancier options of tipis, a safari tent atop an old Land Rover and a bell tent (all of which can sleep up to four people).

The Algiers, Baltimore | The Algiers

BALTIMORE TO MIZEN
FOOD

THE ALGIERS, BALTIMORE
51.4834, -9.3726
thealgiersinn.ie
One of a few good pubs in this tiny seaside village, the menu here is particularly good. The chefs have over thirty years of travel and cooking experience, bringing influences from California, Mexico and Thailand together with local West Cork produce to create great food.

HUDSON'S WHOLEFOODS, BALLYDEHOB
51.5628, -9.4601
A health food shop and wholesome cafe, with great alternative options. Well known locally for its famous pasties, these savoury bakes are filled with delicious combinations.

SCHULL STREET KITCHEN
51.5262, -9.5453
instagram.com/schull_street_kitchen
A bougie food truck with a very different kind of menu. Choose from both meat and veggie burgers, jerk chicken, lobster rolls and haloumi wraps, among other offerings. Gluten free options and fine side dishes make this a place worth seeking out if you're in Schull.

THE WILD WEST BAR, GOLEEN
51.4950, -9.7113
Great pub grub makes this a good spot to call in to for a feed of food before a feed of pints.

CROOKHAVEN PUBS
51.4691, -9.7248
There are three bars in Crookhaven, all of which serve food. The Crookhaven Inn and O'Sullivan's have good standard fare, Nottage's is a little fancier. No matter which you choose the waterside location is excellent.

BARLEYCOVE BEACH BAR AND RESTAURANT
51.4697, -9.7812
barleycovebeachhotel.com
This bar and restaurant is stunningly situated above one of West Cork's most spectacular beaches. And there is a large outdoor deck from which to enjoy the view if you're lucky enough to visit during fine weather. Both the lunch and dinner options are excellent and more reasonably priced than you'd expect for what feels like fine dining.

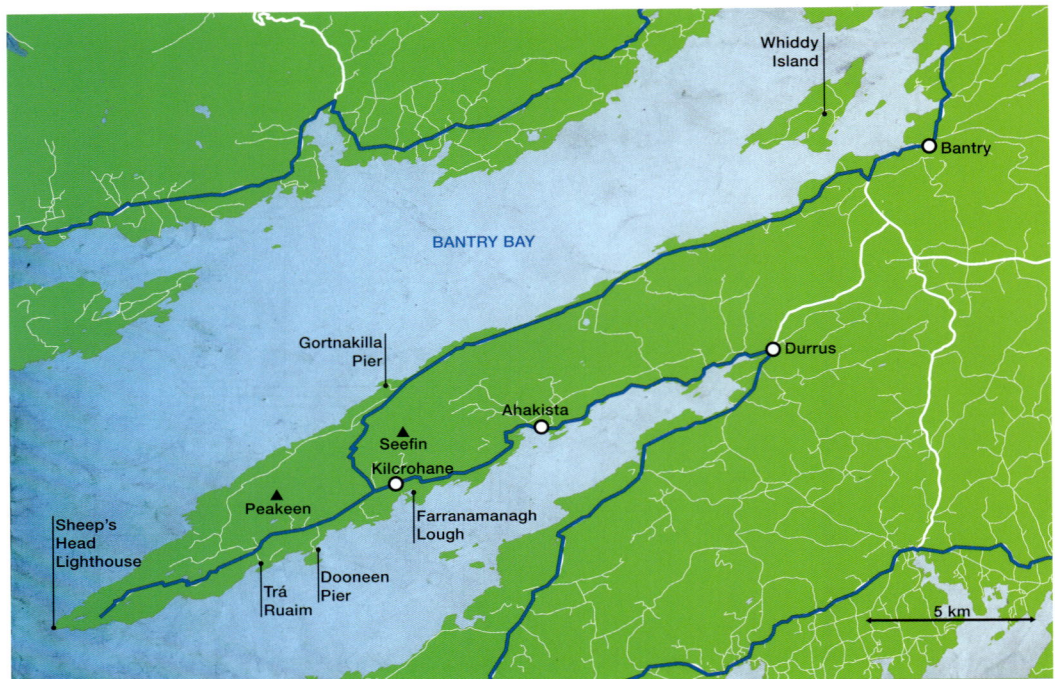

SHEEP'S HEAD AND BANTRY

Sheep's Head is the slender finger of land that stretches out to sea between the Beara and Mizen peninsulas. Only 25km long and never much more than 3km wide, it's a quiet place, perfect for hikers.

There are a large number of signposted walks through the low hills that form the spine of the peninsula. Not every walk has been included but there should be more than enough to keep all but the most avid walkers occupied for a few days.

Its largely traffic-free roads are also well suited to cycling.

See thesheepsheadway.ie for details of all the walking and cycling routes on the peninsula, including The Sheep's Head Way, a multi-day 175km walking route around the peninsula.

DURRUS
The pretty village of Durrus straddles the Mizen and Sheep's Head peninsulas. It is probably best known for the soft cheese that is made locally - Durrus Farmhouse Cheese.

AHAKISTA
This tiny village lies right on the sheltered shores of Dunmanus Bay (*51.6000, -9.6324*). It's a popular stop with the sailing fraternity and every August bank holiday weekend it hosts the Ahakista Regatta.

It's also the starting point for four worthwhile walks: the 4.7km (each way) Mass Path Linear Walk (black arrows), the 9km Barán Loop (green arrows), the 12.1km Seefin Loop (blue arrows) and the 15.4km Glanlough Loop (purple arrows).

The recently restored Ahakista stone circle (*51.5985, -9.6444*) is well worth visiting on the hillside above the village.

KILCROHANE
The small village has a few shops and pubs as well as plenty of self-catering and B&B accommodation. Every Easter weekend it hosts a traditional music festival.

Two walks start from the village: the 3.6km Funeral Path Loop (purple arrows) and the 6km Farranamanagh Loop (red arrows).

DOONEEN PIER
This sheltered harbour has a Green Coast award and is ideal for swimming. It's also a popular place to fish for mackerel and pollock (*51.5636, -9.7305*). Look out for the signposted left turn 2km west of Kilcrohane.

Gortnakilla | RC

BLACK GATE WALKS
There are two loop walks between Kilcrohane and the end of Sheep's Head. They start at the long two-storey stone building on the left hand side of the road about 4km west of Kilcrohane (*51.5647, -9.7567*). They are the 5.6km Caher Loop (green arrows) and 8.4km Cahergal Loop (purple arrows).

SHEEP'S HEAD LIGHTHOUSE
This tiny lighthouse lies in a wild setting at the very end of the peninsula. Accessed via a series of steep steps it offers some wonderful views - to the north is Bantry Bay with Beara beyond, and to the south is Mizen Head and Dunmanus Bay.

The road ends about 2km from the lighthouse, at a cafe, Bernie's Cupan Tae, which opens in summer (*51.5458, -9.8265*). Even though the views from the cafe are brilliant, it's highly recommended that you go the extra mile (literally).

LIGHTHOUSE LOOP
From the carpark follow the well-worn path past Lough Akeen to the lighthouse. The 4.2km loop (blue arrows) returns along a rough track on the north side of the peninsula. If you are looking for a shorter walk then you can just retrace your steps back to the carpark. Note dogs aren't allowed.

POET'S WAY LOOP
A longer (12.4km) version of the Lighthouse Loop that continues further up the spectacular north coast before returning to the carpark via a track along the south coast. Follow the red arrows.

SEEFIN AND PEAKEEN
From Kilcrohane a narrow road, known locally as the Goat's Path, leads over the hills to the north side of the peninsula. At its high point is a carpark with panoramic views (*51.5952, -9.711*).

To the east is Seefin, the highest point of the peninsula at 345m. There are a number of hills named Seefin in Ireland, the name coming from the Irish for the Seat of Fionn. Fionn Mac Cumhaill was the leader of a mythical band of warriors in ancient Ireland and these lookout posts must have been of great interest to him and his men.

PEAKEEN RIDGE WALKS
A 5.5km linear walk traverses west along the spine of the Sheep's Head, starting from the carpark. Decent footwear is recommended as this walk crosses open mountainside and can be wet underfoot. Follow the cream arrows along the ridge to the townland of Letter West. Return by the same route or have a pick up arranged.

There is also a loop walk which may be more suitable for those without a car shuttle, the 11km

Stone waymarker on the north coast | RC

Peakeen Ridge Loop (red arrows). See irishtrails.ie for details.

BEACHES
Unfortunately Sheep's Head doesn't have many beaches of note, which may be why it stays relatively quiet during the summer when other nearby areas are busy.

The strand at Farranamanagh Lough (*51.5802, -9.6911*), just outside Kilcrohane, is rocky but pleasant, and there is another beach at Trá Ruaim (*51.5600, -9.7558*). Both of these beaches are probably more suited to launching a kayak than sunbathing, provided it's calm enough.

There is an impressive puffing hole on the coast close to Trá Ruaim, and there are also a few popular shore fishing spots in this area.

On the north coast of the peninsula is the small, quiet pier at Gortnakilla (*51.5695, -9.7864*). Again, there's no beach, but it's a good place to set out kayaking from, or to head to if you're looking for easy access for a swim, provided it's calm of course. It's also a peaceful place to park up in a van for the night, and the coast beyond the slipway is a great place to wander.

BANTRY BAY
Bantry is a bustling town with all the facilities you might want, with pubs, restaurants, hotels and tourist information. Bantry House (bantryhouse.com) is an elegant 18th century mansion turned B&B (*51.6771, -9.4654*). The beautiful formal gardens that extend across seven terraces are well worth a visit.

It's also possible to go horse riding with Bantry Pony Trekking. See bantrybayponytrekking.com.

BLUEWAY
There are three kayak trails in the Bay. The trails, which start from the pier in Bantry (*51.6806, -9.4618*), are 2km, 6km and 9km in length. The two longer trails cross over to Whiddy Island. Download the excellent pocket guide from bantrybayport.com/pocket_guide.

WHIDDY ISLAND
Not far off the coast from Bantry is the unassuming Whiddy Island. It's a quiet place, with one pub, some self-catering accommodation, a 5km walking trail, and bike hire available on the island.

The Ocean Star III, which operates daily from Bantry Pier, offers guided tours of the harbour as well as crossings to the island. See whiddy.ie for a timetable and more information about the island.

Sheep's Head Lighthouse | RC

Walking the Sheep's Head Way | RC

Dooneen sunset | Patricia Ronan

GUIDED WALKS
Charlie McCarthy is a registered guide and historian and operates a B&B, offering walking and accommodation packages. See seamountfarm.com for more.

CYCLING
The 120km Sheep's Head Cycle Route flanks the north and south shores of the peninsula and is an excellent way to explore this quiet coastline. It is poorly signposted but the OSI maps of the area (85 and 88) show the route. A few roads link the north and south sides of the peninsula so it's easy to make shorter loops. Be warned, it's hilly! Nigel's Bike Shop in Bantry rents bicycles.

WATERSPORTS
Based in Ahakista, Carbery Sailing (carberysailing.com) offer full, half day and evening trips. The sheltered waters of Dunmanus Bay are a great place for kayaking. Based in Durrus, Darren's Kayaks (darrenskayaks.com) offer trips and tuition.

Goat's Path Pod Park | Goat's Path Pod Park

SHEEP'S HEAD AND BANTRY
ACCOMMODATION

PINEWOOD COTTAGE, KILCROHANE
airbnb.ie/rooms/32534694

This beautiful stone farmhouse has been restored with a bright and comfortable interior and is suitable for larger groups, with three bedrooms sleeping up to six people. Seven night minimum stay.

THE ARTIST'S STUDIO, LAHARADOTA
51.5599, -9.7701
theartistscottage.com

Located on the southern coast of the peninsula this luxury rental is split between a cottage (sleeps six) and a studio (sleeps four). The obvious feature is the Greek-styled outdoor pool overlooking Dunmanus Bay, but the more subtle interior details are stunning too.

GOAT'S PATH POD PARK
51.6337, -9.6023
goatspathpods.ie

This campground has six pods (sleep up to five), one of which is set into the hillside for that real hobbit house kind of feel.

Bring you own tent, caravan or campervan too, with all the usual cooking and cleaning facilities, and a BBQ too.

BANTRY BAY CABIN, BANTRY
airbnb.ie/rooms/2429609

A colourful, cosy getaway that sleeps up to five people. Great location looking out over Bantry Bay, but with plenty of privacy in the lush greenery of the garden too.

Organico | RC

SHEEP'S HEAD AND BANTRY
FOOD

DURRUS PUBS
51.6219, -9.5218
All three of Durrus's pubs serve food, and three makes for a sensible number for a pub crawl.

DURRUS CHEESE
51.6455, -9.5285
durruscheese.com
Visit this long established cheese maker to buy some cheeses direct from the source. Book ahead to get a tour of the dairy.

ARUNDEL'S BY THE PIER, AHAKISTA
51.5999, -9.6223
arundelsbythepier.com
A much-loved pub just a stone's throw from the water. As such, the seafood options are excellent, and as is the way around here, most of the meat and vegetables are locally sourced too. On warm days you can enjoy the views from the beer garden that overlooks the pier.

THE WHITE HOUSE CAFE, KILCROHANE
51.5730, -9.7241
thewhitehouse-gallery.com
Lovely lunches and cakes a little west of Kilcrohane, with much of what's on offering being made and produced locally.

ORGANICO, BANTRY
51.6802, -9.4494
organico.ie
A wholefoods and health shop with an excellent deli and bakery attached. A great place to eat something hearty and wholesome in Bantry.

THE STUFFED OLIVE, BANTRY
51.6791, -9.4502
fb.com/TheStuffedOlive
Located on Bridge Street in Bantry, this busy cafe, bakery and deli offers a wide range of really interesting baked goods, sweet and savoury, as well as excellent coffee to wash it down.

BEARA

The hilly terrain and masses of exposed rock give the Beara Peninsula a very wild and rugged feel. Yet there are also sheltered pockets of lush green woodland, offering quiet and refuge and a more welcoming climate. Like the rest of the southwest the weather here is mild, bathing in the relative warmth of the Gulf Stream.

Though not rich in beaches there are a few worth seeking out, and way out on the western end of the peninsula you are unlikely to meet any crowds. There's a quietness here you might not expect. Bring your walking boots and your bike and enjoy the peace and quiet.

GLENGARRIFF
Coming from the Irish for rugged glen (Gleann Garbh), Glengarriff is true to its name, though the town itself is nestled at the foot of the valley and is a lot more hospitable than the wild landscape surrounding it.

GARINISH ISLAND
World famous for its gardens, this small island in Glengarriff Harbour enjoys a balmy climate and is home to some plant species that are very unusual for this part of the world.

The gardens aren't all about the plants; there are a number of unusual historic structures on the island including the Clock Tower, Grecian Temple, Italian Temple and Tea House.

Between April and October ferries run from the main pier in Glengarriff (*51.7506, -9.5424*) and the Blue Pool (*51.7498, -9.5491*). The short cruise passes Seal Island, unsurprisingly home to a colony of quite tame harbour seals. See garinishisland.ie for more information and harbourqueenferry.com for ferry times.

THE BLUE POOL
This beautiful sheltered harbour is well signposted from the centre of town. It's a convenient swimming area as there are steps leading down into the water. Just be wary of the ferries coming and going.

GLENGARRIFF NATURE RESERVE
Home to some of the last remaining natural woodland in Ireland, the Glengarriff Nature Reserve (glengarriffnaturereserve.ie) is an important pocket for biodiversity. The warm, wet climate means the woodland here is classified as a rainforest. Lichens and mosses grow on the old oaks, which also support more than 200 species of insect. The rivers are some of the cleanest in the country and a last refuge for the

Garinish Island Gardens | Shaun Dunphy

Glengarriff Nature Reserve | DF

Hungry Hill | DF

The Healy Pass | DF

freshwater pearl mussel, a slow growing species that can live to 130 years. Bats can be seen at dusk in the summer and if you're lucky you might see other mammals including otters, stoats and red squirrels.

There are five short signposted trails in the reserve. It's possible to combine them into a big loop that takes in the best of the area. The walks all start from the main carpark (*51.7536, -9.5643*), which is well signposted off the N71.

ADRIGOLE

As you travel west from Glengarriff towards Adrigole the craggy profile of Sugarloaf Mountain dominates the skyline, protruding over the layered rocky hillsides to your right, while Bantry Bay stretches out to sea on the left.

Adrigole Harbour is handy for a quick swim and is a safe bay for kayaking (*51.6827, -9.7160*).

The Mare's Tail is the very impressive waterfall that cascades down the lower slopes of Hungry Hill to the west of the harbour (*51.6913, -9.7721*). It's one of the highest waterfalls in Ireland and makes a very impressive sight after heavy rain. Enquire locally if you'd like to see it up close.

HUNGRY HILL

West of Adrigole is Hungry Hill, a looming presence on the Beara Peninsula. Its massive bulk can be seen from many points along the south coast but be warned - the steep, rocky ground and capricious weather mean a trip up the mountain is for experienced walkers only.

THE HEALY PASS

Even if you're planning on following the Wild Atlantic Way along the coast it's worth making a trip up the Healy Pass (see the photo on page 26). This winding mountain road, which links Adrigole and Lauragh, twists and turns its way up through the hills, culminating in a breathtaking viewpoint overlooking Kerry to the north and West Cork to the south (*51.7211, -9.7565*). Once a classic stage in the Circuit of Ireland rally it's not for the nervous driver!

BERE ISLAND

This relatively large, quiet island lies just a short distance off the Beara shore. Measuring just under ten kilometres from end to end makes it a walker's paradise, and thanks to its position at the mouth of Europe's deepest harbour, it has a long and interesting military history.

The island has three signposted walking loops. The Ardnakinna Loop is a 10km round trip starting from the west pier (*51.6389, -9.9003*). It follows minor roads and green tracks out to Ardnakinna Lighthouse (*51.6185, -9.9179*). The Doonbeg Loop is a short (5km) but hilly loop that starts near the Gallán Standing Stone in the centre of the island (*51.6306, -9.8621*). The views are far-reaching and well worth

Lonehort Gun Battery, Bere Island | RC

Sunrise at Dzogchen Beara | RC

Bullig Bay | RC

the walk. The 7km Rerrin Loop starts from the quay at the east end of the island (51.6344, -9.8199) and passes many old military structures as well as some well-marked bronze age sites.

Lonehort Battery, on the eastern end of the island (51.6422, -9.7914), has recently been restored, and excellent guided tours are available to the public. It's an extensive military structure, with a huge dry moat and guns still in place. See the website below for details.

There are plenty of B&Bs and self-catering options for an overnight stay too. Two car ferries operate daily from Castletownbere (bereislandferries.com) and Pontoon (51.6550, -9.8552) (murphysferry.com). Get there early if you want to take the car. See bereisland.net for more general information.

CASTLETOWNBERE

One of the biggest fishing towns in Ireland, with a long maritime history. There are plenty of shops and cafes, and some decent pubs too. MacCarthy's Bar is worth seeking out, as is the book written about its name.

DUNBOY WOOD

This pleasant little sheltered bay with old woodland backing a secluded beach is a little-known gem with a fantastic signposted stroll.

Head west from Castletownbere along the Wild Atlantic Way. After 3km turn left (signposted 'Puxley and O'Sullivan Bere Castles') and take a right at the fork in the road soon after. Take the second left and park at the entrance to the woods (51.6301, -9.9328).

The starting point for this walk has moved recently, but if you follow the gravel road past the barrier in the carpark you soon pick up the purple arrows of this 4km loop. The walk goes through the forest that reaches down to the shores of Bullig Bay and back inland at Piper's Point after a great view of Bere Island.

DZOGCHEN BEARA

Situated in a stunning position overlooking the entrance to Bantry Bay this Tibetan Buddhist retreat centre is unique in Ireland (51.6148, -9.9799). There are daily meditation classes and longer weekend breaks for those who want to delve deeper into their soulful side. The cafe is quite pleasant and there is a hostel too, offering affordable rooms in a quaint converted farmhouse. You might not want to leave. See dzogchenbeara.org for details.

CAHERMORE AREA

The southwestern corner of Beara between Castletownbere and Allihies is a quiet one. There are small quays at Cahermore (51.6035, -10.0446) and Black Ball Harbour (51.5964, -10.0410) for those looking to get into the water. In suitable sea conditions a paddle between these two piers makes a great day, taking in the impressive cliffs of White Ball Head.

Dursey Island Cable Car | Ilaria Leschiutta

Allihies | RC

GARINISH
Out near the end of the peninsula is this nice safe Green Coast beach (*51.6173, -10.1351*). As it's tucked in behind Garinish Island it's quite sheltered and ideal for families. Dursey Boat Trips (durseyboattrips.com) run trips out to the amazing Bull, Cow and Calf Islands from here, passing Dursey along the way.

DURSEY ISLAND
Way out at the end of the Beara Peninsula Ireland's only cable car links this quiet island (*51.6103, -10.1550*), which is home to only a handful of semi-permanent residents, with the mainland. The cable car runs daily throughout the year. See durseyisland.ie for the details.

There are no facilities on the island so bring food and warm clothes. There is a water tap in the first old village. Camping is permitted but enquire on the island about where is best to stay.

The Beara Way does a 14km loop around Dursey, taking the main road west to the end of the island before returning along the hills. Make sure you allow plenty of time to ensure you don't get stranded on the island. It's worth keeping an eye on the sea for whales, dolphins and seabirds.

The Bull, Cow and Calf are three distant rocks with lighthouses in various states of repair off the western end of the island. The Skelligs can also be seen on a clear day and the views to Kerry in the north and West Cork in the south, are superb.

The cable car station on the mainland is also the starting point for a lovely 4km loop which hugs the high coastline from here to Garinish and returns along a nice green road.

ALLIHIES
Allihies is the biggest of the colourful villages along the north shore of Beara. There is a hostel, B&Bs, a shop, restaurants and pubs, as well as the Allihies Mine Museum (*51.6390, -10.0460*). Copper has been extracted from the mountainsides here for at least 3,500 years and the remains of the last working mines are visible on the hills above the village. The museum is open daily from April to October and intermittently for the rest of the year (acmm.ie).

ALLIHIES LOOP WALKS
There are three fantastic loop walks around Allihies, which start from the Mine Museum (*51.6390, -10.0460*). They mix coastal paths with mountain tracks and give great views of the sea and landscape of this beautifully rugged area. They are the 7km North Engine Loop (green arrows), the 10km Kealoge Loop (blue arrows) and the 18km Ballydonegan Loop (purple arrows).

Kilmackillogue Harbour, Lauragh | Alan Cronin

BALLYDONEGAN BEACH
This is a very nice beach which is partly man-made. Sand was a by-product of the mining and the river swept it down to the shore where it has stayed. There is a campsite, sauna and coffee truck beside the carpark (*51.6334, -10.0611*).

EYERIES
The road between Allihies and Eyeries winds its way through some spectacular landscape. Eyeries is another vibrant village along the quieter north coast of Beara, with a few nice pubs, a post office and shops.

There is a lovely marked coastal trail that starts and ends in the village also. From O'Sullivan's shop follow the blue arrows to enjoy the 6km Creha Quay Loop.

Pallas Strand is a nearby beach, a little west of the village. Parking is very limited (*51.6848, -9.9723*).

ARDGROOM
Ardgroom is a good base for three things: fishing, walking and cycling. In nearby Glenbeg Lough (*51.7222, -9.8806*) brown trout fishing is open between the 15th of February and the 12th of October.

Ardgroom stone circle is also worth a visit, and is just a short distance from the village (*51.7359, -9.8698*).

Beara Boat Tours (fb.com/bearaboattrips) run angling and sightseeing tours from nearby Ballycrovane Pier (*51.7136, -9.9493*). Also nearby is Europe's tallest Ogham stone, standing over five metres high. Enquire at the closest house for permission to enter the field it's in (*51.7138, -9.9446*).

PULLEEN LOOP
Starting from the small pier at Cuas (*51.7517, -9.9034*) is a good 5km loop that makes a circuit of the boggy coastline. The caves at the start of the loop make for a great place to swim when it's calm.

CYCLE LOOP
This 20km cycling loop isn't signposted but is easy to follow and isn't too strenuous. From the village head west on the R571 for just over 3km and turn onto the L4910 at a sign for the Ring of Beara. You soon pass Lough Fada, and then An Cailleach Bheara, an old stone said to once have been a woman of which many stories have been told. Continue along the coast road, passing quiet harbours with great views north to the Ring of Kerry.

LAURAGH
This small hamlet is beautifully situated at the head of Kilmackillogue Harbour, not far from the peaceful surroundings of Glanmore Lake.

Gleninchaquin Waterfall | Alan Cronin

Beara Coast Road | RC

RABHACH'S GLEN
A little inland of Lauragh is the spectacular valley of Coomeengeeragh, also known as Rabhach's Glen. Parking can be had at the end of the road, for a small fee (51.7371, -9.8039). The Rabhach was an infamous man who lived in one of the houses deep in the back of the valley and murdered two people in the 1800s. Bring your boots and head up into the valley for a look around this incredible mountain landscape.

COORNAGILLAGH BEACH
This pebble shoreline (51.8257, -9.740) may not compare terribly well to the many sandy beaches along Ireland's west coast, but it's a lovely secluded spot all the same, made more enticing recently by the newly installed Sunset Sauna and Coorna Café (instagram.com/sunsetsaunakerry). Ormond's Island lies just offshore and is easily reached by kayak/SUP, or a fit swimmer.

GLENINCHAQUIN
A family owned hill farm and parkland (gleninchaquin.com) set at the back of an impressive, remote valley (51.8021, -9.6607). The main feature is the massive waterfall spilling down the mountainside but there's plenty more to be seen in the area, like the wonderful woodland and restored famine cottages.

There are six trails, from gentle strolls around the farmland to long hikes in the surrounding hills. All are well signposted and very worthwhile. There is a small charge for parking.

Uragh Stone circle is signposted on the way into the valley and is worth a diversion, framed against the waterfall in the distance (51.8129, -9.6979).

THE BEARA WAY
The Beara Way is a signposted walking trail that travels around the peninsula in a loop from Glengarriff. It's approximately 200km long and usually takes 8-10 days to complete. For the fit walker there is no better way to see this part of the world. You see a lot more of the landscape than you would from a car. For information see bearatourism.com.

THE BEARA WAY CYCLE
A 138km route covers the whole peninsula but shorter variations are also possible. A clockwise circuit from Castletownbere to Allihies and back via the north shore of the peninsula is a good long day out with plenty of hills. Allihies to Dursey Sound is a little less punishing. ■

Wild Atlantic Glamping | Wild Atlantic Glamping

BEARA
ACCOMMODATION

GYPSY WAGONS, GLENGARRIFF
airbnb.ie/rooms/27594851
Two traditional gypsy wagons high in the hills above Glengarriff. There's space for tents too. Compost toilet, basic outdoor kitchen, firepits and a pond for bathing. No electricity and you'll need to walk or have a 4x4 for the last 1.5km of track. This won't be for everyone, but it's certainly unique, and very affordable.

WILD ATLANTIC GLAMPING, BERE ISLAND
51.6394, -9.8282
wildatlanticglamping.ie
Luxury bell tents on a waterside location on Bere Island. Options available for two to five people, and local activities such as kayaking, snorkelling and foraging can be organised from the campsite.

THE BEARA BUS
51.6090, -9.9957
bearabus.ie
A converted double-decker perched on a high cliff overlooking the open Atlantic. Full kitchen and bathroom facilities, and an outdoor BBQ area and hot tub. On the higher end of the price range but there's very little else like it anywhere in Ireland. Sleeps two.

CREATIVITY CABIN, KILCATHERINE
51.7136, -9.9809
thecreativitycabin.com
A lovely self-contained cabin overlooking Coulagh Bay. Fully equipped with kitchen, bathroom and wood burning stove, and Wi-Fi is available.

GLANMORE COTTAGE
airbnb.ie/rooms/16366964
An old stone cottage tucked into the remote Glanmore Valley. Renovated to a comfortable standard with authentic old style charm. Sleeps six across three bedrooms.

CHEZ SHEA WAGON, LAURAGH
airbnb.ie/rooms/2643072
Idyllically situated in a remote spot outside of Lauragh, this two person wagon is perfect for couples. No kitchen but breakfast is included, and there's a kettle for tea/coffee.

Glengarriff Food Trucks | RC

BEARA
FOOD

GLENGARRIFF FOOD TRUCKS
51.7500, -9.5490
The carpark beside Quill's Woollen Market offers a variety of options from various food trucks. Take your pick from pizza, waffles, crepes and toasties. There are plenty of places to eat in the pubs of the village for those who'd rather eat inside.

CHEF'S TABLE, CASTLETOWNBERE
51.6506, -9.9126
fb.com/thechefstablewestcork
Seriously good seafood takeaway prepared with imagination and flair. Nothing wrong with the land-based fare either. Open seasonally, food can be eaten indoors in Twomey's Bar opposite.

THE TEA ROOM CAFÉ, CASTLETOWNBERE
51.6502, -9.9135
thetearoomcastletownbere.com
Great spot in Castletownbere for breakfast and brunch, with lots of delicious homemade dessert options available too.

BEARA NECESSITIES, EYERIES
51.6923, -9.9552
instagram.com/beara_necessities
Breakfasts, lunches and dinners with flair, with plenty of focus on local provenance food and organic coffee and wine. The main restaurant is in Eyeries, with a food truck often on show at the beach in Allihies (*51.6336, -10.0601*) and also three days a week at The Urhan Inn (*51.6720, -10.0007*).

AN SÍBÍN, LAURAGH
51.7656, -9.7708
ansibinkenmare.com
An establishment that started in the 18th Century, with the current restaurant under the care of two very experienced chefs.

CORK

Sybil Head on the Dingle Peninsula (see page 100) | RC

KERRY

Known in Ireland as The Kingdom, Kerry could indeed be a seat of royalty. It has a richly varied coastline, spread around the southwest corner of the country. Kerry has some of the finest mountains in all of Ireland, and they form the spines of each peninsula, dividing and providing a backdrop to the north and south coasts of each. There are plenty of well-known tourist traps, but even more places to escape the summer crowds.

Though we've included the entire Beara Peninsula in the Cork chapter, the northeastern corner of Beara actually flies the Kerry flag, and as is common in much of the county, the landscape is truly wild.

Coming into Kenmare, an attractive town tucked into the head of a long sheltered bay, the famed Ring of Kerry begins. This route overlaps the Wild Atlantic Way at the coast, and along this seaboard there are plenty of stops worth taking; the quiet bays and beaches along the Kenmare River, the paradise that is Derrynane and the awesome otherworldliness of the Skelligs are just a few.

The Dingle Peninsula, with its world-class scenery and thriving music scene, is understandably popular. Its landscape appears to have been designed to please the human eye, and few who travel west of Dingle Town are left unimpressed.

Humble North Kerry is a place far from the madding crowds, but with enough hidden gems to make it a worthwhile destination for anyone who wants to do more than just tick the usual boxes.

IVERAGH

Iveragh is the largest of Kerry's three main peninsulas and as such, has a huge amount to offer the visitor. As well as some of the most famous attractions in the country, such as the Skelligs and the Ring of Kerry, there are numerous small headlands and hills worth seeking out.

The mountainous interior is never far from the coast and it makes a worthy diversion as well as an impressive backdrop. There you will find a lifetime of empty peaks to climb and mountain lakes to swim in.

THE RING OF KERRY

The Ring of Kerry is a 180km driving route around the Iveragh Peninsula that starts and finishes in Killarney. The Wild Atlantic Way follows most of the route with the exception of the inland section. There is so much to see it's better to take your time, spending at least one night along the way, rather than rushing around it in a day.

The many tour buses that travel along its narrow roads do so in an anti-clockwise direction. To avoid getting stuck behind them it's preferable to travel clockwise around the ring (which is south to north along the Wild Atlantic Way). Be warned the route can get congested in the summer and many sections follow small, winding roads. If you aren't a confident driver you may find it a little nerve-wracking.

RING OF KERRY CYCLE ROUTE

There is a variation of the Ring of Kerry for cyclists. It's over 215km long and around two-thirds of it avoids the busy main road. The route is reasonably well signposted and it is also marked on the relevant OSI maps (sheets 78 and 83).

KENMARE

This attractive small town is the first one you meet on the Iveragh Peninsula when coming from the south. It's a good base for exploring the Beara Peninsula (see page 68) and the mountains of Iveragh.

COASTEERING AND KAYAKING

Coasteering - scrambling around the rocky coast and jumping into pools, gullies and sea caves - is an exhilarating way to experience the shore. It's the perfect activity for a rainy day as getting soaked is going to be the least of your worries. See eclipseireland.com for details.

Emerald Outdoors (emeraldoutours.ie) run kayaking trips in the area, including night time trips to try see bioluminescent plankton.

Rossdohan | RC

White Strand, near Sneem | RC

The Milky Way above the Skelligs | Michele Cati

ROSSDOHAN
Though not signposted, a short walking or cycling loop around this little known peninsula is worthwhile and should help you forget about the busy Ring of Kerry road.

Park at the church at Tahilla (51.8304, -9.8225). Heading west, take a left after the church, down a quiet country road and follow this to Rossdohan Island, passing small lakes and attractive cottages on either side of the rich hedgerows. Retrace your steps after reaching the pier and take a left at the next crossroads, following a quiet, winding road before a right turn onto the Kerry Way. A lovely green road leads you back to the start.

SNEEM
The pleasant village of Sneem is a popular stop on the Ring of Kerry. Two signposted walks start from the North Square.

- The 14km Fermoyle Loop follows a mix of minor roads and open ground, passing plenty of sites of historical interest (white arrows).
- The 11km Lomanagh Loop takes a slightly shorter route across gentle hillsides and through forestry plantations (red arrows).

If you're looking to explore more of this area bikes can be hired from M. Burns Cycle Hire in the village.

For the past few years Sneem has hosted a storytelling festival which attracts storytellers from all over the globe. It's usually held in November, offering something for the winter tourist.

WHITE STRAND
West of Sneem there are a number of small sandy beaches, at least two of which are known as White Strand. Some are right beside the main road, while others lie at the end of one of the many minor roads that lead south to the sea. Grab a map (OSI sheet 84) and explore. Though some are popular local spots, there are plenty of quiet, sheltered coves to be found on all but the busiest of days.

KERRY DARK SKY RESERVE
Due to the lack of light pollution, the western part of the Iveragh Peninsula has been designated as an International Dark Sky Reserve. While the landscape is certainly impressive during the day, the show doesn't stop once the sun goes down, at least not if you're lucky enough to get clear skies.

The winter is the best time to stargaze as the nights are long and it gets dark early. Grab some warm clothes and a flask and head out into the night. In high summer the sun is never too far from the horizon so it doesn't get as dark, though it's still worth looking up if you find yourself outside in the small hours.

Derrynane Beach | RC

O'CARROLL'S COVE
Just off the road before Derrynane is O'Carroll's Cove, with a beach bar and caravan park (*51.7603, -10.0806*). It's a lovely sandy beach although it can get busy in the summer.

DERRYNANE
With lush woodland, gently sloping hills and a collection of beautiful beaches Derrynane isn't too far from paradise (at least on a sunny day). If you are happy to walk, lounge on the beach, snorkel in the sea or fish from the rocks you'll never be short of things to do.

Derrynane is situated around the small village of Caherdaniel. Lamb's Head (*51.7440, -10.1356*) is a quiet cul-de-sac, favoured by shore fishermen and walkers. The Blue Flag beach extends around the east and north shores of the bay, and there are lifeguards in the summer. In the woodland bordering the bay is the historic Derrynane House and gardens.

A local artist has developed an interactive smartphone app which guides you along a nature trail around the beach, providing information, pictures and videos of Derrynane's rich biodiversity. See vincenthylandartist.com for more information.

The beach at the old quay (*51.7604, -10.1434*) is very safe for swimming and Derrynane Sea Sports (derrynaneseasports.com) offer equipment rental for a variety of water-based activities.

There is a sauna (kingdomsauna.ie) a little further east along the bay that operates in summer (*51.7605, -10.1369*).

WALKING
The following 12km walk takes in the best of the area and can be finished with a drink in Caherdaniel.

Heading west out of the village, pass an Ogham Stone and take a left off the road at the signs for Nature Trail and Carpark. Leave the carpark through a short wooded section and come out on a flat, grassy area behind the beach. Having reached the beach walk west along the strand, admiring the surrounding views. As you come to a wooden house on a small headland follow the track up to the road or you can keep going along the beach if the tide is low enough. Abbey Island is a worthy detour from here, for those with the time (*51.7574, -10.1446*).

Just up the road from the small stone quay is a yellow signpost pointing past a small shed. The path twists along heathery slopes with great views over the harbour and a pleasant little bay, ideal for a quick swim. From this little beach follow the well-worn grooves in the rock to find the path along the coast again, eventually arriving at a more modern pier. Follow the winding road up the hill and take a right at signs for the Kerry Way at a sharp bend. Continue straight at the next Kerry Way sign, passing over a stile shortly after it. The next sign guides you up

Derrynane Woods | RC

Sea spaghetti | RC

and left from the track along a very pleasant upland section. You soon reach a road where you turn right and almost immediately left again. There are two tracks in the woods; take the upper one, eventually leaving the shaded forest to follow signs for the Kerry Way back to Caherdaniel.

DERRYNANE HOUSE
For those looking for a shorter stroll, Derrynane House and the surrounding woodland are worth a visit (*51.7630, -10.1305*). The house was the ancestral home of Daniel O'Connell, famous for his political defence of local customs at a time when the natives were being persecuted for their beliefs. There is a small entrance fee for the museum.

ATLANTIC IRISH SEAWEED
In times gone by seaweed was a valued resource along the Irish coast. Its use as a nutritious food is known worldwide, but seaweed extracts are also used in many everyday products, from beer and ice cream to toothpaste.

At one point seaweed was one of the biggest exports from Ireland, but these days it's an undervalued resource which has the potential to provide opportunities in many dwindling rural areas.

Atlantic Irish Seaweed (atlanticirishseaweed.com) is a company based in Caherdaniel offering foraging

KERRY

Saint Finian's Bay | RC

trips to budding hunter-gatherers. These excursions are highly informative and hands-on, and the fruits of your labour will be cooked up afterwards for a delicious, self-sourced meal.

WATERVILLE
The road from Caherdaniel to Waterville is cut into the mountains, culminating in the pass at Coomakista. Further north is Waterville, which has a Green Coast beach, shops and restaurants. There is also plenty of accommodation.

Sea Synergy (seasynergy.org) is a locally based ocean-awareness group that has a small office based in the town with an interesting exhibition. They also run kids clubs and watersports for much of the year.

FISHING
Behind the town lies Lough Currane, which is well known for its sea trout and salmon fishing. If you fancy your chances, Neil O'Shea, a fourth generation ghillie, is the man to talk to (oshealoughcurrane.com). Note that fishing permits are required by law. They can be purchased online at store.fishinginireland.info.

WALKING
There is a 24km walk starting and ending in Waterville. A long day out, it would make a decent challenge for the adventurous runner.

Starting at the The Lobster Bar (51.8271, -10.1720), follow the Kerry Way north, soon leaving the village to follow the track up a pleasant ridge. After 5km along the ridge take the signposted right turn down towards Lough Currane. Follow the markers up over a shoulder of mountain and back down to a forestry track. When you meet the road turn right to return to Waterville.

INNY STRAND
This fine stretch of sandy beach is a 10km drive north of Waterville (51.8456, -10.2317). It's good for swimming and walking, with an easy 6km loop walk taking in part of the beach and the bog behind it, as well as a 1.5km clifftop walk. Coming from Waterville, the beach is on the left, marked by a sign for the Emlagh Loop Walk.

BALLINSKELLIGS BEACH
This is a fantastic Blue Flag beach, suitable for swimming, and popular with walkers (51.8209, -10.2734). There are lifeguards on duty daily in July and August and on weekends for most of June and September.

Both Skellig Sauna (skelligsauna.ie) and The Fire and Ice Sauna (fire-and-ice-sauna.com) operate near the beach, and as the name of the latter suggests, allow easy access to both elements.

Kerry Cliffs | Alan Cronin

Gannet | RC

Walking near Bolus Head | RC

The unmissable McCarthy Mór tower house dates back to the 16th century, and is believed to have been built to protect the coast from pirates and to perhaps charge a tariff on passing ships.

There are two walking trails starting from the carpark, the 2.6km Monks Way Loop and the 11.9km Skellig Way, a linear route to the far side of Bolus Head.

Skelligs Watersports (skelligsurf.com) offer a variety of watersports camps and rental in the summer months.

BOLUS HEAD

Bolus Head is the hilly promontory that guards the south arm of Saint Finian's Bay. The Skelligs are a near constant presence in the corner of your eye, drawing your gaze west again and again. There is an excellent signposted 9km loop walk, with high cliff scenery and beautiful views. Follow the purple arrows.

Coming from Ballinskelligs, take a left off the R566 at the sign for the Bolus Head trailhead. Park at the U.S. Navy Liberator Monument (*51.8141, -10.3371*), dedicated to the eleven lost airmen who crashed into the Atlantic here in 1944.

SAINT FINIAN'S BAY

This small, picturesque beach has good views to the Skelligs and decent surf when conditions align (*51.8463, -10.3353*). Beside the road, not far from the

Steps to the Monastery, Skellig Michael | Alan Cronin

The Monastery on Skellig Michael | Valerie Hinojosa

An Atlantic puffin | RC

beach is Skelligs Chocolate (skelligschocolate.com), a chocolate factory and cafe (*51.8458, -10.3299*).

Skellig Sauna (skelligsauna.ie) can also be found here.

PORTMAGEE
The Wild Atlantic Way continues north from Saint Finian's over Coonanaspig, a steep climb with incredible views to the north (*51.8562, -10.3670*).

Before Portmagee there are signs on the left for the unimaginatively named Kerry Cliffs, described as the most spectacular in the county (*51.8696, -10.3797*). This is a bold statement in a county with such an impressive coastline, but nonetheless, it's worth paying the small fee to park the car and make the short walk west for what is indeed a magnificent view.

Portmagee, a charming fishing village with many pubs and restaurants, is the embarkation point for most of the boats to the Skelligs. It is also connected to Valentia Island (see page 86) by a bridge.

THE SKELLIGS
There are few places in the world quite like the Skelligs, and words do little to convey the feeling of the place. The two rocky islands, Skellig Michael and Little Skellig, lie 10km off the coast of Portmagee, their sharp summits pointing to the sky.

Skellig Michael is a UNESCO world heritage site, owing to the monastic site established there between the 6th and 8th centuries. The monastery stands testament to the dedication of the monks, who must have had a tough existence out on the fringe of society with little in the way of food and shelter.

The stone dwellings on the island were all made using a technique known as corbelling, a system that has kept the inside of the cells dry since they were first constructed. The monks levelled flatter areas near the monastery for use as gardens and built sophisticated water catchment systems as there is no fresh water on the island. Over 100 stone crosses have been recorded, and the last family to live in the lighthouse were still using the oratory as their church during the 19th century.

The ridges that make up these summits could rival similar scenery from any mountain range in the world, only these precipitous cliffs rise out of the ocean, taking the brunt of the bad weather that this area often sees. The cliff scenery and exposure are second to none in Ireland.

In recent years the islands became even more famous thanks to their appearance in two Star Wars films.

The Little Skellig is the biggest gannet colony in Ireland, home to over 25,000 pairs. It's an incredible sight during the summer breeding season.

Skellig Michael is home to a large population of seabirds, including kittiwakes, storm petrels, Manx shearwaters and everybody's favourite, Atlantic puffins.

Ancient remains and Little Skellig | RC

Little Skellig with Skellig Michael behind | RC

Autumn colour on Valentia | RC

Bray Head, Valentia | RC

Be warned, the steep nature of the island has been known to cause vertigo and there have been accidents in the past. The steps to the monastery are unguarded and uneven, and are slippery when wet. All that said, unless you are particularly afraid of heights this is an experience not to be missed.

A limited number of boat tours are permitted to the island between May and October, see skelligexperience.com for a list of boatmen. They sail from Portmagee and Ballinskelligs. Bear in mind that landing on Skellig Michael is very much weather dependent. Book well in advance and pray for a calm sea.

VALENTIA ISLAND

In the northwest corner of the Ring of Kerry sits Valentia, a large hilly island with two contrasting shores. The south side is the relatively calm and low-lying coast bordering the Portmagee Channel. The north side is a totally different place, with high cliffs along much of the coast and an open, exposed aspect.

The island was the site of one end of the first transatlantic telegraph cable in the mid nineteenth century. The cable, which landed at Newfoundland, was replaced regularly until the sixties. The Valentia Island Heritage Centre houses an exhibition about the cable as well as plenty of other fascinating exhibits

Valentia Lighthouse | RC

(51.9254, -10.2943). See valentiaisland.ie for the opening hours.

It is possible to drive onto the island from just outside Portmagee (51.8863, -10.3630). Between March and September a car ferry links Knight's Town, on the eastern end of the island with Reenard Point, near Cahersiveen (51.9291, -10.2777).

The island's proximity to the mainland dulls its overall sense of remoteness but there is still plenty to be seen. A cycle around the island's main road is a good hilly challenge. Cycling or not, it's well worth stopping off at Glanleam Bay (51.9238, -10.3171). The beach is beautiful, and as it faces northeast it's often relatively sheltered. Bear in mind there's no access for cars on the slip road down to the beach, but a few laybys to pull into higher up.

BRAY HEAD LOOP WALK

Coming from Portmagee, take a left after crossing the bridge and follow the signs for the Bray Head loop walk. This 5km walk takes you out to the island's western end, past the old signal tower and up past high cliffs. There is a small charge for parking (51.8920, -10.3965).

CULLOO

Following the northern road east there is a sign to the left for Saint Brendan's Well. Follow the rough road to the signs for Culloo Rock and park here if your car makes it that far (51.9087, -10.3970). This is the starting point for a short but worthwhile walk. Head further along the road to the holy well and two old crosses. Having crossed the stile to see the second cross it is possible to follow a reasonably dry track to the shore. It's a lonely, pleasant stretch of coast, ideal for a picnic on a sunny day in May when the sea thrift is blooming in profusion. Walk east to Culloo Rock (a popular, but exposed fishing spot) and follow the track beside the stream back to the car to complete the circuit.

GEOKAUN MOUNTAIN

Well signposted at the eastern end of the island is Geokaun Mountain (51.9158, -10.3501). As with many places along The Ring of Kerry, there is a small charge for parking, but for this place in particular, the few euro is well spent. There are three stopping points along the road to the summit. The first is at a short walkway that leads to the huge Fogher Cliffs, which fall away to the sea from the north side of the mountain.

The second stop is at the beginning of a mile-long path around the hill, which shouldn't be missed. It's not exactly adventurous but well worth it for a quick fix of scenic inspiration. The views are extensive, with the Dingle Peninsula to the north, the stately rise of Cnoc na dTobar to the east, the rounded hills of South Kerry inland and the distant Skelligs to the west. The top of the mountain has picnic benches and dotted along

The Beentee Loop | RC

White Strand | RC

Kells Bay | RC

Walking trail on Seefin | Denis Dineen

the track are information boards about the natural and cultural heritage of the area.

SLATE GROTTO
On the lower slopes of Geokaun Mountain is a slate quarry that operated for much of the 19th century (*51.9249, -10.3427*). It's open again these days, though on a much smaller scale. The grotto became a site of pilgrimage after 1954, which explains the religious statues in the top of the main cave. The place has a strange air of industry in a very rural setting, with a bit of religious devotion thrown in for good measure.

TETRAPOD TRACKWAY
Another popular feature at this end of Valentia is the tetrapod trackway, the world's oldest in-situ record of a vertebrate walking on land (*51.9295, -10.3458*). The tracks, which date back 385 million years, belonged to one of the first vertebrates to leave the sea and colonise the land.

The story these fossilized footprints tells us is far more inspiring than the sight itself, which, after reading the information board, is a little underwhelming. Still, it's worth a quick visit.

CAHERSIVEEN
At the foot of Beentee mountain is the busy market town of Cahersiveen.

CYCLING
Casey's Cycles (bikehirekerry.com) do rentals, and cycling is an ideal mode of transport for exploring the surrounding area. They also provide maps of four cycling routes in the area, from 29km to 53km. Each of these routes takes you on a different journey through the surrounding countryside, along quiet back roads and stunning seaside paths.

BEENTEE LOOP
There is an information board at the Fairgreen carpark (turn right after the petrol station if coming from the south) where a number of walking routes start and finish (*51.9467, -10.2203*). The 10km Beentee Loop is an excellent walk for those looking for a panoramic view. It takes you to the summit of Beentee (376m), from where you can take in Cahersiveen and Valentia, the Macgillycuddy's Reeks and the Dingle Peninsula. The 13km Carhan Letter Loop is a longer variation that takes a different route off the summit.

LAHARN BOG LOOP
This walk is a longer (15km) loop around the base of the mountain that avoids the steep climbs of the previous route.

Rossbeigh | DF

WHITE STRAND

Just north of Cahersiveen is an area known as 'Across the Water' by locals. This area has some sites of historical interest and a gorgeous Blue Flag beach.

Take a left after the church in Cahersiveen, and cross the bridge. Heading left, there are signs for Leacanabuaile and Cahergal stone forts (*51.9555, -10.2615*), as well as Ballycarbery Castle (*51.9495, -10.2595*), all worth a visit if you have an interest in history.

Continuing past the carpark at Cahergal, you come to a T-junction at a stony bay. White Strand is at the end of the left turn (*51.9451, -10.2759*).

Not too far offshore is Beginish Island, whose quieter beaches are an enticing sight. Those with kayaks and some experience should have little trouble getting out there on a calm day.

CNOC NA DTOBAR

Cnoc na dTobar (Hill of the Wells) is the prominent peak north of Cahersiveen. The walk to the top is a great way to spend a few hours on a nice day. The mountain is a site of pilgrimage and crosses have been erected most of the way up to the summit to guide the devout.

The carpark at the start of the walk is only a few minutes drive from Cahersiveen (*51.9785, -10.2115*), there is a small charge.

Follow the crosses (not always easy to find) or one of the many paths below the southwest ridge to the summit at 690m. The views on a clear day are extensive (see the photo on page 6). Return by the same way for a 7km round trip.

Because of the mountainous nature of the walk you should carry a map (OSI sheet 83) and compass (and know how to use them), as well as spare clothing, rain gear and plenty of food and water.

KELLS BAY

This very pleasant bay is tucked between the mountains and the open water of Dingle Bay to the north (*52.0246, -10.1041*). The Blue Flag beach is beautiful, and there is a campsite just behind it.

ROSSBEIGH BEACH

Rossbeigh is a expansive Blue Flag beach backed by impressive sand dunes. It's safe for swimming, surfing is possible when conditions are right, there's a mobile sauna (instagram.com/rossbeigh_sauna) and the strand is long enough for a decent walk (*52.0552, -9.9760*). Burke's Horse Riding offer treks on the beach as well as trips around the area. See beachtrek.ie for details.

GLENBEIGH

The village of Glenbeigh has a few pubs and restaurants as well as a campsite (campingkerry.com).

Looking down the Hag's Glen from Carrauntoohil | Denis Dineen

There is a nice 12km loop around Seefin that starts from the church in Glenbeigh (*52.0560, -9.9400*). Follow the quiet road west from the church as far as a picnic bench opposite two bungalows. Turn left here and follow the yellow walker signposts up to Windy Gap. After taking in the view descend to the left along a track overlooking Lough Caragh. This track eventually meets a quiet road and then the main road, which takes you back into Glenbeigh.

KILLORGLIN
This town is the last or first port of call on the Iveragh Peninsula as you travel along the Wild Atlantic Way. It's famous for the Puck Fair, which is held every August. The three-day event is the oldest traditional fair in Ireland and has been running for over four hundred years. A wild goat is taken from the hills and the Queen of Puck traditionally crowns the goat King Puck, as he is paraded around town.

INLAND
It would be a shame to miss out on the mountains and lakes that comprise the interior of Iveragh.

KILLARNEY
Killarney is probably the busiest tourist town in Ireland, with tens of thousands visiting every year. The town has plenty of pubs, cafes, restaurants, hotels and hostels and is an excellent, if a little busy, base for exploring the Iveragh Peninsula.

KILLARNEY NATIONAL PARK
This, the oldest national park in Ireland, is a beautiful area of wild mountains, ancient native woodland and sprawling lakes. In and around the park's boundaries you will find popular attractions such as Torc Waterfall (*52.0028, -9.5059*) and Mountain (*51.9977, -9.5196*), Muckross House and Gardens (*52.0183, -9.5024*), and the Lakes of Killarney.

There are various walking and cycling routes in the park which take you through some of the oldest natural woodland in the country. It is home to our oldest population of red deer, and a huge range of other wildlife. It's also possible to take a boat trip on the lakes. See killarneynationalpark.ie for more.

THE MACGILLYCUDDY'S REEKS
The Reeks, as they're known locally, are the highest mountain range in Ireland, with 10 of the 12 highest points in the country including the highest of them all, Carrauntoohil. While small by international standards, the Reeks are rugged and rocky and prone to unpredictable weather. They should only be approached by experienced walkers with good navigation skills. If you're unsure of your ability Kerry Climbing (kerryclimbing.ie) offer a guiding service, including not just Carrauntoohil, but the many other less well known mountains in the area. ∎

Dromquinna Glamping | Dromquinna Manor

IVERAGH
ACCOMMODATION

CAMOMILE COTTAGE, KENMARE
airbnb.ie/rooms/1113562137353468322
A comfortable apartment set in gorgeous, lush gardens, with full kitchen and bathroom. Just a few miles from Kenmare and only a few hundred metres off the Kerry Way walking trail. Sleeps up to three.

DROMQUINNA GLAMPING
51.8743, -9.6445
dromquinnamanor.com
Luxury camping for those reluctant to stay anywhere but a hotel. The coast nearby is good for kayaking, with sheltered water and plenty of small wooded islands to explore out in the bay.

SHEPHERD SKY HUT, CASTLECOVE
airbnb.ie/rooms/897094920742915012
Cosy, bright and roomier than it looks from outside, this wooden hut is great for couples. There are cooking facilities and the outdoor space is a wonderful place to relax in.

KINGDOM OF THE HARE, ST. FINIAN'S BAY
airbnb.ie/rooms/1017264181551466495
A nicely refurbished stone cottage retaining much old style character - the flagstone floors are particularly charming. As it's hidden down the end of a secluded mountain valley there is no internet, but that's just another selling point in this case. Only fifteen minutes walk to the beach. Sleeps five across three bedrooms.

VALENTIA ISLAND ESCAPE
51.9070, -10.3542
valentiaislandescape.com
Located in the centre of the island and with multiple options to choose from, this place makes for a great base for exploring the wider area. Choose from a traditional stone farmhouse with full facilities or a range of smaller, unusual options like a converted bus, an old boat and a number of quirky little caravans.

KELLS BEACH PODS
airbnb.ie/rooms/36260432
These wooden pods sleep three and are just a stone's throw from the beach at Kells Bay. The kitchen and bathroom are located in a shared building on site, maximizing the space in each camping pod.

Emilie's | RC

Maison Gourmet | RC

The Oratory Pizza and Wine Bar RC

IVERAGH
FOOD

MAISON GOURMET, KENMARE
51.8796, -9.5835
The baked goods here are among the best anywhere. Great brunches too, with the usual mix of hot drinks, again done to a high standard. Can be busy in summer, but so is everywhere else in Kenmare at that time of year.

THE VILLAGE KITCHEN, SNEEM
51.8384, -9.9002
No illusions of grandeur, just simple food done right and fairly priced. An excellent lunch option in Sneem.

DRIFTWOOD SURF CAFÉ, ST. FINIAN'S
51.8475, -10.3352
You won't find many restaurants with a better view, and the food is good too, with an ever-changing menu adapted to the seasons. The main restaurant is ideal for those who'd like to dine indoors, while An Bothán (the adjacent shipping container) is a more casual outdoor setup, perfect for eating out on a fine summer evening.

THE LOBSTER, WATERVILLE
51.8269, -10.1720
thelobsterwaterville.com
One of the longest established restaurants in this book, The Lobster has been feeding and watering tourists on the Ring of Kerry for over 60 years. Not a place to live in the past though, its food is up to the best of modern gastropub standards, and as the name suggests, lobster is on the menu.

THE ORATORY PIZZA & WINE BAR, CAHERSIVEEN
51.9452, -10.2288
theoratorywinebar.com
Excellent quality pizza in the unique setting of a 19th century church. Outdoor seating for fine summer evenings and plenty of room in the atmospheric interior for all other weathers.

EMILIE'S, GLENBEIGH
52.0564, -9.9392
A stone oven kitchen serving up delicious sourdough pizza, as well as sweet and savoury baked treats to eat in house or take away.

KERRY

THE DINGLE PENINSULA

Many people would argue that the Dingle Peninsula (Corca Dhuibhne in its native language) is the most beautiful corner of Ireland. This Irish-speaking region certainly has a lot going for it, with wonderful beaches, mountains, rolling green fields, a rugged coastline, lonely islands and a treasure of heritage. All of Ireland's clichés can be found here, but it's easy to love it.

INCH STRAND

The first port of call for most people coming from the south is the fine strand at Inch (*52.1422, -9.9813*). This is a surfer friendly Blue Flag beach, popular with seasoned locals and visitors alike. The Offshore Surf School (offshoresurfschool.ie) and Kingdom Waves (kingdomwaves.com) offer rentals and lessons.

If surfing isn't your thing, then a walk might be, and there's enough beach here to keep you on your feet for hours. On sunny days when the carparks get full people park on the sand. If you are driving on the beach watch out for others, especially children, and remember the tide. Every year somebody parks on the sand and heads out for a walk, only to come back and find the flood tide washing out their engine bay.

Inch Beach Campsite is just the other side of the road from the strand, with tent and campervan pitches available (inchbeach.com/campsite).

SOUTH COAST BEACHES

Between Inch and Dingle Town are a few quiet beaches that are worth seeking out.

- Minard is a pleasant beach near a 16th century castle (*52.1268, -10.1092*).
- Kinard occasionally has surf. Look out for the iconic sea stack known as An Searrach offshore (*52.1213, -10.2064*).
- Dún Síon is a lovely beach (*52.1257, -10.2168*). There are strong currents so swimming in the sea is dangerous, but it's possible to swim in the river.
- Binn Bán is a small cove on the outer edge of Dingle Harbour (*52.1212, -10.2495*).

DINGLE TOWN

The animated town of Dingle is usually thronged with tourists during the summer. This is a place that knows how to attract visitors, and even during the winter there are festivals and events. There are plenty of great places to eat and drink and many pubs have traditional music in the evenings.

For nearly 40 years a lone bottlenose dolphin known as Fungi hung around the harbour mouth, but he hasn't been seen since 2020. Nonetheless, it's worth making a boat trip around the harbour to see

Minard | RC

Riding in Smerwick Harbour | Dingle Horseriding

Kayaking along the cliffs west of Dingle Town | RC

the lighthouse and impressive cliffs beyond. There are multiple different tour companies operating around the marina (52.1391, -10.2745). See page 96 for details of longer trips out around the Blaskets.

There are plenty of accommodation options in Dingle, from hotels and self-catering to B&Bs and hostels (see the list below). During the summer it's wise to book in advance.

- Lovett's, The Grapevine Hostel (grapevinedingle.com) and The Hideout Hostel are all located in town.
- The Rainbow Hostel is less than 2km outside town (52.1478, -10.2888). It's a quieter hostel with camping available rainbowhosteldingle.com.

HARBOUR WALK
This walk follows the coast east from the town. Follow the narrow road opposite Moran's petrol station to the shoreline of Dingle Harbour. If you carry on along the coast you eventually reach the lighthouse and the pleasant beach at Binn Bán. After the beach a path climbs to Ceann na Binne (52.1172, -10.2480), a lofty place to take in the views over Dingle (4km each way).

WATERSPORTS
The rugged coastline south of Dingle Town is best appreciated from the water, with impressive high cliffs and sea caves either side of the harbour mouth.

Various different kayaking trips can be booked with Irish Adventures (irishadventures.net) in Dingle Town, and both Dingle Surf (dinglesurf.com) and Wild SUP Tours (wildsuptours.com) offer Stand Up Paddleboarding trips in the area.

HORSE RIDING
There's something romantic about travelling through a wild place on horseback, and the following operators will help you do just that. See dinglehorseriding.com and burnhamhorseridingdingle.com for trips from Dingle, and longsriding.com for treks from Ventry.

SLEA HEAD DRIVE
This winding coastal drive takes in many of Dingle's most compelling sights. The road west of Ventry has been carved into the seaward side of Mount Eagle and each turn reveals new views over the Blasket Islands and the sea beyond.

Once around Slea Head itself the views of Coumeenoole open up and with the steep green fields, black cliffs, golden sand and emerald ocean, it's surely one of the best views in the country. And that's only a small section of the 57km route.

Most people drive the route but it is also very enjoyable on a bike. There are a number of places to hire a bike in Dingle Town, including Paddy's Bike Shop (paddysbikeshop.com), and Dingle Bikes (dinglebikes.com).

KERRY 95

Dingle Bay | Matt Gillman

It's possible to make the cycle shorter or longer, depending on fitness and time. The shortest variation leaves the main road at Dunquin and crosses Mám Clasach (52.1417, -10.4255), the narrow road that passes between Mount Eagle and Cruach Mhárthain, to drop down to Ventry. It's a gruelling climb but the views are spectacular and the descent back to Ventry is fun.

Another option is to do the route at a more leisurely pace, over two days. This allows plenty of time for savouring and exploring the landscape along the way.

VENTRY

As you travel west from Dingle towards Slea Head you will soon reach Ventry, Ceann Trá in Irish. Set in a picturesque bay the Blue Flag beach is more sheltered than most nearby and is safe for swimming and good for snorkelling. Park beside the caravan park (52.1326, -10.3639), where you can jump in Sona Sauna (instagram.com/sonasaunaventry) after a swim, or at Páidí Ó Sé's pub, a bar owned by the legendary local footballer (52.1277, -10.3805).

CRUACH MHÁRTHAIN

Not far inland from Ventry is a prominent hill known as Cruach Mhárthain (52.1496, -10.4309). It's a fairly straightforward walk to the summit and there are spectacular views over West Kerry.

As you arrive at Páidí Ó Sé's from Dingle turn right at the crossroads. Follow the road to the top of the pass and park near the signal tower (52.1417, -10.4255). Cruach Mhárthain is the small conical peak north of the road. Follow the fence behind the tower to the summit. Descend by the same route. It's a 2km round trip.

COUMEENOOLE

Just around the corner from Slea Head is undoubtedly one of the finest beaches in the country (52.1099, -10.4653). At high tide the sea comes all the way up to the cliffs, but at low water the beautiful golden sand stretches across the bay.

The water can be very rough so be careful if swimming. Don't assume that the sea will be calm just because the sun is shining and the wind has dropped.

It's worth following the well-worn path from the carpark to the end of Dunmore Head (52.1111, -10.4750). There you will find one of the most famous views in Ireland. Come at the end of the day to see the sun set over the Blasket Islands.

THE BLASKET ISLANDS

Way out at the end of the Dingle Peninsula, right on the very western edge of Europe, lie the Blasket Islands. Made up of six larger islands and numerous

Slea Head | DF

The view from Cruach Mhárthain | RC

Dunmore Head | RC

Camping on the Great Blasket | RC

smaller rocky outcrops, this is the finest archipelago in Ireland.

It was the home to a hardy community of islanders until the last inhabitants left the Great Blasket in 1954. These days nobody lives on any of the islands year round, but the Great Blasket is a popular destination for day-trippers during the summer, with ferries operating from Dingle, Ventry and Dunquin.

A trip out to the Great Blasket is well worth doing, especially if you stay overnight. The island is over 6km long and hilly, making it an excellent place to go walking. Once you leave the ruins of the village the atmosphere becomes lonely, with great views west to the other islands. See the photo on page 18.

The island's high ground offers an excellent vantage point to observe the abundant marine wildlife. Keep an eye on the sea to the south and you may see basking sharks, whales and dolphins.

Hundreds of grey seals haul out on the beach below the village (An Trá Bán) and they make a fine sight. Don't disturb them - they're totally wild animals and a bite from one of them would be quite serious.

Camping is permitted on the island and there is a water tap in the village. While the island may be busy with tourists during the day, peace descends with the evening. During the night you might hear the low howling of the seals and the eerie calls of Manx shearwaters, seabirds that come ashore to their burrows at night to avoid predators.

If there is a clear sky take a look outside your tent in the middle of the night. The lack of light pollution this far west makes for a brilliant display of stars. The only alternative to camping are the self-catering cottages that open for the summer season (greatblasketisland.net).

Numerous boats offer trips to the island, greatblasketisland.net depart from Dingle and for a shorter trip from the iconic pier at Dunquin (52.1253, -10.4598) see blasketislandferry.com.

BOAT TOURS

Many boat operators offer trips out to the Great Blasket and beyond to get a look at some of the more distant islands. There are plenty of tour companies in Dingle all vying for your custom. Far from the madness of town, there are also tours available from Ventry Pier (52.1317, -10.3600) with an option to combine a landing on the Great Blasket with a sea tour afterwards (marinetours.ie). Highlights include the incredible architecture of Cathedral Rocks on Inishnabro and the puffins around Inishvickillane.

If you're lucky you might get to see some of the wildlife including grey seals, dolphins, whales, basking sharks and a variety of birds. Gulls, gannets, auks and tubenoses all fish in the waters around the Blaskets, and in large numbers can provide as good a show as the bigger species. Don't forget your binoculars. Trips last between 2.5 and 4 hours. Booking is essential

Cathedral Rocks, Inishnabro | RC

Common dolphins | RC

and naturally all trips are subject to the sea conditions. Trips depart from Ventry Pier (*52.1317, -10.3600*).

DUNQUIN

Dunquin, Dún Chaoin in Irish, is the most westerly village in mainland Europe. It's an open and exposed townland, with commanding views of the Blaskets. This is the edge of the world.

Dunquin Pier (*52.1246, -10.4602*) is the point of departure for the Blasket Ferry, and is one of the most well-known viewpoints in all of Ireland.

The Blasket Centre (*52.1332, -10.4612*) is popular with tourists, offering an insight into island life back when the Blaskets were inhabited (blasket.ie).

SIÚLÓID NA CILLE

The Blasket Centre is the starting point for a great 5km coastal and mountain walk. It takes you past the old school built for the film Ryan's Daughter and across open countryside where the wind will chill you or the sun will shine down, or both in the same day.

CLOGHER

A short journey north from Dunquin the main road bends right at Clogher Head (*52.1501, -10.4663*). There is a layby here with room for half a dozen cars and it's worth pulling in to have a proper look. The view from here (on a clear day at least!) is one of

KERRY

Wave watching at Clogher Head | RC

the best around. Take a stroll out to the end of the headland and take in the surroundings.

Just to the north is the wild beach at Clogher Strand (52.1568, -10.4595). The soft grass behind the sand is a nice place for a tent. There are dangerous currents here so swimming is best avoided. Cosán Cuas na nEighe is a good 3km walking trail that starts and ends in the carpark, follow the blue arrows.

FERRITER'S COVE

Just before you arrive in Ballyferriter from the west there's a sign for a golf course. This road leads to Ferriter's Cove, another pleasant bay with the tall cliffs of Sybil Head looming to the north (52.1743, -10.4395).

It's possible to walk to the summit of Sybil Head, which offers incredible views. Just carry on along the road, take a left at the T-junction and park near the last house. Be respectful as this is private farmland.

BALLYFERRITER

Ballyferriter, Baile an Fheirtéaraigh in Irish, is real West Kerry; you're more likely to hear Irish being spoken than English, and students of the Irish language flock here to improve their native tongue. There is a shop, hotel, a few pubs and a museum (westkerrymuseum.com) in the village.

SMERWICK HARBOUR

The southern shores of Smerwick Harbour form an almost continuous beach. This is a good place for a swim in the summer, and for long walks in any weather. Coming from Dunquin, follow the signs for the beach at Smerwick (52.1795, -10.4054), which has a Green Coast award, or Wine Strand (52.1789, -10.3861).

Not far from Wine Strand is the site of an old monastic settlement at Riasc (52.1676, -10.3872). Here you will find a number of beautifully carved standing stones within the remains of a walled enclosure.

Overlooking Smerwick Harbour is the old church at Kilmalkeader (52.1847, -10.3368). The obvious feature is the 12th century church but the ogham stone, high cross and sundial outside the church are older monuments well worth stopping for.

GALLARUS ORATORY

This early Christian church dates back over a thousand years (52.1727, -10.3494). Its beautiful, gently curving stone walls are reminiscent of an upturned boat. It's located near An Mhuiríoch and is well signposted on the Slea Head Drive. There is a small charge for admission and parking at the visitor centre, which is closed in winter though access to the church remains open.

Sunset at Smerwick Harbour | RC

Gallarus Oratory | Shaun Dunphy

Clogher Head | RC

Close by is Campail Teach an Aragail, a camping and caravan park open from April to September (52.1730, -10.3559). See dinglecamping.ie for more.

SEAWEED FORAGING
Local man Darach Ó Murchú gives seaweed foraging workshops in the West Kerry region throughout the year, where you can learn what species are useful as food or cosmetics, and then cook up what you've collected on stoves brought for the occasion. Call 087 2153758 if you're interested in booking a course.

AN MHUIRÍOCH
The beach at An Mhuiríoch can be accessed at the far end of the football pitch (52.1834, -10.3638) and is a nice spot for a stroll and a swim.

BALLYDAVID
The road that leads northwest along the coast from An Mhuiríoch will take you to Ballydavid, or Baile na nGall, another Irish language stronghold. Tigh TP and Tig Beaglaoic are good pubs overlooking the small beach at the pier (52.1905, -10.3759).

SIÚLÓID NA FAILLE
A 6km signposted (red arrows) loop starts from the pier. It follows the coastal path towards Feothanach before returning along a quiet country road. It's a good way to build up an appetite for the pub.

KERRY

Peddler's Lake | Pauric Ward

Standing Stone, Mount Brandon | RC

Winter on the east side of Mount Brandon | RC

BRANDON CREEK

Just over 4km north along the Wild Atlantic Way from Feothanach is the small, steep-sided cove known as Brandon Creek. In 535 AD Saint Brendan set sail from here and reportedly reached the North American continent, long before the Vikings or Columbus.

In 1976 Tim Severin and a small crew set sail from the creek in a boat made of wood and leather to prove that the voyage was possible. They followed the route that Saint Brendan described and reached Newfoundland just over a year later.

The creek is a deep natural harbour, good for a swim (*52.2378, -10.3097*).

MOUNT BRANDON

Steeped in history and beautifully situated, Mount Brandon is a must-do for any hill walker in Ireland. There are few more spectacular summit views for those lucky enough to reach the top on a rare clear day. The longest beach on the Wild Atlantic Way, Brandon Bay, and the iconic coastline of West Kerry are but two of the many inspiring sights.

Anyone planning to venture up the mountain should carry a map (OSI sheet 70) and compass as it is frequently shrouded in thick mist. They should also pack rain gear, plenty of food and warm clothing.

There are two approaches, from the west and east, and both are very different in character.

FROM THE WEST

The western route is the easiest way to the top, offering a gentle slope for most of the ascent.

The carpark for the western ascent of the mountain is at Baile Breac (*52.2148, 10.2923*).

The route follows a clear, well marked path to the top. There are 14 crosses along the way, with white marker posts between these. The path zigzags up steep ground near the summit, and care is required on a few short rocky steps. Descend by the same route. The round trip is 7km with 780m of ascent.

FROM THE EAST

The climb from the east side passes through some steep and dramatic mountain scenery, and is a little more challenging than the previous route.

From the village of Cloghane head north. There is a sign for Mount Brandon not far outside the village. Follow this to the carpark at the end of the road (*52.2393, -10.2057*). From here follow the well-worn track, taking the lower of two paths after about half an hour. After passing through the jumble of small lakes and outcrops on the floor of the glaciated valley, the path becomes much steeper as it winds its way up the intimidating back wall. Take your time along this section, it's tricky but not nearly as intimidating as it looks from the distance.

When you reach the ridge, follow it left for a short distance to the summit, which is marked by a wooden cross. Savour the view if you're lucky enough to

Overlooking Sás Creek | RC

get one. Descend by the same route. The route is 10km with 950m of ascent, making for a long day for anybody not used to hiking.

CONOR PASS

The Conor Pass is one of the highest and most scenic roads in Ireland, but it's unsuitable for nervous drivers or big camper vans. It's the most direct route over to the north side of the peninsula from Dingle Town.

At the highest point of the pass there is a carpark with great views in all directions. Just over 1.5km down the pass towards Cloghane is another carpark beside a small waterfall (*52.1868, -10.1903*). It's worth stopping here and following the stream uphill for a short distance to Peddler's Lake (*52.1863, -10.1888*). The picturesque lake sits in a very impressive mountain corrie and is a great place for a wild swim.

CLOGHANE AND BRANDON

The two small villages of Cloghane and Brandon are signposted shortly after dropping down from the top of the Conor Pass. Both are the antithesis of Dingle Town; a toned down version of a west of Ireland seaside settlement, with enough facilities for most tourists, and a quietness that will appeal to many. The Mount Brandon Hostel is open all year round (mountbrandonhostel.com).

There are some pleasant beaches nearby including: Cappagh Strand (*52.2494, -10.1614*), Brandon Pier (*52.2648, -10.1628*) and An Trá Bháin (*52.2768, -10.1574*).

SÁS CREEK

At the northern tip of the Dingle Peninsula the mountains run down directly to the sea. Here you will find Sás (pronounced Sauce) Creek, a beautiful steep-sided bay.

No roads cross this remote stretch of coast and Sás Creek can only be reached on foot (or by boat!). A hilly 14km walk, Siúlóid a' Sás, will take you there and back in a loop. The walk is signposted (red markers) but it can be hard to follow where it crosses open ground. As the area is prone to mist and changeable weather walkers should be equipped with a map (OSI sheet 70) and compass.

Starting in Brandon village (*52.2682, -10.1616*) follow the red markers along the small roads west of the village. As you gain height you emerge onto open hillside and the road becomes a track. Look out for the signposted turn right, which leads to the edge of the Creek. If the visibility is bad or you aren't confident in your navigation then you should retrace your steps.

If you decide to continue then follow the signs along the edge of the steep slopes, down across the hillside, and through a small valley. A final slog to a stony track leads to Brandon Point (*52.2878, -10.1606*). From here the road leads back to the village.

Brandon Bay | RC

BRANDON BAY

The eastern and southern curves of Brandon Bay are fringed by a 12km stretch of sand which can be accessed along the Wild Atlantic Way between Fermoyle and Castlegregory at four points (from west to east):

- Fermoyle Strand (*52.2431, -10.1252*)
- Kilcummin Strand (*52.2445, -10.1016*)
- Gowlane Strand (*52.2481, -10.0855*)
- Stradbally Strand (*52.2547, -10.0696*)

The beach is exposed and windswept, offering little shelter, but great tracts of privacy. Dingle Surf (dinglesurf.com) run surf lessons on some of these quieter beaches.

CASTLEGREGORY

A popular summer spot, especially for watersports enthusiasts. There are vast sandy beaches either side of the narrow spit, which extends north from the mainland for over 7km. Of note is the Blue Flag beach at Magherabeg (*52.2795, -10.0259*) on the more sheltered east side of the headland. A little further up on the west side of the peninsula Brandon Bay Sauna (brandonbaysauna.com) operates outside Spillane's Bar (*52.3031, -10.0409*).

Jamie Knox's watersports centre offers surfing, windsurfing and paddleboarding lessons and rentals (jamieknox.com). Waterworld also offer surf rentals and lessons, as well as diving courses off the Magharee Islands and Brandon (waterworld.ie).

There is a pleasant walk around the north end of the peninsula. Starting from the grassy carpark at Magherabeg (*52.2795, -10.0259*) it's just a matter of following either coastline north to Scraggane Bay and returning south along the opposite side.

THE MAGHAREE ISLANDS

The Magharee Islands, also known as The Seven Hogs, are the collection of small islands north of Scraggane Bay. They will be of interest to the experienced sea kayaker. Enquire locally about boat trips to the islands.

GLANTEENASSIG

This spectacular mountain valley, with its conifer forest, steep cliffs and waterfalls, could be somewhere in the Swiss Alps (*52.2117, -10.0194*).

There are three signposted walking trails. Unfortunately they are all quite short (300m, 1.1km and 2km), but they provide easy access to some very dramatic mountain scenery.

Coming from the west, the area is signposted to the right just as you enter the village of Aughcasla.

Glanteenassig | RC

TRALEE BAY
The stretch of coastline between Castlegregory and the mouth of Tralee Bay is mostly made up of long stretches of sand. The Wild Atlantic Way runs parallel to the coast and pretty much every road north of it ends at a sandy beach.

Near the mouth of the bay is Derrymore Island. A nature reserve, it supports many rare salt marsh plants as well as wigeon and brent geese who graze on the eastern side of the spit.

THE DINGLE WAY
The Dingle Way is a multi-day walk that starts and finishes in Tralee, and follows the coast around the western end of the peninsula. The 162km trail takes about a week and features a mix of mountain tracks, coastal paths and quiet roads.

There is plenty of accommodation along the route so it's straightforward to plan each day's walk. There are also lots of wonderful places to wild camp.

TRALEE
The large town has all the modern conveniences you will need after a few days in the countryside.

BLENNERVILLE WINDMILL
Just west of Tralee is Blennerville Windmill. The tall white building was used during the 19th century to grind corn and is the tallest of its kind in Europe (52.2566, -9.7371). There is a visitor centre and cafe as well as guided tours of the five-storey windmill.

TRALEE BAY WETLANDS CENTRE
Tralee Bay Wetlands Centre has something for everybody, from bird hides, guided nature tours and a wildlife exhibit, to a watersports centre, a cafe and a viewing tower with great views over the bay (52.2611, -9.7162). See traleebaywetlands.org for more.

FENIT
West of Tralee is the lighthouse at Fenit. A local landmark with the mountains of Corca Dhuibhne serving as a backdrop, it's a favourite with photographers. The Blue Flag beach is very family friendly, with a playground, toilets, lifeguards in the summer and plenty of parking (52.2758, -9.8651).

Fenit is the end (or starting) point for the Tralee to Fenit greenway, a 13km cycle path along the old railway line (kerrygreenways.ie). Wild Water Adventures (wildwateraventures.ie) offer guided watersports activities in the area also, and there are a few food and drink options too.

BARROW BEACH
This gem of a beach is worth seeking out. Follow the signs for Tralee Golf Club and pass through the golf course to the carpark (52.3038, -9.8629).

The Blue Boat, Brandon | Clodagh Edwards

THE DINGLE PENINSULA
ACCOMMODATION

DINGLE WAY GLAMPING, ANNASCAUL
52.1513, -10.0566
dinglewayglamping.ie
Choose from a number of different cosy cabins and huts, all of which are beautifully finished and sleep up to four. There's also a two-person timber pod, and an apartment available for those who want a little more room (sleeps four).

GRANVILLE HOUSE, BALLYFERRITER
52.1648, -10.4102
granvillehouse.ie
Here was the site of a once legendary hotel, recently refurbished for a new lease of life. Stay in a gorgeous self-catering apartment known as The Butterfly House, or a plush yurt or bell tent (with shared kitchen and bathroom facilities). New for 2024 is a sauna, and Ballyferriter's pubs are only a short stroll up the road.

ATLANTIC BAY REST, SMERWICK
52.1934, -10.4142
atlanticbayrest.com
A truly unique collection of clifftop hideaways. There are five different self-catering options available, suitable for solo travellers and groups. All a little rustic, but where else would you find somewhere to sleep almost directly above the sea in a cosy wood cabin? Sauna on site, and access to very secluded beaches, with an outdoor hot shower.

BLUE BOAT, BRANDON
airbnb.ie/rooms/1192253973041555589
Yes, it's literally a blue boat, wonderfully converted with an outdoor deck and separate covered-over outdoor bathroom area. There's a small kitchenette inside, and a bed for two in the bow. Brandon Pier is a short walk away, great for a swim and home to Murphy's pub (see opposite).

STRADBALLY COTTAGE
airbnb.ie/rooms/12924993
This stone cottage has been renovated with upcycled and sustainable materials where possible. Tastefully done, with a wood-burning stove as a centrepiece beneath the two bedrooms, full kitchen facilities and a sauna for warming up after a day outdoors. Sleeps four.

Juice for Thought | RC

Milesian | RC

Báinín | RC

THE DINGLE PENINSULA
FOOD

KITTY'S FOOD TRUCK, INCH
52.1428, -9.9809
A handy one for a day at the beach, from breakfast through to dinner. Burgers, pizza, steak sandwiches and fish and chips on offer, and one of the few places on the west coast you can get the Irish fast food phenomenon, the spice bag (or a spice box as they call it here).

BÁINÍN, ANNASCAUL
52.1523, -10.0522
fb.com/BaininCoffee
Award winning cafe serving great coffee, toasties and baked treats. The Annascaul special, with locally produced black pudding, is a local favourite.

DINGLE - JUICE FOR THOUGHT, REEL DINGLE
Food and drink options in Dingle are very plentiful, from simple takeaways to the finest seafood dining. Many of the pubs do food, and music is a regular feature too. Seafood options are extensive, Reel Dingle Fish is still our favourite (52.1394, -10.2709). Juice for Thought (52.1395, -10.2727) is a great option for a healthy lunch, with delicious soups, sandwiches and sweet treats to go with cold pressed juices and hot drinks.

DOBEY'S FOOD TRUCK, SLEA HEAD
52.1051, -10.4100
Look out for the signs for coffee and lobster if taking the trip around Slea Head. The seafood is as fresh as it gets, being supplied by a local boat from the waters you can sit looking out on while sitting for lunch.

MURPHY'S, BRANDON
52.2685, -10.1599
murphysbarbrandon.com
This pier-side bar is very popular with holidaymakers to this quieter corner of the peninsula, and with good reason. It's a great place for a pint on a summer's evening, and the dinner menu is very good too.

MILESIAN, CASTLEGREGORY
52.2550, -10.0224
instagram.com/milesianrestaurant
One for the fine diners. The set menu isn't extensive, but the options are exquisitely prepared and presented, and good value for what you get.

NORTH KERRY AND LIMERICK

While not as well known as the Iveragh or Dingle Peninsulas, North Kerry has much to offer, including spectacular seascapes, some of the finest beaches in Ireland and many ancient sites, churches and field monuments.

The Wild Atlantic Way follows the coast north into the Shannon Estuary to the ferry terminal at Tarbert. The car ferry links North Kerry with Loop Head in Clare, offering a convenient and novel shortcut between the two counties. Most visitors opt for this short crossing rather than tackle the 207km drive around the Estuary via Limerick City.

From Tarbert a branch of the Wild Atlantic way continues east along the southern shore of the estuary to the port of Foynes in County Limerick. However, as this stretch also forms part of the Shannon Estuary Way it has been included as part of that route, see page 114 for more information.

BANNA STRAND
This is a nice long sandy Blue Flag beach, popular with families, great for walks and a beginner-friendly surfing venue (*52.3384, -9.8346*). There are lifeguards on duty in the summer months.

BALLYHEIGUE
Ballyheigue is a pleasant town that enjoys expansive views of the mountains of the Dingle Peninsula. The Blue Flag beach is a great place to swim or wander the dunes. Further south the long stretch of sand is interrupted by The Black Rock, a tiny island that is ideal for a picnic at low tide. Just make sure that the tides don't cut you off. There is a lifeguard during the summer months and a playground in the carpark (*52.3879, -9.8344*).

KERRY HEAD
A popular fishing spot with a good, remote coastal walk. From the end of the headland there are great views to the south of Tralee Bay and north to Loop Head. A section of the North Kerry Way loops around the roads but a better alternative is to walk to the cliffs on the tip of the headland.

Coming from Ballyheigue, drive north along the Wild Atlantic Way and take the second left (about 5km from Ballyheigue). Ask permission to park in the farmyard (*52.4101, -9.9362*) and follow the rough track to the coast. Be very wary near the cliffs as they are exposed to very big swells and there have been accidents in the past.

Banna Strand | RC

Wild Water Adventures (wildwateradventures.ie) offer coasteering and wild swimming trips along the coast near Kerry Head.

RATTOO MONASTERY

A few miles south of Ballyduff is the 6th century monastic settlement at Rattoo, which consists of a cemetery, an old church, an abbey and a 28m high round tower (*52.4425, -9.6504*). It's signposted about 1km south of Ballyduff on the R551 to Tralee.

BALLYBUNION

Kerry's traditional seaside town is often bustling in the summer time. On the edge of the town is a fine Blue Flag beach that stretches south. In the other direction a path runs along the top of the cliffs, which are full of caves and gullies where seabirds nest and great flocks of starlings roost in the autumn evenings.

The beach at Ballybunion occasionally has good surf. Ballybunion Surf School (ballybunionsurf.com) runs kids camps in the summer time.

Collins's Seaweed Baths was established in 1932 and is still going strong (*52.5137, -9.6749*). The baths are situated on Ladies Strand and are highly recommended.

KAYAKING

One of the best ways to appreciate the coastline is to see it from water level. The coast north of Ballybunion has many epic caves that have to be seen to be believed. Some are connected by tunnels and there is even a skylight in one. Other must-see sights for the kayaker include the Nun's Beach below the convent and the impressive sea arch at The Virgin Rock.

Bottlenose dolphins are common in the area. If you encounter any treat them with respect, they're big animals.

Only take to the water when the conditions are calm and the forecast is good. The sea can get quite rough and big swells are particularly treacherous around the cliffs.

Just south of the main beach, seperated by the River Feale, is Kilmore (*52.4795, -9.6958*), a small, quiet sandy beach.

BROMORE CLIFFS

About 3km north of Ballybunion are the Bromore Cliffs. The cliffs' soft rock has been carved by the sea into impressive caves and sea stacks. There are fantastic colours in the cliffs, abundant wildlife and a few waterfalls spilling into the ocean below.

The landowner has a wealth of knowledge on the history and folklore of the area, and if you don't meet him you can still learn plenty about the area from the information boards. There is a small charge for the carpark (*52.5361, -9.6663*).

Ballybunion sea cave | RC

Rattoo Monastery | RC

Ballybunion Beach | RC

BEAL STRAND
With a name derived from the Irish word for mouth (béal), this gorgeous stretch of sand overlooks the mouth of Ireland's longest river. It's not nearly as popular as some of Kerry's other beaches, but the long empty strand is the perfect place for a walk.

There are strong currents not too far from shore, so swimmers should stay close to the beach. Keep an eye on the water off the strand in the summer months when bottlenose dolphins hunt salmon on the rising tide. Has a Green Coast award. Park at the west end (*52.5739, -9.6312*).

LITTOR BEACH
A very quiet Green Coast beach that looks directly across the estuary (*52.5732, -9.5799*). Parking at the end of the lane is a little tight.

CARRIG ISLAND
Carrig Island is a historic place. The gun battery on the western point was strategically placed; opposite a similar one on Scattery Island. The narrow channel between the islands was well guarded and would almost certainly have prevented Napoleon's ships from sailing any further up the Shannon. In the end the French invasion never came. Going further back in time however, there were other attacks.

Carrigafoyle Castle was built in the late 15th century, and was partially destroyed in a siege in 1580. The west wall, now rebuilt up to the level of the first floor, crumbled under cannon fire and this marked the beginning of the end of the Desmond rule in the area.

Visitors can tour the castle, and it's worth walking around the island itself, taking in the views over the lower estuary. Follow the signs from the village of Ballylongford to the carpark (*52.5695, -9.4948*).

SHANNON FERRY
The Wild Atlantic Way skips across the mouth of the Shannon River between Tarbert in Kerry and Killimer in Clare, saving a long drive around the estuary. The roll-on roll-off car ferry takes 20 minutes to cross and leaves hourly throughout the day. Check sailing times on shannonferries.com.

The Shannon Estuary Way is a new touring route that explores the estuary, see details on page 114. ∎

Thatched Cottage, Ballyduff | RC

NORTH KERRY AND LIMERICK
ACCOMMODATION

WILD ATLANTIC WAY CABIN, BALLYHEIGUE
airbnb.ie/rooms/43893263

This two bedroom timber chalet is located in the village of Ballyheigue, making for a great base for North Kerry. There's a small kitchenette and a single bathroom, as well as a small outdoor seating area for fine mornings and evenings. Sleeps up to four.

THATCHED COTTAGE, BALLYDUFF
airbnb.ie/rooms/50456445

This 18th century thatched cottage has plenty of old world charm. Run as a B&B rather than a rental property, and makes for a great getaway for a couple. The owners run an organic farm, specialising in herbal teas and natural skincare products, which are available to guests. Sleeps two, in a four poster bed.

LAKE LODGE, BALLYBUNION
airbnb.ie/rooms/667835076327662883

A very unique accommodation offering a short distance inland from Ballybunion. Built out into a small lake surrounded by woodland, this circular structure is ringed with wrap-around windows and a timber deck so no matter what the weather you can soak up the light and atmosphere of your surroundings. Inside there's one double bedroom, a full kitchen/living room and a bathroom. Pet friendly, sleeps two.

SCATTERY VIEW COTTAGE, BALLYLONGFORD
airbnb.ie/rooms/20664617

A small and simple stone cottage roughly half way between Ballylongford and Tarbert. There's a compact but fully equipped kitchen, one bathroom and a nice living room with a solid fuel stove. The garden is a good size, ideal for kids to play in, and with great views overlooking the Shannon Estuary. Sleeps up to six across three bedrooms (two doubles and one twin).

Kate Browne's | RC

NORTH KERRY AND LIMERICK
FOOD

KATE BROWNE'S, ARDFERT
52.3261, -9.7802
A fine pub restaurant in a traditionally kept building full of rustic appeal. The lunch and dinner menus are varied and high quality, without the price tag of more high-end restaurants. Well worth a visit if you're anywhere nearby.

SEAN'S STREET PIZZA
52.3388, -9.8240
instagram.com/seansstreetpizza
A mobile pizza truck that is usually found in the carpark at Banna Beach. Keep an eye on their social media as they occasionally run bottomless pizza evenings in Tralee!

THE COAST CAFÉ, BALLYBUNION
52.5114, -9.6727
There are plenty of dining options in Ballybunion, from takeaways to hotel restaurants. The Coast Café is a nice middle ground, offering good breakfasts and lunches at reasonable prices.

BAKING WAVE CAFE, BALLYBUNION
52.5114, -9.6745
fb.com/bakingwavecafe
This small cafe on Lower Main Street in Ballybunion serves coffee and home bakes as well açai bowls and their signature dish - mini pancakes. Closed Tuesdays.

FINUCANE'S BAR, BALLYLONGFORD
52.5464, -9.4755
An honest and authentic country pub with a great historical interest, being the birthplace of The O'Rahilly, a prominent figure in the Irish fight for independence in the early 20th century. No food, but a great place for a pint, without the hordes of tourists.

THE SHANNON ESTUARY WAY

The Shannon, Ireland's longest river, enters the sea via the Shannon Estuary, which stretches 100km from the open water of the Atlantic to Limerick City. Bordered to the south by counties Kerry and Limerick, and to the north by County Clare, the estuary is a vast expanse of constantly ebbing and flowing salt water. For nearly a thousand years it has served as a vital trade route and remains as such to this day, its banks are home to a number of ports, power plants and large factories.

The car ferry that runs between Tarbert in Kerry and Killimer in Clare is part of the Wild Atlantic Way and most visitors opt to make the crossing and continue along the coast effectively bypassing the inner estuary.

The Shannon Estuary Way, which was unveiled in 2017, is a 207km touring route that was created to encourage visitors to explore the estuary. It starts in Tarbert, following the shore of the estuary east before passing through Limerick City and then turning west to regain the north bank of the river, eventually finishing in Kilrush.

Along the way the route passes through over a dozen smaller villages, the large town of Ennis and the city of Limerick. This is a much quieter route than the Wild Atlantic Way, overlooked by the vast majority of visitors to the west coast. It's generally more peaceful and pastoral, and while the scenery is less spectacular than the Wild Atlantic Way, the sights along the Shannon Estuary Way have their own distinct charm.

For more information about the route see shannonestuaryway.ie.

VIEWING POINTS

The eleven Shannon Estuary Way viewing points are located at:

- Glin Pier (*52.5752, -9.2835*)
- Kilteery Pier (*52.5943, -9.2245*)
- Boland's Meadow (*52.6126, -9.1297*)
- Ballysteen Pier (*52.6493, -8.9742*)
- Ringmoylan Pier (*52.6693, -8.8784*)
- Tullyglass Point (*52.6943, -8.8892*)
- Clarecastle Pier (*52.8130, -8.9592*)
- Covraghan Pier (*52.6881, -9.0685*)
- Killadysert Pier (*52.6695, -9.0998*)
- Labasheeda Quay (*52.6224, -9.2462*)
- Knock Pier (*52.6281, -9.3324*)

Askeaton Abbey | RC

GLIN
The small village of Glin has a rich heritage, and its centrepiece is the 13th century castle. The town square is of Georgian design and was built in the 18th century. Three signposted walks start at Saint Paul's Heritage Centre (52.5687, -9.2866).

The Knight's Walk is a pleasant 4km loop (red arrows) through woods and farmland to the highest point in the area, giving great views over the River Shannon. There is a fairy trail for kids near the start of the loop.

The Path (green arrows) is a 4.5km there-and-back walk west along the riverside.

The 8.5km Knockeranna Way (blue arrows) travels a similar distance along the river east from the village. See glin.info for details.

FOYNES
The town of Foynes on the southern shore of the Shannon Estuary has a rich maritime and aviation history. In the 1930s it was the point of departure for flying boats crossing the Atlantic. The Flying Boat Museum (in the old terminal building) exhibits a full-size replica of the Boeing B-314 Flying Boat and is well worth a visit (52.6116, -9.1093). See flyingboatmuseum.com for details.

Foynes Wood (52.6139, -9.1255) has a 1km multi-access trail that twists through woodland on the river bank. Keep an eye on the river for bottlenose dolphins and enjoy a picnic overlooking the water. See coillte.ie/site/foynes for details.

ASKEATON
This town on the River Deel has two main historical attractions, the castle (52.6002, -8.9738) built in 1199, now in ruins, and the much more intact and beautiful 14th century friary (52.6036, -8.9745). Get the most out of a visit by taking a guided trip with Anthony Sheehy (+353860850174), a retired local butcher who's been offering tours since 1964. His knowledge and enthusiasm for the place is infectious.

Askeaton has free campervan parking with facilities, a rare case in Ireland. Find it west of the river opposite the abbey (52.6027, -8.9752).

BEAGH CASTLE
The pier and slip at Beagh (52.6605, -8.9490) is a nice riverside spot with a castle, built around 1260. Beside the castle are five restored coastguard cottages available for rent as well as a cafe (castlecottages.ie).

RINGMOYLAN PIER
A short distance off the Shannon Estuary Way route this is a great place to watch winter flocks of birds probing the muddy shores (52.6692, -8.8784). On the southern shore of the estuary opposite Shannon airport.

Beagh Castle | RC

Clarecastle | RC

Curraghchase Forest Park | RC

Knock Pier | RC

CURRAGHCHASE FOREST PARK
This 300 hectare forest park (*52.5912, -8.8689*) was planted by the de Vere family and is now managed by Coillte. There are playgrounds, public toilets and a cafe in the summer months. The grounds near the old house have lots of green space and some magnificent old trees.

The park has four permanent orienteering courses, a short, medium and long as well as a 2.5km Wheel-O course (orange arrows) which is suitable for those with limited mobility. And there are also three signposted trails on good surfaces throughout the park, suited to both mountain bikes and walkers - the 1.1km The Lake Trail (white arrows), the 2.4km Curragh Trail (blue arrows) and the 3.6km Glenisca Trail (green arrows).

Entry to the carpark is €5, and the park is closed at night. See coillte.ie/site/curragh-chase-forest-park for more information.

CARRIGOGUNNELL CASTLE
A crumbling shell of a castle built on a natural promontory that offers strategic views in all directions, from Limerick City to the Kerry mountains (*52.6452, -8.7419*). Dirty and potentially dangerous (don't fall out of the windows) but worth a visit despite, or maybe because of all that.

LIMERICK CITY
Limerick has all the amenities you can expect from a modern city, and while the bustle might not be to everybody's taste it's reasonably small and easy enough to navigate. Highlights include King John's Castle (*52.6699, -8.6248*), a site that has been occupied for over 800 years and changed hands many times through the ages. The interactive exhibit is a must if in Limerick.

The Hunt Museum (*52.6663, -8.6241*) is another great spot for lovers of antiquity, holding over 2,000 objects spanning over 10,000 years of history. The Milk Market (*52.6635, -8.6224*) is a good stop for a bite to eat, with many different food, drink and craft stalls all under one roof.

If you are a rugby fan then a tour of Thomond Park (*52.6733, -8.6422*), thomondpark.ie, shouldn't be missed.

CRATLOE WOOD
While this 700 hectare forest (*52.7076, -8.7596*) a short distance west of Limerick City doesn't have any signposted trails there is a maze of forest tracks to explore. There is a large playground beside the carpark. Visit coillte.ie/site/cratloe-wood to download a map.

Bunratty Castle | Taylor Floyd Mews

BUNRATTY CASTLE AND FOLK PARK

This large 15th century castle has been carefully restored to its former splendour. Its great hall hosts banquets that feature a meal as well as medieval music, song and dance. The folk park contains over 30 buildings recreating rural and village settings. Surrounding the castle are a few pubs, a hotel and even a winery where mead, a traditional sweet wine containing honey, is made. There is also a pet farm, playground and fairy trail. See bunrattycastle.ie for details.

SHANNON

Home to Ireland's second largest airport and a popular arrival point for visitors to the west coast.

Just outside Shannon Town is the Shannon Aviation Museum (*52.7134, -8.8701*) which delves into the history of aviation with plenty of aircraft on display and a Boeing 737 flight simulator. There are daily guided tour as well as a self-led interactive tour. See shannonaviationmuseum.com for details.

WALKING TRAILS

There are a number of paths that run along the shore between the town and the airport giving really nice views over the river. There are two signposted loops, the 9.5km Shannon Town Estuary Loop (purple arrows) and the 4.5km Illaunmanagh Loop (yellow arrows).

CLARECASTLE

This small village lies downstream of Ennis on the bank of the River Fergus. It was once a busy port, but large vessels can no longer make their way this far up the estuary. The large quay lies quieter now but offers nice views over the river and across to the beautifully restored barracks. Nearby is Ballybeg Woods (*52.8163, -8.9972*), a nice place for a stroll among the trees.

ENNIS

Ennis is a large market town, and the capital of County Clare. There are great pubs and a very strong traditional music scene, plus plenty of shopping, accommodation and food. Of historic interest around the town are Clare Abbey (*52.8289, -8.9693*) and Ennis Friary (*52.8461, -8.9814*), built in the 12th and 13th centuries. Clare Abbey is free to enter, whereas there is a small fee to visit Ennis Friary, but there are guided tours available to enhance a visit.

Ballyalla Lake (*52.8747, -8.9706*) sits just north of Ennis has a Green Coast award and is popular with swimmers. Clare Water Sports (clarewatersports.com) rent stand-up paddleboards and kayaks during July and August.

Canon Island Abbey | DF

LIZZY'S GLAMPING, LISSYCASEY
Though a little ways off the Shannon Estuary Way these glamping lodges are a worthwhile option for anybody looking for lodgings in the general area (52.7394, -9.1726). The design of the lodges themselves is quite unique, like something from a fantasy film. Each one is equipped with a basic kitchen, though the adjoining pub also does food if you'd rather a break from cooking. There's also outdoor seating, a wood-burning stove and private hot tub with each of the lodges. Toilet and shower facilities are communal. See fannyodeas1790.com for details.

LISSYCASEY CASCADES
A 2.6km figure of nine walk starts in the village (52.7488, -9.1480) and heads up a lane, passing an alternative parking (52.75277, -9.1492), before looping around the well-maintained woods crossing the stream via a metal bridge. See sportireland.ie for details.

THE FERGUS ESTUARY ISLANDS
There are over a dozen small uninhabited islands in the broad estuary where the Shannon and the Fergus rivers meet. A wild place, the islands were once home to a thriving population, but nowadays they are only visited by a small number of farmers who keep cattle on the islands.

At the northern end of one of the larger islands, Canon Island, is an Augustinian abbey (52.6790, -9.0372). Most of the extensive buildings date from the 15th century and the stonework remains in excellent condition. It's a wonderful place to explore, all the more compelling for its isolated island setting.

The islands are a magical place and while the currents can be strong, and there are vast mudflats at low tide, they are popular with sea kayakers. Enquire locally about boat trips.

SHANNON ESTUARY WAY RETREAT
A short distance inland from the pretty village of Ballynacally is the Shannon Estuary Way Retreat (52.7238, -9.1020). This centre hosts classes in yoga, reiki and sound baths, among other kinds of treatments (shannonestuarywayretreat.ie).

KILDYSART
This large village is centred on a triangle crossroads. The nearby pier (52.6699, -9.1014) encourages camper vans to park up and is only a short stroll from the village.

Kilkerrin Fort | RC

CROVRAGHAN
A narrow boreen leads down to this small slip at the water's edge (*52.6880, -9.0685*). A busy place, it is a popular departure point for the islands of the Fergus Estuary. At mid-tide there is often plenty of coming and going, with farmers heading out to tend their cattle on the islands.

LABASHEEDA
This small village has its riverside quay and a nice little cafe, Charm Bee (*52.6246, -9.2461*), which doubles as a pottery and craft shop (charmbee.ie).

The beautiful name of the village (in Irish it translates as 'beds of silk'), apparently originated from a poetic sailor who found the bay very sheltered and likened it to sleeping in a bed of silk.

KILKERRIN BATTERY FORT
The best preserved of the dozen Napoleonic forts that line the estuary. The sturdy limestone tower is surrounded by a dry D-shaped moat and commands an excellent view up and down the river. Park at the end of the rough lane (*52.5983, -9.3347*) and follow the shore line west for 125m and cross the field to reach the battery.

BEDS OF SILK, LABASHEEDA
52.6252, -9.2458
bedsofsilk.com
These beautifully crafted huts sleep two, with full bathroom facilities and a kitchenette in each. There's also bike hire available from the owners, as well as BBQ, sauna and hot tub rental (bedsofsilk.com).

SHANNON ESTUARY GLAMPING
A short distance inland between Labasheeda and Kildysart this quiet campsite (*52.6284, -9.1962*) overlooks the tranquil waters of the Shannon and offers a range of accommodation, including a number of luxury tents, a cabin and wooden pods which sleep between two and five (shannonestuaryglamping.com).

KNOCK PIER
This viewing point is at the small working pier, a common feature along the Shannon Estuary Way. Opposite is a pub, The Fisherman's Hut, and a pop-up food truck, Rosie's Coffee. ■

CLARE

Clare has some of Ireland's best known coastal scenery, as well as some of its least known treasures. The Cliffs of Moher need little introduction, but there are breathtaking stretches of coastline all along this county; from the sea-washed, sandstone cliffs of Loop Head to the terraced hills of the Burren.

Music and surfing feature heavily in Clare's modern culture, with professionals from both disciplines travelling to the county in search of both sea and sound waves. There are wildlife sanctuaries too; the Burren, so distinct as to almost be a county in itself, is a wildflower garden known to botanists all over the world. The Cliffs of Moher and Loop Head are important seabird colonies, and the mouth of the Shannon is home to Europe's largest group of resident bottlenose dolphins.

LOOP HEAD

This southwestern promontory of County Clare is often overlooked but it has no shortage of attractions, particularly for those interested in wildlife and exploring the jagged coastline. The Loop Head area has managed to provide for tourists while maintaining an unspoilt feel. It's a quiet place, but it's every bit as impressive as the more famous parts of the Wild Atlantic Way.

While the karst landscape of the Burren in the north of Clare may attract all the plaudits, Loop Head also has some very interesting and impressive cliffs where the contortions and turmoil of the earth's movements can be clearly seen.

The many miles of cliffs are home to a diverse population of birds, however they aren't the only wildlife to be found here. The Shannon Estuary is home to around 200 bottlenose dolphins, as well as plenty of other marine wildlife such as seals and sunfish.

One of the best times to visit is late May, when the coastal wildflowers are in full bloom and the bird colonies at Loop Head are at their busiest.

See loveloophead.com for plenty of useful information.

KILRUSH

After crossing the Shannon the first town you will meet along the Wild Atlantic Way is Kilrush. It has plenty of shops, pubs and a very nice bakery (Considine's - it's well worth a visit). The Shannon Dolphin & Wildlife Foundation has a visitor centre (*52.6356, -9.4959*) near the marina where you can learn about Irish marine life (shannondolphins.ie).

Just outside the village is Cappa (*52.6285, -9.4989*) which has a small rocky beach that is nicely sheltered.

The West Coast Aqua Park (westcoastaquapark.ie) is a giant, floating, inflatable obstacle course in the marina during the summer, providing great fun.

VANDALEUR WALLED GARDEN

Vandaleur Walled Gardens are set over 70 hectares of woodland and include a hedge maze (*52.6363, -9.4733*). Also has a cafe that serves soup, sandwiches, hot drinks and sweet treats. See vandeleurwalledgarden.ie for more information.

SCATTERY ISLAND

About 1.5km off the coast of Kilrush is Scattery Island, a compact area of low-lying land with a long and varied history. The island has a strong association with Saint Senán, who was local to the area, and many

Dolphin watching | RC

Loop Head | RC

saints who followed after him. There are the remains of six churches on the island, as well as a lighthouse, a gun battery, the old village and Ireland's second tallest round tower. The island was sieged many times down through the ages and was finally abandoned in the seventies.

Throughout the summer there are free guided tours of the island. The ferry to the island is operated by Scattery Island Tours (scatteryislandtours.com) from the marina in Kilrush.

QUERRIN
A small village on the shore of the Shannon Estuary with good beach walking, horse riding and a very worthwhile campsite, see page 130.

HORSE RIDING
Carmen's Riding School offers horse riding camps for children during the summer months and full and half day treks for those looking to see the area on horseback. Different abilities are catered for, from beginners to more experienced riders (carmensridingschool.ie).

CARRIGAHOLT
This picturesque fishing village has a nice Green Coast beach, and a few good pubs.

DOLPHINWATCH
The Shannon enters the sea between Loop Head and North Kerry, ending its 360km journey south of Carrigaholt. From here you can sail out to the mouth of the river to see the wildlife, scenery and history of the area.

The highlight of most people's trip is in the name, the area is home to approximately 200 wild bottlenose dolphins. But there's a lot more to these tours than just the dolphins. There are plenty of other wild animals, local heritage and beautiful scenery along the Clare and Kerry seaboards. The trip is fully guided, making for a highly informative few hours at sea.

There's a real emphasis on responsible tourism and the encounters strike a good balance between respect for the wildlife and satisfying the customer.

Of course wild animals being wild, sightings cannot be guaranteed, but there are few other boat tours around the world that can compete with this one's encounter record. Advance booking recommended. For more see dolphinwatch.ie.

COLLEGE STRAND
Another quiet shingle shore, with sand at low water and some interesting clefts in the cliffs at the northern end (*52.5882, -9.7046*). Watch out for the oyster cages at the southern end if swimming.

Kilbaha Coast | RC

Wave Watching at Loop Head | RC

THE BRIDGES OF ROSS
Close to the small townland of Ross is a very interesting section of coastline. The Bridges of Ross (52.5913, -9.8731) are well signposted from the main road to Loop Head.

Only one of the sea arches remains intact (there were three not so long ago) and it's an impressive sight. There are also plenty of other natural features to marvel at nearby. In the bay below the carpark is an interesting cleft in the coast, which leads to a tunnel under the cliffs. The passage opens up at a small stony beach where the ground has caved in. The tide doesn't reach the roof of the tunnel so it's possible to swim through, once the sea is calm of course.

Further west, close to the bridge, are a few sea caves that can be accessed from the land at low tide. Be extremely careful when scrambling around the cliffs here; it's all too easy to get down to places that are difficult to climb back out of. But with care it's possible to get to some otherworldly caverns that are submerged at high tide.

The water beneath the bridge is a good place for snorkelling, but a calm sea is needed as the easiest way to get in and out is where the inlet opens out to the Atlantic. It's possible to jump from the bridge on a high spring tide, but isn't necessarily recommended!

Heading east from the carpark brings you to some more fascinating places, with sea arches, caves, cliffs and blow-holes, enough to make the mind boggle.

This stretch of coastline is also a Mecca for birdwatchers, particularly in August.

KILBAHA
The little village of Kilbaha has a small beach and a playground, as well as a pub that serves good food (see page 131). Just over a kilometre west of the village is a gallery and cafe that specialises in local crafts (kilbahagallery.com).

LOOP HEAD
A circuit walk around the cliffs surrounding Loop Head lighthouse (52.5610, -9.9300) is a must. There are great views over to County Kerry, a pleasant ledge for picnics known as The Hanging Garden, and the famous sea stack, Diarmuid and Gráinne's rock. Keep an eye on the water for bottlenose dolphins, minke whales and seals. Guided tours of the lighthouse grounds are available between April and October.

WAVE WATCHING
Wave watching is one of Ireland's most under appreciated pastimes. Our western seaboard is wonderfully exposed to an enormous stretch of ocean and the prevailing winds carry the weather towards us in a never-ending tide. When the sea is wild it is these western extremities that take the brunt of the storm and sitting to watch the drama unfold as sea meets land is entertainment that most people never tap into.

Castle Point Cave | RC

The very end of Loop Head is a superb place to witness the awesome power of the sea. The shallow shelves below the high cliffs force the cavernous emerald waves to smash upwards, revealing their immense force. The skies that accompany the rough weather are often worth watching in their own right.

The dangers of hanging around a high cliff on a windy day hardly need mentioning but with due care and common sense there is no reason why you can't enjoy this spectacle when the conditions are right. Wrap up warm, bring a packed lunch and prepare to be amazed.

NORTH SHORE WALKS
The north coast of the Loop Head Peninsula is one of high, steep cliffs and wide open views. These two walks give a good flavour of this quiet but remarkable coast.

LOOP HEAD TO FODRY
This walk starts at Loop Head lighthouse (*52.5610, -9.9300*). From the carpark beside the lighthouse follow the northern coastline east. You will soon pass a striking sea arch near the bird colonies. There are more islands and arches further east until the cliffs gradually decrease in height and you reach the rocky beach at Fodry (*52.5798, -9.8810*). Either retrace your steps or have a pick up arranged. It's 4.5km each way.

TULLIG TO GOLEEN
Heading west from Carrigaholt take the second right after the church in the village of Cross. A rough track leads to a quarry on the left. Park considerately here (*52.6105, -9.8026*).

Follow the coastline east, with views over the offshore islands, imposing precipices and remarkable caves and gullies. The cliffs increase in height towards Knocknagarhoon before a gentle descent leads to another quarry at Goleen Bay (*52.6410, -9.7350*). Walk back along the coast or have a car shuttle organized. It's 8km each way.

CASTLE POINT
The sign at Castle Point (*52.6559, -9.7204*) welcomes you to Kilkee Cliffs, a seemingly made up name. The old name for this headland was Dunlicky (Fort of the Flagstones) and the remains of the fort can just about be made out past the carpark.

It's a popular spot for mackerel fishing though unfortunately there is often a terrible mess left behind. If you fish here please take your rubbish home.

There is a very impressive sea cave in the cliffs below the carpark, but it's quite tricky to get into and is flooded at high tide. It would be a very dangerous place to get stuck. Those who can get in and out won't be unimpressed.

The Pollock Holes | RC

KILKEE

Kilkee is a popular seaside holiday village, with a long tradition of tourism. Holidaymakers have been coming here since the early 19th century, and continue to flock to the town in the summer months. The Blue Flag beach is the best in the area (*52.6834, -9.6474*).

CLIFF WALKS

Starting and ending at the beach in Kilkee are two signposted loops that are well worth the effort. There is a 5km circuit (blue arrows) and a longer 8km variation (red arrows), both of which take in the dramatic coastal scenery on the southern side of Moore Bay.

The cliffs at the east end of town can be easily reached by a short walk from the beach. There are no signposted trails but it is a beautiful area worthy of exploration nonetheless. Byrne's Cove (*52.6921, -9.6543*) is a popular swimming spot, though it can be wild.

COASTEERING/KAYAKING

There are plenty of opportunities for kayaking, swimming, snorkelling and coasteering in the bay. So get out and explore yourself or if you need instruction and equipment contact Nevsail Watersports (nevsailwatersports.com).

There are diving boards at the west end (drive out towards the Diamond Rocks cafe and look for the small gap in the wall).

THE POLLOCK HOLES

If you aren't an experienced snorkeller and want a safe place to give it a go with plenty to look at then head for the Pollock Holes (*52.6832, -9.6659*). The huge rock pools retain seawater after the tide has retreated. With starfish, sea anemones, urchins and various fish and crustaceans, this is a shoreline safari that couldn't be more accessible. It's the perfect place to start exploring the underwater world.

Get stuck in and investigate the edges, take a peek behind the seaweed and marvel at the colours. Just remember to treat the wildlife with respect.

The best pools are closest to the sea, at the furthest corner from the carpark. The pools remain uncovered about two hours either side of low tide. If there is a large swell the outer pools will be affected by waves and are best avoided. Keep an eye on the sea conditions and leave as soon as the sea starts spilling back in. The lie of the land means the incoming tide approaches from the sides so be careful not to get cut off.

Moore Bay, Kilkee | RC

BEACHES

While the Loop Head Peninsula isn't famous for its beaches there are a few that are worth checking out.

- Doonaha (*52.6163, -9.6504*) is a pleasant sandy beach, good for swimming.
- Haugh's Strand (*52.6155, -9.6775*) is secluded, with access via a quiet farm track. Best approached by bike as you need to cross private land to reach the beach and parking is very limited.
- At Rinevella (*52.5868, -9.7323*) there is a sand and shingle beach which is good for swimming.

Querrin | RC

Sunset on the Kilkee Coast Road | RC

Sea kayaking near Rinevella | RC

GUIDED WALKS
Martin from Loop Head Walking Tours offers a number of different walking tours, long and short, see loopheadwalkingtours.ie for details.

KAYAKING
The sea kayaking around the Loop Head Peninsula is among the best in Ireland, though it's not a place for the inexperienced. The north coast of the peninsula is very exposed, with few safe landings, and the southern side - where the Shannon meets the sea - is prone to strong tides.

That said, there are options for good weather days that don't require a lifetime of experience. On calm days the coast around and outside of Moore Bay (Kilkee) is worthy of exploration, see page 126. Kilbaha is another safe place to launch when the weather allows. Just west of the bay you can see the Reading Room, a small tower built on the cliff edge by a landlord's agent in the 19th century.

Rinevella is another good area to embark from. Just east of here the lighthouse and caves at Kilcredaun are best seen from sea level. Be aware of the strong tides in this area. The sea is squeezed in and out at this narrow gap between Clare and Kerry, creating fast currents.

Carrigaholt is generally quite a sheltered place to kayak. There are great views of the 15th century tower house from the water and the small caves to the south are interesting.

CYCLING
Loop Head is best explored by bike. Unlike some of the more popular tourist areas along the coast there are no tour buses clogging the roads and the peninsula is compact and flat enough that most areas can be seen in a long day. However it could be worth slowing down and allowing yourself more time to explore the stunning coastline in this quiet corner of West Clare.

Starting and ending in Kilkee the 65km Loop Head Cycleway brings you along the coast of the peninsula, off the busiest roads and within striking distance of some of the famous sights like Carrigaholt Castle, Loop Head Lighthouse and the Bridges of Ross. Bikes can be hired at Williams Hardware in Kilkee.

Pure Space, Querrin | Pure Space

LOOP HEAD
ACCOMMODATION

COLOURFUL COTTAGE, BREAGHVA
52.6310, -9.715
noharmfarm.ie
A cheerfully renovated cottage centrally located on the Loop Head Peninsula. The decor is all bright pastel colours, and a full kitchen and cosy living room make this a great base for a larger group or family. Attached to the No Harm Farm, meaning fresh produce is often available too. Sleeps five across three bedrooms.

PURE SPACE, QUERRIN
52.6313, -9.5982
purespace.ie
This is a campsite like you've never visited before. It has all the usual stuff: like space for tents and camper vans, toilets, showers and laundry services. And then there are the things you're not likely to find in most other campsites. Like a sauna. Or yoga classes. There's a pizza oven. And a communal 12m dome tent for chilling in.

If you don't have your own tent you can stay in one of the luxury bell tents, with bed linen provided and a mini wood-burning stove. There's a four hectare native woodland on the site and plenty of walking in the surrounding area. A place worth seeking out.

BRENNAN'S OLD HOUSE, CROSS
airbnb.ie/rooms/5088517
This 130 year old cottage has been well restored and still maintains a quite old-style feel, though not through sacrificing modern comfort. It's quiet, private gardens will appeal to many, and it's centrally located on the peninsula, making a perfect base for larger groups to get to know the area. Sleeps six across three bedrooms.

WILDHAVEN CABIN, MOYASTA
airbnb.ie/rooms/19923678
This renovated mobile home is roughly half way between Kilrush and Kilkee, and ideal for a couple or small family. A particularly big plus is the enclosed garden, ideal for visiting pets, who are welcome. There's a full kitchen, wood stove in the living room and a covered outdoor deck. The interior design might not be to everybody's tastes but it's certainly unique!

The Long Dock | The Long Dock

LOOP HEAD
FOOD

THE JELLYFISH MARKETPLACE, KILRUSH
52.6365, -9.4896
fb.com/JellyfishMarketplace
Housed in a restored flour mill overlooking the marina on Frances Street. They serve breakfast and lunch with a brunch on weekends. The menu is varied with staples such as granola and French toast, as well as more creative options like brioche lobster rolls and breakfast focaccia. Their coffee is their own signature blend and they also produce a range of freshly-baked breads

THE LONG DOCK, CARRIGAHOLT
52.6039, -9.7107
instagram.com/thelongdock
Excellent pub grub, with as many fresh ingredients from as close as possible used in their hearty meals. Nice gift shop too, with lovely homemade breads, sauces, chutneys and desserts to take away.

KEATING'S, KILBAHA
52.5693, -9.8630
Another great west of Ireland pub within a stone's throw of the sea. The food is unpretentious, traditional grub, and good value for money.

THE PANTRY, KILKEE
52.6790, -9.6482
pantrykilkee.ie
A great deli with a fine selection of wholesome options to choose from. Either eat in or take it out and go sit on the seafront in Kilkee.

POLLOCK & PORTER, KILKEE
52.6800, -9.6463
pollockandporter.com
A higher end restaurant in Kilkee, but well worth the money if you want to treat yourself. Food that's sourced, cooked and presented very, very well, and with a wine and cocktail menu to match.

DOONBEG TO LAHINCH

The stretch of the Atlantic coast between Loop Head and Lahinch is renowned for its traditional music and expansive beaches. There's probably nowhere else in Ireland that attracts more surfers than Lahinch and likely no better town than Milltown Malbay for aspiring musicians. What could beat a visit to a pub with good tunes after a few hours of thrashing around in the sea or walking a long Atlantic strand?

BALTARD
The cliffs at Baltard are very tall, very steep and very impressive. They aren't signposted, but are worthy of an evening's exploration. Take care at the cliffs and respect the signs regarding trespassing (*52.7331, -9.6075*).

DOONBEG
A small village with an iconic ruined castle where the Doonbeg River meets the Atlantic. It is the trailhead for two signposted trails, the 8km Doonbeg Loop (green arrows) and the 20km Tullaher Loop (purple arrows). Just outside the village is a campsite (strandcampingdoonbeg.com) with all the usual facilities in a pleasant location.

WHITE STRAND
The small Blue Flag beach lies to the northwest of the village. There is a lifeguard on duty on weekends in June and September and daily during July and August (*52.7477, -9.5508*).

DOUGHMORE BAY
A classic west coast strand, open to the Atlantic and backed by sand dunes. A great place for a long evening walk. It is signposted to the left as you travel north from Doonbeg. The carpark (*52.7456, -9.5041*) is beside the golf course.

QUILTY
The little village of Quilty is flanked to the north and west by Green Coast beaches, all of which are best when the tide is out.

Southwest of Quilty is the Green Coast beach at Seafield. There are actually two beaches either side of the headland. The beach inside the quay (*52.8088, -9.4904*) is sheltered, while the other is west-facing and takes the brunt of the elements.

Further south is Carrowmore (signposted 'Carrowmore Point' off the main road), another open beach (*52.7745, -9.4827*).

Spanish Point | RC

A session in Milltown Malbay | RC

Surfing in Lahinch | RC

SPANISH POINT
Spanish Point is a popular Blue Flag beach (*52.8431, -9.4328*), best at low tide when the sand is exposed. Celtic Surf School (celticsurfschool.ie) offer rentals and lessons, one of Clare's more well known surf spots.

MILLTOWN MALBAY
Just inland from Spanish Point is the village of Milltown Malbay, renowned as one of the hubs of traditional Irish music in the country. Every July it is packed with the best musicians during Willie Clancy week (scoilsamhraidhwillieclancy.com). Students of Irish music from all over the world come for workshops and to take part in sessions in the many excellent pubs. The sight and sound of up to twenty musicians of all ages sawing fiddles and squeezing accordions to the same tunes is fairly special. Even when the festival isn't on there are few other towns in Ireland with better music.

WHITE STRAND
This pleasant little bay (*52.8687, -9.4279*) offers safe swimming, kayak rental (clarekayakhire.com and clarewatersports.com) and has a campsite behind the beach for tents and mobile homes. It has a Blue Flag and is patrolled by lifeguards during the summer. Sauna Suaimhneas have a mobile sauna at the beach here (saunasuaimhneas.com).

LAHINCH
During the summer Lahinch is a bustling town with cafes, pubs and shops. Known to local watersports enthusiasts as Surf City, the Blue Flag beach (*52.9348, -9.3488*) is ideal for board riders of all abilities. There are at least six surf schools in Lahinch so there's no problem finding somewhere to hire gear or get lessons.

Walkers will be happy too, with 2km of golden sand to stretch the legs on. It's possible to swim at the beach, but there are rip tides and the water is often packed with surfers. There is a lifeguard during the summer.

Sauna Suaimhneas (saunasuaimhneas.com) also operate a sauna on the beach here, as well as at Clahane Shore (*52.9324, -9.4216*), a popular swimming spot a little to the west near Liscannor.

ENNISTYMON
Just a little ways inland from Lahinch is the picturesque village of Ennistymon, based around the stepped cascades of the Cullenagh River. There are a few excellent pubs, cafes and restaurants, and the walk through the Glen, which starts from the Falls Hotel (*52.9404, -9.2977*) is well worth doing. ∎

Skippy's Shack | Patrick Cross

DOONBEG TO LAHINCH
ACCOMMODATION

GRANDA'S HOUSE, DOONBEG
airbnb.ie/rooms/54178845
Set on a working dairy farm, this 200 year old cottage has been entirely modernised, with a huge open plan ground floor and two bedrooms above. Sleeps up to four across a double and two single beds.

SEA-RENITY COTTAGE, QUILTY
airbnb.ie/rooms/1155762070831275505
A recently renovated cliffside cottage in the small village of Quilty, on Clare's west coast. The interior is bright and decorated in a bold, colourful style, with original windows expanded to take in the close sea views. The garden is so close to the sea it gets sprayed by salt water in wild weather, but makes for a great place to hang out when the sun shines. Sleeps two.

COSY CABIN, MILLTOWN MALBAY
airbnb.ie/rooms/49088010
A simple, but beautiful, wooden cabin on an elevated site, with distant sea views and plenty of peace and quiet. There's one double bedroom with adjoining bathroom, a kitchen/living area and a small outdoor deck for time outside. Perhaps a little basic for some tastes, but a welcome retreat for those not looking for luxury. Pets welcome.

SKIPPY'S SHACK, LAHINCH
airbnb.ie/rooms/598331180867268428
A small but super-cool stay for two, this solar powered converted shipping container is just two minutes from the beach at Lahinch. It has a king-size bed, full kitchen facilities, a stove, and enough clever design features to make the small space feel as comfortable and uncluttered as possible. There's a gated garden for when the sun shines too, so you needn't spend the whole stay indoors.

Pot Duggan's | Patrick Cross

DOONBEG TO LAHINCH
FOOD

MORRISSEY'S, DOONBEG
52.7310, -9.5244
morrisseysofdoonbeg.ie
Good for a pint, great for a meal, this gastropub goes a little beyond your average pub grub to serve up delicious dinners.

LUNA, MILLTOWN MALBAY
52.8567, -9.4012
instagram.com/thelunafoodco
Just around the corner from the busy main street of Milltown, this cafe serves great breakfasts and lunches, with a healthy mix of salads and sweet treats in a bright and airy building.

POT DUGGAN'S, ENNISTYMON
52.9390, -9.2933
potduggans.com
A superb pub with an exceptional menu. The pizzas are particularly good, but then so is everything. Beautiful riverside outdoor area too, not to be missed for food and drink if you're in the area.

MOY HILL
52.8959, -9.3323
moyhillfarm.com
Buy direct from the growers at this roadside farm shop. Seasonal vegetables and produce from a regenerative farm, you can't eat much better than this stuff, and it's doubly good knowing that the farming practices help restore soil fertility.

DODI, LAHINCH
52.9323, -9.3460
fb.com/dodicafe
This popular cafe on Main Street serves Middle-Eastern inspired brunches and lunches. Expect queues on weekend mornings as people crowd in for luxurious hangover cures.

HUGO'S DELI, LAHINCH
52.9333, -9.3448
fb.com/HugosDeliLahinch
Probably the best bakery in Ireland, bar none. Great mix of sweet and savoury, and the sourdough is delicious. Get there early, often sells out fast.

THE BURREN

The Burren is an area of exposed limestone covering the northwest of Clare. The unusual and fascinating landscape, known as karst, was formed around 340 million years ago, when this part of the earth's crust was the bed of a shallow tropical sea.

The terraced hills of the Burren are composed of limestone pavements with intersecting cracks known as 'grikes', which leave isolated slabs of rock called 'clints'. The barren landscape was once described in rather morbid terms as *"a country where there is not enough water to drown a man, wood enough to hang one, nor earth enough to bury him."*

A flying visit to the Burren cannot do it justice. There is a lifetime of learning and discovery to be had in this surprising, rocky land.

While obviously of great interest to geologists, the Burren landscape is also world famous for its botany. There is a curious mix of Arctic-Alpine and Mediterranean species, which rarely appear side by side. The summer meadows are a blanket of colour and even areas of extensive limestone pavement can be dotted with thousands of wildflowers growing from the cracks in the stone.

The Burren also has a rich archaeological heritage with monuments of all types from the last 6,000 years. One of Ireland's most famous ancient structures, the Poulnabrone Dolmen, lies in the heart of the Burren but there is evidence of man's engagement with this landscape in every valley and on each hillside.

Though the Cliffs of Moher aren't of the same geological formation as the Burren, they are interesting enough and close enough to have been grouped together as the Burren and Cliffs of Moher Geopark. This international designation aims to promote sustainable tourism and livelihoods for those living in the region. See burrengeopark.ie for more information.

CLIFFS OF MOHER

The world famous Cliffs of Moher are Ireland's most popular natural attraction. Stretching for 8km and reaching up to 214m high, there are astonishing views in all directions.

The visitor centre is located almost midway along these spectacular cliffs, set into a grassy hillside (52.9719, -9.4262). Nearby is the 19th century O'Brien's Tower and a stretch of protected cliff side path with viewing areas. Entry costs €6 per person and it can be very busy. Please be careful near the edge and obey the warning signs.

An excellent alternative way to experience the cliffs is to walk the Doolin to Liscannor coastal walk (see page 140).

Looking towards O'Brien's Castle, Cliffs of Moher | Jennifer Boyer

Burren coast| RC

AILEEN'S
A specific combination of wind and swell can create a huge wave near the foot of the cliffs. As it's hidden from view and lost in the scale of its surroundings it was only discovered relatively recently by big wave surfers. The wave, known as Aileen's, can get up to 10m and attracts surfers from across the world.

Near the northern end of the cliffs there is a steep path that leads down to sea level. The steep descent is well worn by surfers who use it to access Aileen's. Seeing the cliffs from below is a humbling perspective, one that's only suitable for those comfortable with the adventurous descent.

DOOLIN
Though it can get busy during the summer, Doolin is an excellent base for exploring the Cliffs of Moher, the Burren and the Aran Islands. There is plenty of accommodation, including at least half a dozen hostels, and the pubs in the village are renowned for traditional music. It's also a terrific place to wave watch when the winter storms pound the coast.

The pier at Doolin (*53.0153, -9.4045*) is used by ferry companies to take people to the Aran Islands and the Cliffs of Moher from March to October. Book well in advance during the summer. See doolinferry.com for timetables.

Wild Atlantic Seaweed Baths (wildatlanticseaweedbaths.com) run their much-loved whiskey barrel hot tubs from the pier here too.

CYCLING
The village is the hub for the four signposted routes of the North Clare Cycle network. With both coastal and inland routes, there is plenty to see, including Atlantic views, ancient portal tombs and picturesque villages.

- Loop 1 the shortest tour (18km), goes from Doolin south towards the Cliffs of Moher.
- Loop 2 (39km) passes through the villages of Liscannor, Lahinch and Ennistymon. A shorter 26km variation is also possible.
- Loop 3 (43km) heads inland towards Kilfenora passing by the Poulnabrone Dolmen.
- Loop 4 (47km) travels north from Doolin along the coast road, with spectacular views of the Aran Islands. A shorter 21km variation is also possible.

Bikes are available to rent in Doolin (doolinrentabike.ie).

DOOLIN CAVE
A few kilometres north of the village is Doolin Cave, home to the largest known stalactite in Europe (*53.0411, -9.3449*). The tour of the cave is well worth a go, especially on a wet day. There is a cafe and

Exploring the Burren's backroads | DF

Dog Rose | RC

Scurvy Grass | RC

Blackthorn | RC

Bloody Crane's Bill | RC

Fanore | RC

nature trail on the premises, and even a sunny day discount! Open daily from March to October.

DOOLIN TO LISCANNOR COASTAL WALK
This walk is arguably the best way to experience the Cliffs of Moher. At 18km it isn't short, but there aren't many more easily accessible, spectacular coastal hikes anywhere in Ireland.

The walk starts in Doolin and is marked with blue arrows. Heading southwest out of the village you soon leave the road and hug the coastline above increasingly tall cliffs. Before long the route meets the northern end of the massive Cliffs of Moher.

Continuing south, the cliffs rise and projecting stone slabs at the edges make for perfect, if worrying, natural viewing platforms. The famous O'Brien's Castle is soon reached and you can either stop at the visitor centre or rush through the crowds depending on your inclination. Most people miss out on the scenery south of here but there is no shortage of interest with sea arches, caves and huge bird colonies in the summer months. Gradually losing height, you eventually arrive at Hag's Head before turning east towards the small village of Liscannor.

THE DOLMEN CYCLEWAY
Starting and finishing in Lisdoonvarna this signposted 45km loop takes in many of the interesting inland sights including the steep hairpins of Corkscrew Hill.

AILLADIE
Along the coast road north of Doolin (*53.0693, -9.3582*) is a convenient layby. It's a good place to stop and admire the sheer cliffs at Ailladie, a climber's paradise (see page 145).

FANORE
The main beach along the Burren coastline has beautiful rich sand and hilly dunes (*53.1173, -9.2872*). It has a Blue Flag and there are lifeguards on duty during the summer. Aloha Surf School (surfschool.tv) offers surf and kayak lessons during the summer.

WALKING TRAILS
The Black Head Loop is a tough 26km loop (purple arrows) but it's a great way to experience the bizarre landscape of the Burren up close. There are great views over the ocean from Black Head, as well as inland to the green valleys and iconic flat-topped hills. The shorter loop, back through the Caher valley, is about 14.5km (red arrows). Both loops start and finish in the carpark at Fanore beach (*53.1173, -9.2872*). The 21km Fanore Ballyvaughan Trek (green arrows) links the two villages along a green road around the hilly slopes of Black Head.

BALLYVAUGHAN
This small harbour village lies on the sheltered southern shore of Galway Bay.

The cliffs at Ailladie | RC

Caving in The Burren | Terry Casserly

Fertile rock | RC

BALLYVAUGHAN HERITAGE TRAIL
One of the Burren Geopark Heritage Trails, this easy 2.3km walk explores some of the historical sites of interest in the village of Ballyvaughan (*53.1172, -9.1520*). Follow the green footstep arrows. See burren.ie for more information.

BALLYVAUGHAN WOOD LOOP
This 8km loop follows quiet roadways and green lanes through the countryside behind the village. There are splendid views of the distinctive limestone layers of the surrounding hills. It's not that well signposted so keep your eyes peeled for the purple arrows.

BISHOP'S QUARTER
This pleasant stretch of strand about 2km north of Ballyvaughan (*53.1295, -9.1287*) has a Green Coast award. Look out for the signposted left turn.

THE FLAGGY SHORE
At first glance the Flaggy Shore might seem an unspectacular length of coastline, but the interest here is in the finer details. This region is like a natural outdoor geology classroom. There are fossils in the rocks, left over from when this area was the bed of a tropical sea. There are also signs of more recent (in geological terms at least) activity too - there are granite boulders that were dragged here from Connemara by glaciers, and the marks from that slow

Poulnabrone Dolmen | Nicolas Raymond

Corcomroe Monastery | RC

Slieve Carran Nature Reserve | DF

grinding process can still be seen on the ground. The area is best accessed from the small beach between New Quay and Finavarra Point (53.1570, -9.0864).

The Flaggy Shore Heritage Trail is an 8km loop (green footprint arrows) around the Finavarra Peninsula which passes a number of sites of geological and historical interest (53.1569, -9.0882). See burren.ie for details.

CORCOMROE MONASTERY

Close to Ballyvaughan is the ruin of this 13th century monastery. It is noted for its unusual ornamentation and carvings. There is a legend that the king who ordered the construction executed the five masons once it was completed, to ensure no similar structure could be built for his rivals. It is signposted off the Wild Atlantic Way at Bell Harbour (53.1265, -9.0543).

AILLWEE CAVES

During the guided tour through the caverns (53.0894, -9.1436) you will cross over bridged chasms, under weird formations, and alongside the thunderous waterfall (aillweecave.ie). There is also a bird of prey centre which offers displays of birds including eagles, falcons, hawks, and owls.

AN RATH FAIRY FORT

Close to the turn for the caves is Ballyallaban Ring Fort (53.0900, -9.1585). This fort consists of an earth wall and deep trench. It is in good condition and is in a very pretty setting surrounded by beech trees.

POULNABRONE DOLMEN

This ancient portal tomb is one of the most famous landmarks of Ireland, and attracts a few hundred thousand visitors each year (53.0487, -9.1401). When the tomb, which was built almost 6,000 years ago, was excavated in 1986 the bodies of 16 adults and 6 children were found buried inside.

CARRON TRAILS

The small village of Carron is the trailhead for three nice walks. The longest one, the 9km Carron Loop (purple arrows), follows minor roads, animal tracks and grassy lanes, taking in the Clab Valley, Saint Fachtnan's Holy Well and part of Termon Hill. It traverses fields of stone slab and passes a 'turlough' (an area which floods in winter but is dry in summer).

The 5km Carron Turlough Loop (red arrows) makes a circuit of the large turlough on minor roads. Another shorter route, the 5km Templecronan Loop (green arrows), visits Termon Cross and Teampall Chrónáin to the north of the village. The walks start opposite Cassidy's Pub (53.0353, -9.0768).

Just down the road is Clare's Rock Hostel (claresrock.com).

The trail at Lough Avalla | Conor Lawless

LOUGH AVALLA FARM LOOP

A must do for anybody looking to stretch their legs in the Burren's magical landscape. The 6km walk passes through both wood and farmland and offers great views of Mullaghmore, the National Park's signature hill. It's very well signposted and local hazel was used to make the beautiful gates and stiles along the walk.

The trail starts and finishes at Mullaghmore Crossroads, which is also the trailhead for the National Park trails (*52.9966, -9.0376*). Walk up to the crossroads and turn left to start the walk following the purple markers.

After your walk you should call into the Lough Avalla Tea Room (*53.0036, -9.0467*), a delightful cafe run by the family who owns the farm. The homemade cakes and hot drinks will be well deserved after the walk. On the east side of the lake is a jetty. Follow the wide track beside it for a short distance to reach the cafe.

BURREN NATIONAL PARK

Though the Wild Atlantic Way hugs the coast, it's worth deviating inland to the Burren National Park. The roads are narrow and winding but it's a captivating place to explore.

The trailhead for five of the Park's seven signposted trails around Mullaghmore is on the southeastern side of the Burren. From Corofin head north along the R476. Turn right in Killnaboy (signposted 'Kilnaboy Church & School') and follow the road for 5km.

Just before the crossroads is a lay-by on the right (*52.9966, -9.0376*).

Alternatively, avail of the free bus to the crossroads from the National Park Information Point in Corofin (*52.9450, -9.0628*) which runs through the summer.

A number of walks start from the crossroads including: the 1.3km Knockaunroe Turlough (orange markers), the 1.5km Nature Trail (green arrows), the 6km Mullaghmore Traverse (red markers), the 6.5km Mullaghmore Return (green markers) and the 7.5km Mullaghmore Loop (blue markers).

Two more walks begin in the Slieve Carran/Keelhilla Nature Reserve (*53.0764, -8.9988*), the 2km Yellow Route and the 2.5km Brown Route. They are not serviced by the bus.

Download a trail map from burrennationalpark.ie. There are guided walks during the summer months, see the website for details.

NATIONAL PARK INFORMATION POINT

This information point is on the ground floor of the Clare Heritage Centre on Church Street in Corofin (*52.9448, -9.0626*). It is open to the public from April until the end of September, providing information on the flora and fauna of the National Park. ∎

Burren National Park | RC

Rock climbing at Ailladie | Pat Nolan

Burren wildflower | RC

Typical Burren landscape at Oughtdarra | RC

Exploring by bike | DF

WALKING
There is such a wealth of interest in the Burren that a knowledgeable walking guide can significantly enhance your experience. See burrenguidedwalks.com for details.

ROCK CLIMBING
The sea cliffs and inland crags of the Burren are very popular with rock climbers. Ailladie, on the coast road north of Doolin, is one of the best climbing areas in Ireland. See climbit.ie or burrenoec.com if you are interested in giving it a go.

CAVING
The Burren landscape is a hollow one. As limestone is a relatively soft rock it is constantly being eroded by rivers and rain at a much faster rate than other types of stone. Most of this water finds its way underground where it gouges out incredible subterranean caves and caverns.

There are a few famous caves in the Burren that are established tourist attractions (Aillwee and Doolin) but if you want a real caving experience you can book a few hours with the Burren Outdoor Education Centre (burrenoec.com). Their trips are an excellent introduction to a pastime that is usually reserved for a select few experts. The outings are tailored to your personal ability so there is a challenge available for everybody.

SEA KAYAKING
Sea kayaking is a great way to get a different perspective of the coast. North Clare Sea Kayaking (northclareseakayaking.com) offer guided tours of this world famous stretch of the Wild Atlantic Way. There are plenty of options to make the most of the given weather, from the sheltered bays around Ballyvaughan to the tall cliffs further south. If you're lucky you might even see dolphins, seals and seabirds. See the photo on page 18.

CYCLING
The dense network of small roads around the Burren are ideal for cyclists, whether you're a training fanatic or a leisurely explorer. Some of the routes starting at the Doolin Cycle Hub (see page 140) venture inland to the Burren, as does the Dolmen Cycleway (see page 136). For more suggested routes see *Cycling in Ireland* by Three Rock Books.

Carley's Cottage | Carley's Cottage

THE BURREN
ACCOMMODATION

WILD MEADOW HUTS, DOOLIN
wildmeadowhuts.ie
Small, but luxurious, glamping huts in a gorgeous meadow outside Doolin. Each comes with a king-size bed, kitchen facilities and a bathroom, and guests can book a session in a private hot tub during their stay.

DOOLIN GLAMPING
53.0165, -9.3797
doolinglamping.com
This campsite has pitches as well as a few quirky accommodation options: a luxury bell tent (sleeps 2-5), a Mongolian yurt (sleeps 2-6), a Native American tipi (sleeps 2-3) or a tiny vintage caravan (sleeps two).

BURREN GLAMPING
52.9861, -9.1923
burrenglamping.com
A tastefully renovated horse truck (sleeps six) on a working farm in the Burren's heartlands. Treat yourself to some free-range pork or chicken direct from the source. On the pricier end of the scale but well worth it.

CARLEY'S COTTAGE, CAHER VALLEY
airbnb.ie/rooms/6137764
This carefully restored cottage has plenty of original character. The stone floors and original walls of the living room shows the bones of what was a cow house over a hundred years ago, while the full kitchen, two bedrooms and two bathrooms are all modernised for comfort. Sleeps five.

CHALET ON THE HILL, BALLYVAUGHAN
airbnb.ie/rooms/31289104
This beautiful timber chalet is located above the village of Ballyvaughan There's a double bed in the loft and the couch on the ground floor can pull out to sleep two. With lots of light to feel close to the outdoors while remaining cosy, even if the weather isn't.

THE CROW'S NEST, NEW QUAY
53.1545, -9.0692
airbnb.ie/rooms/641266875292415857
Built from recycled timber under the shade of a fine old tree, this raised timber cabin makes for a cool getaway. There's no much in the way of a kitchen, with just a toaster, kettle and fridge, but Linnane's Bar (see opposite) is within walking distance. Sleeps two.

Linnane's | Linnane's

THE BURREN
FOOD

MOHER COTTAGE, LISCANNOR
52.9529, -9.4211
mohercottage.com
A gift shop and cafe serving excellent coffees and sweet treats, and a wide range of Irish made gifts.

THE IVY COTTAGE, DOOLIN
53.0127, -9.3852
theivycottage.ie
A tasty menu and good outdoor seating options make this a worthy alternative to the usually-thronged pubs of Doolin. No reservations taken, so be prepared to wait in high summer.

BURREN FINE WINE & FOOD
53.0903, -9.1733
This cafe lies a few kilometres south of Ballyvaughan at the foot of Corkscrew Hill. Situated in a renovated stone stable they serve homemade, local, seasonal lunches and afternoon teas. They also offer cycling tours. Check burrenwine.ie before visiting to confirm it will be open.

O'LOCLAINN'S, BALLYVAUGHAN
53.1161, -9.1503
oloclainnsbar.com
For six generations this small one-room pub has been serving locals and visitors in the seaside village. And while from the outside it doesn't look like anything special, inside you will find the walls covered with shelves packed with over four hundred different whiskeys from across the world. A must-visit.

LINNANE'S, NEW QUAY
53.1559, -9.0758
linnanesbar.com
If you're looking for seafood you can't do much better than this pub restaurant right on the pier at New Quay.

JULIA'S LOBSTER TRUCK
instagram.com/juliaslobstertruck
Barbecued lobster, grilled fish, mussels, oysters. If you're into eating what the sea provides follow Julia on Instagram to see where the food truck will be next. Generally based in North Clare and not to be missed for seafood lovers.

GALWAY

The vast majority of the coastline of County Galway lies within Connemara, a region which due to a lack of an official definition, has boundaries that are a little unclear. Everyone agrees on the northern border, Killary Harbour, and the Atlantic defines it in the south and west. The uncertainty relates to the eastern border - some say it stretches to the edge of Galway City while others draw a line from Killary Harbour to Kilkieran Bay. Either way, Connemara is one of the most popular tourist areas in Ireland.

Compared to the most rugged parts of Ireland's Atlantic coast Galway's coastline is reasonably low-lying, and as a result the area between land and sea is easily accessed. This coupled with the extremely jagged, indented nature of the coastline means that it is home to a massive number of tiny bays, rocky coves and sandy beaches.

Galway City, the only city on the Wild Atlantic Way, is a vibrant, youthful place. With plenty of pubs and restaurants it's the ideal place to spend some time before heading back into the wild.

It's worth noting that from a geological point of view the Aran Islands have much more in common with the rocky landscape of the Burren in Country Clare, but they are part of County Galway. They are the strongholds of island life in Ireland, still relatively well populated after most other offshore communities have dwindled. Their combination of sea-locked isolation and lunar landscape is enough to keep attracting tourists for many years to come.

The predominantly flat terrain near the coast, particularly south of Clifden, is ideal for cycling and there is a network of many hundreds of kilometres of small, very quiet roads (known as boreens) to explore.

ARAN ISLANDS

While each of the three Aran Islands (Inis Mór, Inis Meáin and Inis Oírr) have their own distinct character, they all share a rugged karst landscape and an intense sense of culture and place. A visit is a chance to experience the distilled essence of Ireland's west coast.

During the summer the islands, particularly Inis Mór, can get busy, but it's always possible to escape the crowds. The rest of the year is much quieter and the islands are an amazing place to be during a winter storm. The only way to properly experience them is to stay overnight. Even on the two smaller islands there is too much to see in a day and you will miss out on that essential Irish cultural experience - a night in the pub.

Like many of the other islands off Ireland's west coast, the Irish language is still in daily use and you will hear plenty of it spoken in the shops and pubs.

The islands are very exposed to the prevailing wind and there is little shelter so it can feel raw. However, the clouds often pass over before releasing their payload on the mainland so they stay relatively dry.

With very little in the way of trees or vegetation they are a barren and sometimes bleak, but very beautiful place. One of the most distinctive visual features are the stone walls. Approximately 1600km of hand-built dry-stone walls divide the arable land into thousands of tiny plots.

There are three ways to reach the islands. Either fly (see page 162 for more information) or take the ferry (aranislandferries.com) from Rossaveal (see page 162) in County Galway. Those prone to seasickness might be tempted to pay a little more for the spectacular eight minute flight to the islands from the small airport near Inverin (53.2316, -9.4695). See aerarannislands.ie for more information on timetables and scenic flights in the region.

The other option, between March and October, is the shorter ferry crossing from Doolin in County Clare (see page 138).

INIS MÓR

The largest and most popular of the Aran Islands. Inis Mór is basically a huge slab of limestone that rises gradually from north to south, terminating at the huge cliffs (up to 100m in height) that run without interruption along the full length of the south coast. During the summer months it is a lively place where the busy pubs serve late into the night.

There are a number of B&Bs, hotels, and a hostel (kilronanhostel.com) in the main village, Kilronan. There is also a small supermarket, an ATM, a few restaurants, a cafe and plenty of pubs.

The cliffs of Inis Mór | RC

WALKING TRAILS

Three signposted trails start and finish in Kilronan. As they all follow small roads and lanes they are also suitable for bikes.

The 16km Cill Mhuirbhigh loop (purple arrows) follows wonderfully quiet roads and lanes through Gort na gCapall before turning east at the Blue Flag beach at Cill Mhuirbhigh and returning along the northern coast. This is a great way to get to Poll na bPéist or Dún Aonghasa as it avoids the (relatively) busy main road.

The two other routes, An Chorrúch 12km (blue arrows) and Dún Eochla 10km (green arrows), are shorter variations of the Cill Mhuirbhigh loop.

CYCLING

The most popular mode of transport on the island is cycling. There isn't much traffic and barring a few short steep hills, the roads are pretty flat so it's a great way to get around. As you arrive off the ferry you will be met by representatives from the various bike hire companies. Their prices are all similar but it's worth haggling.

It is possible to take in most of the island's sights in a 26km loop. From Kilronan follow the Cill Mhuirbhigh walking trail, passing through Gort na gCapall before diverting to visit Dún Aonghasa. Then head west along the main road to the end of the island before following the quiet coast road back to Cill Mhuirbhigh beach. From the beach return to Kilronan along the second half of the Cill Mhuirbhigh loop.

BEACHES

There is a beautiful Blue Flag beach at Cill Mhuirbhigh (*53.1307, -9.7498*) just off the main road between Kilronan and Dún Aonghasa. The cove is very sheltered and it's one of the few beaches on the island without dangerous currents. There is a lifeguard on duty at weekends in June and September, and every day in July and August.

Just east of the airport is Trá Mhór, a long, secluded sandy beach (*53.1040, -9.6409*). Behind the beach is a massive tidal lagoon. If you decide to swim remember that there is no lifeguard and watch out for jellyfish and strong currents. Follow the road east past the airport to the end of the island and then head north to reach the beach.

Trá na bhFrancach is a small roadside beach just north of Kilronan (*53.1259, -9.6599*).

DÚN AONGHASA

The spectacular Iron Age cliff top fort (*53.1249, -9.7661*) is the most popular sight on the island and day visitors usually make a beeline straight for it. The fort is enclosed by three massive dry-stone walls and a 'cheval de frise' (tall slivers of limestone set

GALWAY   151

Poll na bPéist | Nicole Johnson

vertically into the ground to deter attackers). Perched precariously at the edge of a long line of 100m tall cliffs, its setting is impressive to say the least.

Mystery surrounds the fort's origins. It's not clear who built it or why. Its elevated position suggests that it may have been built for ceremonial rather than military or tactical purposes. One possibility is that it was used by druids for seasonal rites involving bonfires.

To get there either take a mini-bus from Kilronan or cycle. There is a small admission charge and be warned that the path from the visitor centre and cafe to the fort is quite steep and rocky, but short enough.

It's a sheer drop from the cliff edge to the Atlantic and there is no guardrail so be very careful, especially when it's windy. It can get very busy on summer days so try and visit early in the morning or late in the evening when the day trippers have left.

POLL NA BPÉIST

At the foot of the cliffs east of Dún Aonghasa the sea has cut a perfectly rectangular section of rock from the flat limestone terrace to leave an astonishing swimming pool shaped hole (*53.1216, -9.7547*). Its name translates as the Serpent's Hole and it's often referred to as the Wormhole.

This remarkable piece of natural architecture has twice hosted a cliff diving competition in which the divers plunged 27m into the deep water of the Poll.

Once a little visited sight, the diving competition has raised its profile and it's now quite popular. You must be extremely careful as people have been washed into the water by rogue waves that, even on seemingly calm days, can sweep the terraces without warning.

It's a tricky walk over rough and often slippery ground and the route is a little indistinct but it's well worth the effort. Either follow the Cill Mhuirbhigh loop, or take the main road west (turn left just before Cill Mhuirbhigh beach) to the tiny village of Gort na gCapall. At the junction beside the shrine (*53.1231, -9.7409*) take the road south and look for a narrow path on the right that runs between the stone walls. Follow this path, which is marked intermittently with red arrows, down to the coast and walk west along the shore until the Poll comes into view.

DÚN DÚCHATHAIR

The Black Fort (*53.1043, -9.6871*) is more remote and much quieter than the world famous Dún Aonghasa, but no less spectacular. A high terraced wall cuts across the narrow headland which is surrounded by water and tall cliffs on three sides. When the fort was built in the Iron Age it may have been much larger but erosion of the cliff edge has left only a portion of the wall intact.

Follow the main road south out of Kilronan and past the beach. You'll see a road that climbs steeply up the hillside to the right (the turn is just past the small lake

Dún Aonghasa | Marcus Murphy

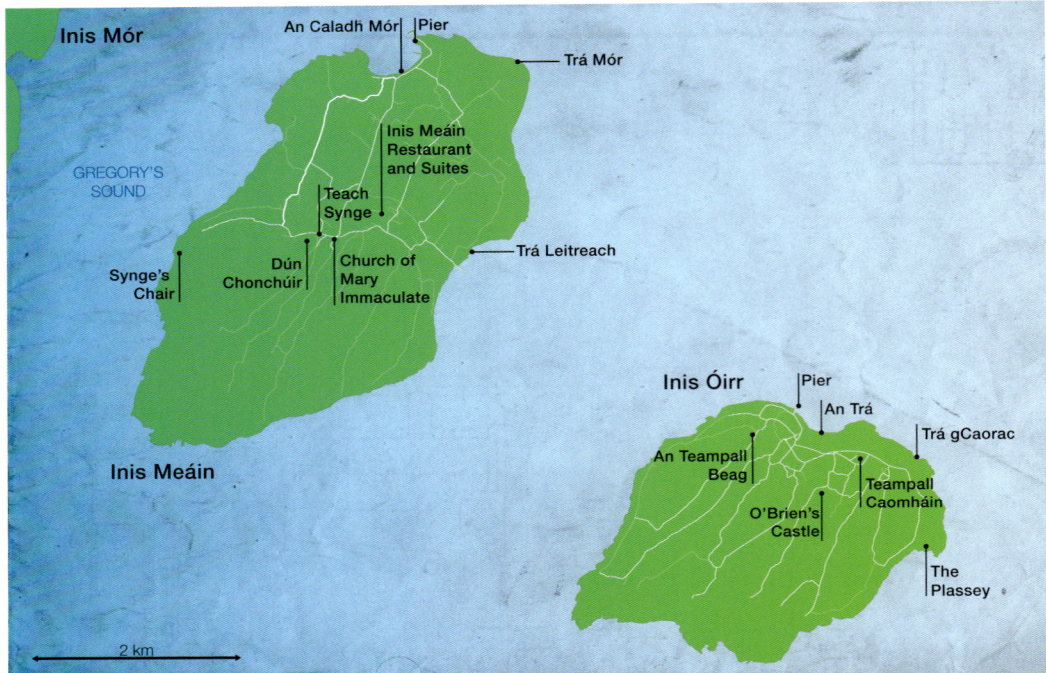

on the right). Turn right and follow this road, which fades to a rough track, up the hill. At the end of the track head directly to the coast and walk left along the top of the cliffs to the fort. Enter the fort through a small opening on the left-hand side of the wall (it's close to the cliff edge so be very careful).

TEAMPALL BHEANAIN
Apparently one of the smallest churches in Ireland, this tiny stone ruin dates from the 7th century and sits on high ground overlooking Killeaney Bay (*53.1023, -9.6661*).

INIS MEÁIN
Inis Meáin, the middle island, is by far the quietest and least developed of the three islands. Depending on your outlook this can be either a good or a bad thing. And even though there is only one shop, one pub and limited accommodation, it is a great place to get away from it all.

The island is home to a small, close-knit Irish-speaking community. The best way to explore it is by walking. It's possible to circumnavigate the island on foot in a day.

The northern half of the island is low-lying and fertile, with a few sandy beaches. As the land rises to the south in a series of terraces, the ground becomes rockier and limestone pavements dominate, culminating in the dramatic cliffs and storm beaches of the southern coastline.

TEACH SYNGE
Irish playwright J.M. Synge spent each summer between 1898 and 1902 on the island and drew a lot of inspiration from its culture. The beautiful thatched cottage (*53.0845, -9.5923*) where he stayed has been restored as closely as possible to the way it was then. The small museum, which has books, photographs and letters on display, is open during the summer months.

SYNGE'S CHAIR
Perched on top of the cliffs on the west coast is a low semi-circular stone wall that offers a sheltered spot to look across Gregory's Sound towards Inis Mór and watch the waves (*53.0820, -9.6136*). A favourite spot of the playwright, it's a short walk from the end of the road on the western side of the island.

DÚN CHONCHÚIR
This large oval ring fort (*53.0834, -9.5947*) dates back to the first century AD. The fort is impressive and well worth a visit. It's one of the highest points on the island and has panoramic views in all directions.

The west coast of Inis Meáin | RC

Teach Synge | Chris Brooks

Dún Chonchúir, Inis Meáin | Andy Haslam

WALKING TRAILS
There are three signposted trails on the island, all of which start from the pier (*53.0999, -9.5772*). The 10km Cill Cheannannach loop (blue arrows) follows the northern coast around the island before returning along the main east-west road, taking in the tiny 8th century church of Cill Cheannannach (*53.0805, -9.5754*), Synge's Chair, Dún Chonchúir and Dún Fearbhaí (*53.0806, -9.5800*).

The Dún Fearbhaí loop (purple arrows) extends the previous route, adding an extra 3km section that crosses the high ground in the southwestern corner of the island.

The best option if you are short on time is the 8km Dún Chonchúir loop (green arrows). It sticks to the west of the island but passes close by Dún Chonchúir and Synge's Chair.

CHURCH OF MARY IMMACULATE
The island's church (*53.0839, -9.5909*) was built in 1939 using stone from the ruins of the much older church opposite it. If you are passing it's well worth popping in to see the beautiful Harry Clarke stained glass windows.

BEACHES
There are three beaches on the northern half of the island:

- An Caladh Mór is the sheltered rocky strand beside the pier (*53.1007, -9.5774*).
- North of the runway is the 1.5km long Trá Mór. The wide open sandy expanse is a great place for a walk on a stormy day (*53.0992, -9.5638*).
- Trá Leitreach is beside the old pier on the east coast and is quite sheltered from the prevailing wind (*53.0829, -9.5693*).

INIS ÓIRR
The smallest of the three islands, Inis Óirr is a mere 3km by 3km. It's only a short crossing from Doolin so it's a good choice for those short on time. However there is plenty to see, including lots of archaeological features with many examples of its Bronze Age, Pagan, Celtic, Early Christian and Norman-Irish history.

There are a number of B&Bs, a hostel (bruinisoirr.ie), a hotel and a campsite. For the latest information on events and accommodation on the island visit discoverinisoirr.com.

Áras Éanna, the island's arts and heritage centre, is housed in the renovated weaving factory (*53.0646, -9.5310*). The centre, which contains a theatre/cinema, two galleries and a cafe, hosts weaving, basket making and quilting workshops (aras-eanna.ie).

The Plassey | RC

THE PLASSEY
In 1960 the cargo vessel M.V. Plassey was caught in a bad storm and ran aground on the rocks off the island's east coast. A group of islanders rescued the entire crew using a breeches buoy (a crude rescue device similar to a zip-line). You can see photos from the rescue on the walls of Tigh Ned's pub. The iconic wreck now rests above the high tide mark (*53.0557, -9.5037*).

TEAMPALL CAOMHÁIN
The ruins of Teampall Caomháin (Saint Kevin's Church) lie sunken into the sandy hill opposite the runway (*53.0639, -9.5140*). Caomháin is the patron saint of the island and the church dates back to the 10th century. It is cleared of wind-blown sand annually by the locals.

AN TEAMPALL BEAG
A tiny ruined church (*53.0659, -9.5292*), known as Cill Ghobnait (Saint Gobnait's Church) or Teampall Beag (small church). It dates from the 10th century and is dedicated to Saint Gobnait. Nearby are the remains of three outdoor altars, two bullaun stones (Neolithic stone bowls), and a clochán (a dry-stone hut).

O'BRIEN'S CASTLE
The island's highest point (*53.0608, -9.5198*) is home to a 15th century church and an 18th century signal tower and has great views over the surroundings.

WALKING
There are two signposted trails on the island. The first, the 8km Ceathrú an Locha Loop (green arrows), explores the eastern end of the island passing An Loch Mór and the Plassey wreck. The second, the 13km Ceathrú an Phoillín Loop (purple arrows), is an extension of the first, adding an extra circuit around the west coast.

Another option is to walk the coastline of the island, a 10km circuit. Much of the southern shoreline is trackless, remote and quite rough, but enjoys beautiful views over to the Cliffs of Moher.

BEACHES
There are two Green Coast beaches on the island. Beside the pier is An Trá, a wonderful, sheltered beach with white sand and clear turquoise water (*53.0659, -9.5198*), it also has a Blue Flag. The other is the smaller, quieter, Trá gCaorach, just east of the runway (*53.0636, -9.5058*). ■

Inis Óirr beach and O'Brien's Castle | Terry Ballard

Currachs at An Trá | Denis Dineen

An Teampall Beag | Allie Couture

The iconic stone walls | Richard O'Beirne

Inis Meáin Island Stays | Andy Haslam

ARAN ISLANDS
ACCOMMODATION

ARAN ISLANDS CAMPING AND GLAMPING, INIS MÓR
53.1244, -9.6621
irelandglamping.ie
A short distance outside Kilronan, right beside the beach, is Aran Islands Camping and Glamping. They have a number of wooden cubes (sleep six) and pods (sleep four) as well as camping facilities.

KILRONAN HOSTEL, INIS MÓR
53.11977, -9.6680
kilronanhostel.com
Located beside the pier on Inis Mór this hostel offers dorms as well as private rooms and has a large kitchen. Tigh Joe Mac's pub is right next door.

ARAN THATCHED COTTAGE, INIS MÓR
53.1306, -9.7053
aranthatchcottage.com
This traditional thatched cottage on Inis Mór was built in 1844. Simply furnished the cottage sleeps four in a double and two singles. It's set on raised ground with great views across Galway Bay.

INIS MEÁIN ISLAND STAYS
53.0866, -9.5844
inismeain.com
This pair of beautiful stone-clad and white-washed buildings blend so well with their surroundings that they are almost invisible. Both boast stylish minimalist interiors with expansive windows that make the most of the views across the island. Teach Boirne (The Karst House) sleeps eight, and Teach na Curraigh (The Currach House) sleeps four.

BRÚ RADHARC NA MARA, INIS OÍRR
53.06810, -9.5247
bruinisoirr.ie
This hostel is a stone's throw from the pier on Inis Óirr. They have dorms, en-suite doubles and family rooms. Open from Easter to the end of September.

RUA CAMPING, INIS OÍRR
53.0645, -9.5208
inisoirrcamping.ie
This campsite, which backs onto the beach, offer pitches for tents as well bell tents to hire (which sleep four).

Minnie's Café | Fionn O 'Flaithearta

ARAN ISLANDS
FOOD

TIGH NAN PHAIDI CAFE, INIS MÓR
53.1315 -9.7573
instagram.com/teachnanphaidis
This quaint cafe operates from a traditional white-washed and thatched cottage located in Kilmurvey Craft village at the foot of road that leads up to Dún Aonghasa. There is also an ice cream shop and seafood cafe next door.

JOE WATTY'S PUB & SEAFOOD BAR, INIS MÓR
53.1239, -9.6705
joewattys.ie
Lively pub at the northern end of Kilronan. Serves seafood and pints of stout.

MINNIE'S CAFÉ, INIS MÓR
53.13047, -9.7003
instagram.com/minniescafe.inismor
This small wooden hut is on the main road across the island near Mainistir. It serves hot and cold drinks, açai bowls, granola and freshly baked goods. Outdoor seating.

TEACH ÓSTA, INIS MEÁIN
53.0846, -9.5833
fb.com/teach.osta
As the only pub on the island it operates as the focal point, where everyone gathers in the evenings. It also serves food between 12.00 and 19.00 daily. There are regular trad music sessions during the summer.

TEACH AN TEA, INIS OÍRR
53.0654, -9.5252
cafearan.ie
This tearoom serves coffee, freshly baked cakes, soup and salad. The eggs used in the baking and the fresh fruit and vegetables come from their own garden.

THE SEAWEED CAFE, INIS OÍRR
53.0638, -9.5176
instagram.com/theseaweedcafe
Set in an elevated position near O'Brien's Castle. This family-run cafe offers plenty of home baked treats, sweet and savoury. Outdoor seating only.

SOUTH GALWAY

This section incorporates Galway City and surroundings as well as South Connemara. Connemara is the largest Gaeltacht (Irish-speaking area) in Ireland and the Irish language, music and culture play a big part in everyday life. You will hear locals and visitors speaking Irish as they go about their daily business. During the summer many Irish schoolchildren spend a few weeks learning their native tongue in the Irish colleges.

The Gaeltacht can be divided into two distinctive parts. The stretch of coast west of Galway City that passes through the villages of Barna, Spiddal, Inverin and Rossaveal is known as Cois Fharraige (which means 'seaside'). And the collection of small islands and bays further west is called Ceantar na nOileán (which means 'islands district').

There is a strong boating tradition in Connemara and the traditional sail boats, known as Galway Hookers, are famous across the world. Hookers, with their tarred black hulls and their iconic red sails, were originally designed as fishing craft, but were mostly used as cargo boats, carrying turf and seaweed between Galway and Clare. Nowadays, many of them compete during the summer in keenly contested regattas.

AUGHINISH

Tucked away in the back of Galway Bay lie a series of small promontories and peninsulas between Kinvarra and Ballyvaughan. The quiet flat roads are suited to leisurely, exploratory cycling. Bring a picnic and head across the causeway to Aughinish Island (*53.16585, -9.0573*) where you can take in the excellent views of the Burren hills.

KINVARA

On the south shore of Galway Bay, a short distance from the Clare border is the attractive seaside village of Kinvara. It was once a thriving port and each summer a festival, Cruinniu na mBad, celebrates the village's maritime tradition when up to a hundred of the region's traditional sailing boats, Galway Hookers, converge on the port to race.

Each Friday between 10.00 and 14.00 there is a farmer's market selling local produce and crafts on Courthouse Road (*53.1390, -8.9374*). See kinvarafarmersmarket.ie for details.

Dunguaire Castle | Bernd Thaller

DUNGUAIRE CASTLE
Just west of Kinvara is this 16th century castle which sits on a small grassy headland right on the shore of Galway Bay (53.1421, -8.9260). It's open to the public from April to October and you can enjoy a four-course medieval banquet in the evenings. See dunguairecastle.com for details.

TRAUGHT
A little north of Kinvara is the Blue Flag beach at Traught, which is safe for swimming and has lifeguards in the summer (53.1721, -8.9851).

BURREN NATURE SANCTUARY
A few kilometres south of Kinvarra lies the Burren Nature Sanctuary, a visitor centre set on a 20 hectare farm (53.1292, -8.9274). Guests are encouraged to interact with and learn about the Burren's unique landscape through walking trails, seasonal events and guided tours.

There is an excellent cafe, playground and comfortable cottage rooms available for overnight stays. See burrennaturesanctuary.ie for details.

RENVILLE PARK
This public park just south of Oranmore (53.2458, -8.9540) has a number of walking trails from 1km to 3.75km. The trails pass though pockets of woodland and take in the playground (53.2494, -8.9636) and Renville Castle, which dates from the 16th century.

It's also possible to access the park from the beach carpark which is slightly further down the road beside the pebble beach (53.2456, -8.9618). The beach is home to Sauna Fiáin, see saunafiain.com for details.

GALWAY CITY
The bustling, bohemian city lies where the River Corrib enters Galway Bay. The city is compact and well suited to exploring on foot. From Eyre Square wander down Shop Street, the main thoroughfare, to the 16th century Spanish Arch on the banks of the Corrib. Along the way you might stop into Tigh Neachtain (tighneachtain.com) to sample their eclectic selection of craft beer or grab an excellent fresh fish and chips from McDonagh's (mcdonaghs.net).

Throughout the year the city hosts a number of festivals including the International Arts Festival and the Film Fleadh in July, and the Oyster Festival in September.

HARE ISLAND
Hare Island is a small tidal island off Ballyloughane Beach in Galway Bay (53.2586, -9.0256). It's possible to walk the 800m out to it during very low tides and make a short loop of its coast before the sea cuts it off again.

Swimming at Salthill | Christopher Tierney

SALTHILL BEACH
The seaside resort on the edge of Galway City has a nice, but busy Blue Flag beach (*53.2566, -9.0923*). At the western end of the promenade is Blackrock Baths (*53.2566, -9.0923*), a great spot for a swim with diving boards, steps into the water and changing facilities.

MUTTON ISLAND
A short walk east of Salthill is a kilometre long causeway that stretches out into Galway Bay connecting Mutton Island with the mainland (*53.2631, -9.0565*). You can't access the actual island, but it's a great spot to catch the sunset.

RUSHEEN BAY
Nearby Rusheen Bay is a great place for windsurfing and kayaking (*53.2585, -9.1196*). The bay is semi-enclosed making it ideal for beginners. There is a watersports school based there that rents equipment (rusheenbay.com). The beach, known as Silver Strand, has a Blue Flag.

AN TRÁ MHÓR
A long sheltered Blue Flag beach with clear water and great views across Galway Bay to the Burren (*53.2426, -9.3582*). The sand slopes gradually into the water so it's a good place to swim. There is a lifeguard at weekends in June and September and daily during July and August. Look out for the signposted left turn 3.5km west of Spiddal.

ROSSAVEAL
While there isn't much to see in Rossaveal itself, it is an important transport hub for the Aran Islands (see page 150). The ferry leaves from the busy fishing port (*53.2659, -9.5600*) and makes regular sailings to all three islands. Consult aranislandferries.com for timetables and fares.

Aer Arann (aerarannislands.ie) flies from Connemara Regional Airport (*53.2316, -9.4695*) near Inverin to all three islands. On a clear day the eight minute flight offers a spectacular view of the islands and isn't significantly more expensive than the ferry. As well as flying direct to the islands they also offer scenic flights that take in the Burren, the Cliffs of Moher, and Dún Aonghasa on Inis Mór.

CARRAROE
The village of An Cheathrú Rua (Carraroe) lies in the heart of the Connemara Gaeltacht. Every year on the first weekend in August it hosts the maritime festival, Féile an Dóilín. Celebrating the region's rich maritime history, the festival revolves around the ancient and beautiful Galway Hooker boat, with races, parades, lectures on maritime history and boat-building exhibitions.

Lettermullan Island | RC

There are two beaches at Spiddal, both with summer lifeguards. The eastern one (*53.2440, -9.2989*) is smaller and just off the road. The western beach (*53.2414, -9.3110*) is divided in two, and sheltered by the quay. A mobile sauna regularly sets up here and at nearby Trá an Dóilín, see driftwoodsauna.ie for dates and details.

TRÁ AN DÓILIN
This Blue Flag beach, also known as Coral Beach, is noted for its sand that consists of very fine coral (*53.2477, -9.6289*). It's usually quieter than the beaches closer to Galway City. There are plenty of small rock pools to explore and some good snorkelling. The water is patrolled by lifeguards at weekends in June and September and daily during July and August.

CARRAROE WALK
An 8km loop on small roads with one short stretch of rocky coastline. Park in the village and follow the main road southwest, after 3km you will arrive at Trá an Dóilin. Continue north along the coast over rough ground. Shortly after passing a small promontory you will meet a small sandy beach and carpark. Follow the narrow road back to the village, passing the football pitches.

CEANTAR NA NOILEÁN
The archipelago of islands at the western end of Galway Bay is one of the quietest parts of Connemara and is characterised by granite drystone walls and a patchwork of small rocky fields.

The five largest islands are linked by bridges and causeways. The Wild Atlantic Way only goes as far as the bridge that connects Lettermore and Gorumna Islands but it's well worth continuing further on to discover more of this hidden gem.

There are numerous small sandy beaches on the islands, particularly on the west shore of Gorumna and the southern shore of Lettermore.

LETTERMULLAN HERITAGE CENTRE
The private collection of local historian John Bhaba Jeaic Ó'Confhaola is displayed in a small cottage on Lettermullan Island (*53.2329, -9.7372*). The collection, which includes old books, tools, instruments and photographs, gives a great insight into life as it once was. See fb.com/ionad.meallain for more details.

WALKING
The islands are covered in a network of narrow roads and boreens, many of which lead down to hidden bays and beaches. Perfect for leisurely cycling and walking, Ceantar na nOileán Teo have details of six walking routes on their website cnnoilean.ie.

Brigit's Garden | DF

SEA KAYAKING
The maze of tiny deserted islands, sheltered bays and sandy beaches is ideal for exploration by sea kayak. Shearwater Sea Kayaking (shearwaterseakayaking.ie) offer kayaking instruction and guided tours, ranging from short evening paddles to multi-day camping trips.

INLAND
While the Wild Atlantic Way sticks close to the coast, the main road from Galway City to Clifden, the N59, runs much further inland, along the foot of the Twelve Bens and Maumturk Mountains. There are a few interesting places that are well worth checking out if you are travelling that way.

LOUGH CORRIB
Lough Corrib, the second largest lake on the island of Ireland, separates the mountains and bogs of Connemara from the fertile grasslands of Mayo.

Internationally renowned for its salmon and brown trout fishing, anglers travel from across the world to fish the lake. Tom Sullivan (tomdoc.com) offers guided fishing trips if you want to try your luck.

The lake is connected to the Atlantic by the River Corrib River which flows through the centre of Galway City. Give it a Go (giveitago.ie) run kayaking trips up the River Corrib from the heart of the city.

BRIGIT'S GARDEN
Enchanting gardens set on 4.5 hectares of native woodland and wildflower meadows. As well as the gardens there is a nature trail, an ancient ring fort, thatched roundhouse, crannóg, a calendar sundial, playground, cafe and gift shop (53.3855, -9.2131). It's not far off the N59 between Moycullen and Oughterard, look out for the signs (brigitsgarden.ie).

WILDLANDS, MOYCULLEN
The centrepiece of this newly opened adventure park in Moycullen (53.3307, -9.1687) is the massive high-ropes course which runs for over a kilometre and reaches up to 15m into the air. It has over 40 obstacles, including a 100m zip line, spread across four circuits of increasing difficulty. At the heart of the course is a 16m tower with a number of climbing walls, a 'freefall' and a Tarzan swing. For smaller kids there is a lower course with twenty obstacles.

Indoors there is an amazing climbing wall with a series of increasingly challenging and very unconventional routes.

Those who want to keep their feet firmly on the ground can check out the fairy trail, adventure playground, disc golf and archery. There is also a restaurant, a food truck and accommodation (see page 166 for more information). See wildlands.ie for further details.

Galway Wind Park | DF

Lough Corrib | DF

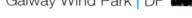
The Twelve Bens | DF

DERROURA MOUNTAIN BIKE TRAIL
Just over 7km west along the N59 from the town of Oughterard is Derroura Mountain Bike Trail (*53.4409, -9.4505*). This purpose-built 16km trail has steep climbs and tricky descents, as well as great views over the Maam Valley and Lough Corrib. See irishtrails.ie for a map of the route.

MAUMTURKS
To the east of the Inagh Valley, opposite the Twelve Bens, lie another range of quartzite peaks, the Maumturks. They form a discontinuous ridge running north to south and are more rounded and less featured than their better-known neighbours.

THE TWELVE BENS
The Twelve Bens mountain range, which dominates the skyline of southern Connemara, is home to the Glencoaghan Horseshoe, one of the great Irish mountain walks. The route takes in six of the range's twelve summits, and while it's not that long (about 16km) it's a very tough walk with plenty of height gain and steep ground.

As the Bens are often shrouded in cloud, which can descend without warning, the ability to navigate with a map (Harvey Connemara 1:30,000 is best) and compass is essential.

GALWAY WIND PARK
The vast area of bog, lakes and conifer plantations, which lies between the mountains of Connemara and the Galway coast, is home to 58 towering turbines that generate enough power for every home in Galway. A large network of gravels roads and tracks criss-cross the area and there are six signposted walking and cycling trails.

The following routes all start from the trailhead (*53.3828, -9.3744*) on the L1311, which links Oughterard and Rossaveal:

- The 4.5km Connemara View Loop (orange markers)
- The 5km Turbine Trail (black markers)
- The 5.5km Peak Ridge Path (purple markers)
- The 10km Seecon Lough Path (green markers)

For cyclists there is a 21km route, the Forest Cycleway (blue markers), as well as lots of scope to create longer routes. There is also a wheelchair and buggy-friendly trail, the 200m long Split Rock Trail (red markers), which starts slightly further down the road from the main carpark (*53.3804, -9.3933*). ∎

Kitty's Camping | DF

Wildlands | Wildlands

Cnoc Suain | Todd Parker

Wild Atlantic Bus, Oughterard | Richard Barton

SOUTH CONNEMARA
ACCOMMODATION

KITTY'S CAMPING, KINVARA
53.0871, -8.9459
kittyscamping.com
Stay in a number of cosy wooden wagons (sleeping from 4-6), a timber cabin (sleeps eight) or bring your own camper or tent. There is a kitchen, fire circle and BBQ area, all with the Burren's hills as a lovely backdrop behind sheltering trees.

WILDLANDS, MOYCULLEN
53.3296 -9.1697
wildlands.ie
This adventure centre has 14 wooden chalets that sleep up to six. They are just a minute's walk from the restaurant which serves great pizza and the adventure hub where you can choose from dozens of activities.

CONNEMARA GLAMPING, INVERIN
53.2336, -9.5036
connemaraglamping.ie
Located on a family farm this site has a number of safari-style tents that sleep six. Some have a private wood-fired outdoor bath. There is also a stone cottage, Teach na mBo, that sleeps four.

CNOC SUAIN, SPIDDAL
53.2893, -9.2645
cnocsuain.com
This 17th century homestead in the bog north of the village of Spiddal runs short sessions on Irish culture, nature and heritage. Their beautifully restored stone cottages are available for rent.

HOUSE BOAT, GALWAY CITY
53.28045, -9.0318
airbnb.ie/rooms/35332397
Moored a twenty minute walk from Eyre Square on the banks of tidal Lough Atalia. The restored Dutch barge sleeps two in a double bed and is very spacious with a large open-plan layout.

WILD ATLANTIC BUS, OUGHTERARD
53.4532, -9.3365
wildatlanticbus.ie
This converted double-decker bus, near the shores of Lough Corrib in Oughterard, is fitted out with a stove, kitchen and bathroom. It's set in lovely grounds with outdoor seating and a shower hut nearby.

Moran's Oyster Cottage | Moran's

SOUTH CONNEMARA
FOOD

MORAN'S OYSTER COTTAGE
moransoystercottage.com
53.2107, -8.8950
Located in a 250 year old thatched cottage on the northern bank of the Kilcolgan River south of Galway City. The menu has a strong focus on seafood and they are renowned for their oysters which come from a nearby natural oyster bed in Galway Bay. Closed Mondays.

GALWAY MARKET
53.2724, -9.0542
galwaymarket.com
A bustling, open air market that has been in operation for centuries, with everything from Asian street food to local cheeses. Open every Saturday from 08.00 to 18.00, and for full weekends in July and August.

PRÁTAÍ, GALWAY CITY
53.2725, -9.0533
instagram.com/pratai_official
From the corner of busy Shop Street they served hand cut, cooked to order skin-on fries with a vast range of sauces, seasonings and garnishes.

TACOS TRAVIESAS
instagram.com/tacostraviesas
Serves Mexican-inspired tacos, tostadas and loaded fries from various locations around Galway City and further afield. Check their Instagram for details.

ÁLAINN, SALTHILL
53.2570, -9.0921
alainn.ie
Located near the Blackrock diving tower on the Salthill seafront this food truck serves coffee and poké, açaí, and protein bowls to hungry sea swimmers.

EDO ON THE ROAD
edoontheroad.com
Contemporary Italian food including homemade pasta and stone-baked pizza from Spiddal Pier (*53.2410 -9.3120*) during the week and Spanish Arch in Galway City (*53.2699, -9.0541*) at weekends.

MID CONNEMARA

As the Wild Atlantic Way follows the rocky low-lying coastline north it leaves the shelter of Galway Bay and is exposed to the full force of the Atlantic. This extremely indented coast is a maze of bays, small islands and coves.

The villages of Carna, Roundstone and Ballyconneely and their surrounds are very popular with holidaymakers. The better-known beaches in the area can get busy on sunny summer days, but as always in Ireland there are many other beaches that you can have all to yourself.

CNOC MORDÁIN

The rocky summit of Cnoc Mordáin (353m) offers great views up and down the coast and inland to the Twelve Bens. The mountain's long, distinctive ridges of granite, known as roche moutonnée, were formed by the movement of a glacier in the last ice age.

Just over 4km north (towards Galway City) along the Wild Atlantic Way from Kilkieran village is a left turn (*53.3542, -9.7048*) marked by a sign for 'Hillside House B&B'. Drive up this narrow road, park at the gate and continue up the track on foot. When, after 1.5km, a forest appears on the left, leave the track and head north up the broad ridge. Cross a subsidiary peak (*53.3675, -9.7290*), descend in a northeasterly direction into a saddle and then steeply up to the summit (*53.3775, -9.7077*). To return to the car retrace your steps for a 10km round trip.

FINISH ISLAND

At low tide it's possible to walk across the sand to the small, uninhabited island of Finish (*53.2996, -9.8029*). A few kilometres west of Kilkieran, turn south off the Wild Atlantic Way and follow a narrow road down to a small pier (*53.3035, -9.7896*). Cross the sand (check the tide and don't get stranded) and follow the rough track to the far end of the island (7km round trip).

MACDARA'S ISLAND

Every year on the 16th of July hundreds of local people travel on boats to Macdara's Island where mass is celebrated at the oratory in honour of Macdara, the area's patron saint of fishermen and sailors. It may be possible to hitch a ride over to the island and take part in this ancient tradition.

The tiny, one room oratory, which was restored in 1975, is considered one of the finest early Christian oratories in Ireland.

Macdara's Oratory | RC

INISHNEE WALK
The small, quiet island of Inishnee is connected to the mainland by a bridge 2km north of Roundstone. A pleasant 4.9km signposted walk follows the island's narrow roads and laneways in a loop starting from the bridge (*53.4144, -9.9082*).

ROUNDSTONE
The small fishing village of Roundstone is a popular stop-off for tourists and has plenty of good pubs and restaurants as well as a spectacular view across Cashel Bay to the Twelve Bens.

From the pier it's possible to take a boat trip out to the beautiful deserted island of Inishlacken with Roundstone Bay Tours (roundstonebayandisland.ie).

ERRISBEG
The rounded, lumpy profile of Errisbeg rises up behind Roundstone village. Even though modest in height, at only 300m, there are amazing views in every direction from its summit. The hill is covered in rocky outcrops, the ground can be boggy and there isn't a well-defined path so the walk is only suitable for well equipped, experienced hikers.

The easiest route (3km round trip) starts from the high point of the Ballyconneely to Roundstone road (*53.3913, -9.9786*). Park at the bend of the road (note dogs aren't allowed) and go through the gate. Then it's just a matter of weaving up through the outcrops and gullies. It's hard going and there is no obvious path, but persevere because the view from the top is very rewarding.

DOG'S BAY AND GORTEEN
Just west of Roundstone village are two of Ireland's finest beaches, Dog's Bay (*53.3809, -9.9633*) and Gorteen (*53.3809, -9.9542*). They lie back to back, joined to the mainland by a thin neck of grassy dunes. Both beaches are sheltered from currents and are popular for swimming, windsurfing and kite surfing. The narrow roads that lead down to them can get very busy in the summer.

The east-facing Gorteen is the larger and more sheltered of the two beaches. It has a lifeguard on duty at weekends in July and August.

The grassy headland past the beaches is a wonderful place to wander, exploring the rocky inlets and hidden coves. Both bays have fantastic seagrass meadows just out from the beaches which make for interesting snorkelling.

Gurteen Bay Caravan Park has camping and caravans for hire a stone's throw from the beach.

ROUNDSTONE BOG
North of the coast road between Clifden and Roundstone lies a vast area of blanket bog, streams and lakes, known as Roundstone Bog. It's remote and lonely, but very beautiful, with fascinating views

Gorteen, Roundstone | DF

Roundstone Bog | RC

of the ever-changing light on the Twelve Bens. Almost completely devoid of trees and with over a hundred lakes there is as much water as land.

The ninety square kilometre expanse is crossed by just one narrow road, the appropriately named Bog Road, which serves as an interesting and very bumpy shortcut between Clifden and Roundstone.

The bog, while appearing barren and lifeless, is in fact home to a wide range of wildlife. You can see carnivorous plants, lizards, sedges, purple moor grass, bog myrtle, wildflowers and rocky outcrops covered with lichens and heather.

THE BOG WALK

Crossing the bog from Ballyconneely to Roundstone is an excellent, but tough walk. It is only suitable for experienced hikers equipped with a map and compass and the ability to navigate across complicated ground in thick mist or fog.

Starting from Ballyconneely village follow the Roundstone road south. After just under 1km turn left and follow the minor road to its end in the heart of the bog (*53.4267, -10.0057*). From there it's a matter of striking out across the heather, weaving around the numerous lakes and ponds, heading for the left-hand shoulder of Errisbeg, the serrated peak to the east. Crossing over the saddle of Errisbeg leads to a laneway (*53.3965, -9.9349*) that will bring you down

Bunowen Bay | DF

Inishnee | DF

Doonloughan | DF

into the village of Roundstone. If you find a fairly direct route through the maze of lakes it's about 15km.

BALLYCONNEELY

The low-lying coast of the Ballyconneely Peninsula is adorned with a number of beautiful sandy beaches. Much of the land near the coast is a complex and highly specialised habitat known as machair, which is characterised by fertile, sandy ground. Machair is found in only a few places along the Atlantic coast of Ireland and in a few areas in Scotland. During the summer the short grass teems with exquisite wildflowers.

BEACHES

The area is packed with sandy beaches and even on the busiest days it should be possible to find your own private beach.

The southern side of Mannin Bay (see page 173) has a series of small sandy coves that are accessed from the narrow road just north of Ballyconneely village.

On the north side of the peninsula is Doonloughan (*53.4478, -10.1348*). It's one of the few surf spots in Connemara and in the summer you can rent boards or get surf lessons. Unfortunately the strong currents and big waves mean that the beach isn't ideal for swimming. The grassy area near the beach is popular with campers.

Mannin Bay | DF

Coral Strand | DF

Pony trekking | DF

Aillebrack, beside Connemara Golf Links, has a number of sandy beaches. The largest one, Trá Mhór (53.4191,-10.1436) has a Green Coast award and is the most popular, but the smaller, quieter beaches further south are just as nice. The tidal flats near the southern tip of the peninsula are a great place to forage for shellfish at low tide.

The small beach at Bunowen (53.4075,-10.1209) is very popular with families and has great views of the Twelve Bens, see the photo on page 12. As it faces east it's reasonably sheltered from the prevailing wind. The Connemara Smokehouse and Café (smokehouse.ie) at Bunowen Pier is well worth a visit (53.4046, -10.1170).

PONY TREKKING

There has always been a strong interest in horses in Connemara. It's the home of Ireland's only native horse breed, the Connemara Pony, which is world renowned for its hardiness and gentle temperament. Legend has it that the Spanish horses that escaped from the galleons of the Armada when it ran aground in 1588 bred with the local feral Irish horses. The breed is very popular in Ireland and every August the Connemara Pony Show takes place in Clifden.

The Point Pony Trekking and Horse Riding Centre (53.4192, -10.1606) beside Connemara Golf Links offers a range of treks on ponies and

Derrigimlagh | DF

horses over sandy beaches and grassy commonage (thepointponytrekkingcentre.com).

MANNIN BAY
Just north of the small village of Ballyconneely is Mannin Bay. From a distance the beach beside the road, known as Coral Strand (*53.4419, -10.0640*), doesn't look particularly interesting, but it's worth stopping for a closer look. The sand, known as maerl, is predominantly composed of delicate shells of coralline red algae, but you may also see pieces of sponge, clam, snail, sea urchin and quartz.

Based on the grounds of the Connemara Sands Hotel (*53.4380, -10.0778*) is Cois Trá Rugged Retreat (ruggedretreat.ie). With a wonderful setting overlooking the beach just west of Coral Strand they offer a sauna, seaweed baths and hot tubs as well as a food truck that serves a range of locally-sourced seafood.

SNORKEL TRAIL
The trail follows a series of rocky pools for 400m north of the carpark. Look out for red algae, wrasse, sea urchins and red kelp. Coral Strand is quite sheltered so the water can be a degree or so warmer than other more exposed beaches.

KAYAK TRAILS
The first of the two kayak trails heads north around the tiny island of Ardillaun before returning along the coastline (4.5km). It's possible to extend this paddle by visiting the bay east of the island (7km).

The second trail follows the shore west, passing many small beaches and rocky coves. Experienced paddlers could continue on around Knock Point and visit Doonloughan (14km).

DERRIGIMLAGH
The small townland of Derrigimlagh in the northwest corner of Roundstone Bog has loomed large in the history of the early 20th century. On Sunday June 15th 1919, the first transatlantic flight ended abruptly in its soft ground. Captain John Alcock and Arthur Whitten Brown had flown their twin-engined Vickers Vimy from Newfoundland, Canada, in just over sixteen hours, before crash landing in the bog within yards of the Marconi Wireless Telegraph Station.

The Telegraph Station was set up by Guglielmo Marconi, the Italian pioneer of wireless telegraphy, in 1905. The first transatlantic wireless message was sent from it to Nova Scotia in 1907.

The 5km trail that loops around the site features a number of interesting installations including radio sets that play recordings from the time of the Marconi station, a tuning fork that experiments with different sound frequencies, and a wind reed that creates sounds based on the wind. A white concrete marker (*53.4465, -10.0223*) lies close to the landing spot of Alcock and Brown. ∎

Fernwood | Emilija Jefremova

MID CONNEMARA
ACCOMMODATION

BEN LETTERY HOSTEL
53.4700, -9.8425
benlettery.ie
Sitting on the N59 with the southern slopes of Ben Lettery rising steeply behind, this independent hostel is ideally located for anyone wanting to hike in the Twelve Bens. They have dorms, double and family rooms. All are very reasonably priced and include breakfast. There is a drying room (vital for hikers) and a full kitchen.

In the warmer months there is also the option to stay in one of their three bell tents, there are two doubles and one triple.

BAYSIDE COTTAGE, CASHEL
53.4186, -9.8198
fb.com/BaySideCottageConnemara
From the front this resembles a traditional thatched cottage, but the back of the spacious building has vast windows to take advantage of the excellent views over Cashel Bay. It sleeps ten in three bedrooms and has a large sitting room which leads out to a wooden deck.

FERNWOOD
53.4797, -10.003
fernwood.eco
Located just outside Clifden in a pocket of woodland on the edge of Roundstone Bay, Fernwood is an ultra-stylish, grown-up glamping destination. The 60 hectare organic farm is home to three exceptional buildings. The Treehouse Dome is a geodesic dome that sits among the trees (sleeps two), the Stilthouse is a very unique structure raised on 57 stilts and the Studio is a very contemporary converted garage that overlooks a private garden.

They also have two cottages in the nearby village of Roundstone -The Quay Cottage sleeps four and the Quay House sleeps six - both have amazing views across the bay to the Twelve Bens.

OLD SHEPHERD'S COTTAGE
53.4974, -9.9742
connemara-cottage.com
While less than ten minute's drive from the bustling town of Clifden this stone cottage is in a very remote setting. Sleeping five in three bedrooms, it has a traditionally decorated interior with excellent views over the Owenglen valley and the Twelve Bens.

Connemara Smokehouse, Ballyconnelly | DF

MID CONNEMARA
FOOD

FISHERMAN'S PUB, BALLYNAHINCH
53.4604, -9.8625
ballynahinch-castle.com
This large estate at the foot of the Twelve Bens is surrounded by woodland and water. The castle is home to a suitably old-world bar that serves lunch, dinner and drinks. The atmospheric room is decorated with evidence of how good the fishing used to be in Ireland and the menu has a strong focus on hearty seafood and meat, but there is also an extensive vegetarian menu.

O'DOWD'S, ROUNDSTONE
53.3964, -9.9190
odowdsseafoodbar.com
An excellent seafood restaurant in the small fishing village of Roundstone, with good alternative options too. Best to book ahead in the summer.

THE BOGBEAN CAFE, ROUNDSTONE
53.3956, -9.9188
bogbeanconnemara.com
Serves healthy breakfasts, lunches and sweet treats throughout the day. Limited opening hours outside of the summer season. Bed and breakfast also available.

CONNEMARA SMOKEHOUSE, BALLYCONNELLY
53.4075, -10.1209
smokehouse.ie
Situated beside Bunowen Pier at the end of the Ballyconnelly peninsula, this family-run business produces a range of wild and farmed smoked salmon, tuna and mackerel using traditional beech-wood smoking techniques. Tours of the smokehouse run during the summer months. There is also a cafe serving lunch and snacks.

STEAM, CLIFDEN
53.4885, -10.0180
fb.com/SteamCafeClifden
A great selection of sandwiches, treats and coffees make this a place worth seeking out for lunch in Clifden. Operates from May to September, closes on Sundays and Mondays.

NORTH CONNEMARA

The area north of Clifden is probably the most popular part of Connemara with visitors. It's easy to understand why, as it has a great concentration of offshore islands, sandy beaches and impressive mountain scenery.

CLIFDEN
The unofficial capital of Connemara, Clifden is a bustling town full of pubs, cafes and restaurants. There is also a wide range of accommodation from fancy hotels to utilitarian hostels. As such it's a great base for exploring this part of the Atlantic coast.

SKY ROAD
The Sky Road is justifiably famous for its incredible views over the islands, mountains and coast of Connemara. While most visitors drive the loop it's a great cycle and you might enjoy the view even more after working hard to earn it. See the facing page for a suggested route.

On your way back to Clifden it's worth stopping off and making the short climb to the top of Monument Hill (53.4870, -10.0324) where there is a stone memorial to the town's founder, John D'Arcy, and a great view over the town towards the Twelve Bens.

Eyrephort Beach (53.5119, -10.1366) is a short detour off the Sky Road. It's a nice quiet beach, but be warned if driving as the road down to it is very narrow.

AUGHRUS PENINSULA
North of Clifden the Wild Atlantic Way leaves the N59 to loop around the Aughrus Peninsula. This undeveloped area has dozens of wonderful sandy beaches connected by a network of quiet roads.

The small fishing village of Cleggan on the north side of the peninsula is the departure point for Inishbofin (see page 178).

Just opposite Omey Island (see page 178) is Clifden Eco Beach Camping (clifdenecocamping.ie), a beautiful campsite with a wild, natural feel, see page 184 for more information.

BEACHES
There is no shortage of great beaches on Aughrus:

- Sellerna is a small beach with plenty of parking (53.5572, -10.1315). It is signposted from Cleggan village, follow the signs for 'Trá'. Just east of the

Clifden Eco Beach Camping | Kris Acton

CLIFDEN CYCLE HUB
The four cycle routes that make up the cycle hub all start and finish in the centre of Clifden. They are signposted at most junctions but not all. Download maps from irishtrails.ie.

All Things Connemara on Market Street have a great range of bikes for hire, including tandems, kids bikes and hybrids, as well as electric bikes if you are worried about your fitness.

All the routes are best done in a clockwise direction.

1 SKY ROAD LOOP
A popular drive, some sections of the 16km route are very narrow and can be busy. There is a slightly shorter variation to the signposted route that offers better views and quieter roads. See goo.gl/V4hGX6 for a map.

2 ERRISLANNAN LOOP
The Errislannan Peninsula is much quieter than its famous neighbour to the north, but the views on this 14km loop are just as good. The Alcock and Brown monument marks the highest point of the route and it's a good place to stop and take it all in.

3 CLEGGAN LOOP
A 33km circuit that follows the coast road around the Aughrus Peninsula. It also passes through Cleggan village. It's well worth making the short detour to visit Omey Island (see page 178). Plan to reach the island at low tide. Be very careful on the busy section of the N59 out of Clifden.

4 BALLYCONNEELY AND ROUNDSTONE LOOP
This 40km route passes plenty of interesting sights including the Alcock and Brown landing site at Derrigimlagh (see page 173), Coral Strand (see page 173), Errisbeg (see page 169) and the beaches of Dog's Bay and Gorteen (see page 169).

Be careful on the road south from Clifden as there are some tight, blind bends. With the exception of the steep climb over the shoulder of Errisbeg, the route is reasonably flat.

Sea thrift on Omey | DF

beach is a small megalithic dolmen that is worth a quick look.
- Rossadillisk is a sprawling, flat beach with a large tidal range and lots of rock pools and tiny islands to explore (*53.5649, -10.1505*). Parking is limited and the access road is narrow. The smaller eastern beach, Trá Bhríde, is more sheltered when a westerly wind is blowing (*53.5630, -10.1453*).
- Aughrusbeg is actually a series of interconnected small beaches, one of which is known as Anchor Beach due to the massive anchor that lies lodged in the sand (*53.5584, -10.1771*). It came from the Verity, a three-masted 1,000 ton barque from Nova Scotia, which was wrecked in a storm in 1890.
- Trá Mhór is a peaceful beach, hidden down a narrow lane (*53.5502, -10.1882*). It must be accessed on foot or by bike as there is no parking at the end of the lane.

OMEY ISLAND

The small island of Omey is connected to the mainland by a vast area of sand, and twice a day, for a few hours around low tide, it's possible to walk, cycle or drive across the sand to the island. Check the tide in Sweeney's shop and pub in Claddaghduff village before crossing. It's easy to get seduced by the tranquillity of the island so keep an eye on the time or else you may end up spending longer there than you had planned.

The island is an incredibly beautiful and peaceful place that is full of wildflowers during the summer. The commonage on the western end is a wonderful place to wander and enjoy the views across the water to Cruagh, Friar and High Islands.

Every August the tidal sands host the Omey Horse Races, complete with bookmakers and crowds of spectators.

OMEY ISLAND WALK

This wonderful 5.5km loop follows the coast around the island. Park in the carpark (*53.5388, -10.1445*) on the mainland overlooking the beach and follow the signposts across the sand to the island. Take the narrow road that leads clockwise around the island to the sandy beach, Trá Rabhach. At the far end of the beach look out for a holy well known as Tobar Feichín (*53.5302, -10.1682*). Now either follow the sunken path through the sand dunes or wander across the grass sticking closer to the coast. Either way you will pass the ruins of Teampall Feichín (*53.5358, -10.1678*). After the church descend to the shore and follow it clockwise, passing the graveyard before retracing your steps across the sand to the mainland.

INISHBOFIN

Like many of the west coast's islands, Inishbofin has two distinct personalities. Its sheltered, lush southern and eastern coasts are where you will find the village

Inishbofin Harbour | RC

St. Colman's Church, Inishbofin | RC

The Green Road, Inishbofin | DF

and the best beaches; while the western and northern coasts are wild and remote, with steep cliffs and windswept, heather-clad slopes.

The island is home to a wealth of wildlife. It's an important breeding ground for many birds including the common tern, Arctic tern, fulmar, guillemot, common gull, greater and lesser black backed gull, Manx shearwater, chough and corncrake.

The island has been inhabited for at least 6,000 years and has a rich history, the remains of much of which can still be seen.

The ferry crossing to the island from Cleggan takes about 30 minutes (inishbofinislanddiscovery.com), during which you have a good chance of seeing bottlenose dolphins.

Camping is available in the grounds of Inishbofin hostel (inishbofin-hostel.ie). Wild camping takes place on the unfenced commonage on the island. Ask locally for advice about suitable places to camp, and leave no trace of your stay.

As well as exploring the island on foot you can pony trek (inishbofinequestriancentre.com), charter a boat (inishbofinribcharter.com), scuba dive (islandswest.ie), go deep-sea fishing (bofinangling.com) or hire bikes at the pier.

See inishbofin.com for lots of useful information and details of accommodation.

WALKING TRAILS

The island has three signposted trails that all start from the pier:

- The 7.5km Cloonamore Loop explores the eastern end of the island. A shorter all-road variation is also possible.
- The 8.1km Westquarter Loop is probably the most interesting of the three walks. It takes in the cliffs, blow holes and sea stacks at the western end of the island (a great place to watch the sun set over the Atlantic).
- The Middlequarter Loop is the shortest walk at 4.9km. It visits the second highest point of the island, where there are great views across to the mainland.

Another option is to combine sections of each of the walks into a complete circuit of the coast of the island. It will be about 15km depending on the exact route you take.

SNORKEL TRAIL

There is good snorkelling at Fawnmore Beach (53.6139, -10.2291) opposite the Doonmore Hotel. Enter the water near the carpark and make your way southwest for 300m. The rocky ground is full of sea life including anemones, limpets, mussels, barnacles,

Trá Gheal, Inishbofin | RC

and starfish. If you are lucky you may see spider and hermit crabs.

CROMWELL'S BARRACKS KAYAK TRAIL
The harbour is very sheltered and remains calm in all but the worst weather, however it can be busy, so watch out for other boats. The trail starts from the stony beach east of the new pier (*53.6134, -10.2104*). Follow the coast clockwise into the inner bay. Continue along the shore past a pebble beach where it's possible to land and explore the star shaped Cromwellian fort (*53.6104, -10.2164*). At the large white navigation beacon loop back to the starting point, avoiding the route taken by the ferry.

BEACHES
There are two Green Coast beaches, Dumhach (*53.6162, -10.1813*) and East End (*53.6216, -10.1889*). Both are wide, sandy beaches on the eastern end of the island.

The other beach of note, Trá Gheal, is on the western end of the island (*53.6160, -10.2472*). It's a picture perfect cove with white sand, turquoise water and views across to the now deserted island of Inishshark. Take care on the steep descent from the Green Road to the beach. It's inadvisable to swim from the beach as there are dangerous currents.

The Westquarter, Inishbofin | RC

CLEGGAN HEAD WALK
Back on the mainland there is an interesting 4km walk to the tip of Cleggan Head which lies on the north side of Cleggan Bay opposite the village. The route passes through a working sheep farm and access is permitted, but under no circumstances are dogs allowed on this walk, even on a lead. The farm has six cottages for rent.

Drive east from Cleggan village following signs for 'Cleggan Head Farm'. Turn left into the farm and park in the small parking area on the right after 600m (*53.5610, -10.0980*). Continue past the farm buildings on foot. Just after the walled garden look out for a small neolithic wedge tomb down by the sea.

Follow the track along the southern slopes of the hill (close all gates behind you) to the small, secluded bay (*53.5733, -10.1174*). From the higher ground it's possible to enjoy views north, to the islands of Inishturk, Clare and Achill and the distinctive profile of Croagh Patrick. Return by retracing your steps.

If you want to explore the caves and coves of Cleggan Head from the water Real Adventures (realadventures.ie) offer guided kayaking trips.

Renvyle | RC

LETTERFRACK
The small village of Letterfrack was developed by a Quaker family as part of the post-Famine relief efforts. The large building beside the green was home to Saint Joseph's Industrial School. It now houses the National Centre for Excellence in Furniture Design and Technology.

Kylemore Abbey | Allan Henderson

Diamond Hill | RC

Letterfrack Bay Water Tours (instagram.com/letterfrack_glassbottom_boat) operate Ireland's only glass-bottomed boat, which offers a unique underwater perspective of the sheltered waters of Ballynakill Harbour. On a good day you will see a large variety of sea and cliff birds, grey seals, otters, and possibly even dolphins and porpoises.

There are two hostels in the village, the Old Monastery Hostel (oldmonasteryhostel.com), which has a unique atmosphere, charming and slightly rough around the edges and the Clover Fox (cloverfox.com) which offers food and accommodation.

The Ecology Centre (theecologycentre.ie) offers hands-on activities such as foraging, bog walks and eco-tours that will help you appreciate and understand the landscape and nature of Connemara.

CONNEMARA NATIONAL PARK
Just south of Letterfrack village is the 2000 hectare Connemara National Park (nationalparks.ie/connemara). The visitor centre has a playground and cafe and an exhibition about the park's landscape.

The centre is also the starting point for four signposted trails (53.5502, -9.9454). The three shorter walks are interesting, but the pick of the bunch is the 6.7km Upper Diamond Walk which will take you to the 455m summit of Diamond Hill. The path is steep but well maintained and the hard slog is more than justified by the amazing 360 degree view from the top. Just follow the red markers.

KYLEMORE ABBEY
The picturesque Kylemore Abbey (kylemoreabbey.com) lies a little inland from the Wild Atlantic Way along the N59 between Killary and Letterfrack (53.5594, -9.8915). As well as the castle and the impressive gardens it offers guided walks along the estate's trails. The walk to the Sacred Heart statue on the hillside high above the Abbey offers stunning views over the estate and into the Twelve Bens.

RENVYLE
The small peninsula of Renvyle is very popular with Irish holiday-makers, particularly Renvyle House (renvyle.com), the long established hotel which lies close to a number of beaches at the northern tip of the headland.

The most popular beach in the area is White Strand (53.6070, -9.9891) which has a Green Coast award. It's quite open so there isn't much shelter when it's windy. Access the beach by taking the turn right after the campsite (renvylebeachcaravanpark.com).

Tully pier (53.6025, -9.9731), to the east of White Strand is home to a mobile sauna, see sweathouse.ie for details.

Glassillaun beach | RC

TULLY MOUNTAIN
While modest in height at only 365m, Tully Mountain (also known as Letter Hill) offers an excellent vantage point with views up and down the coast and into the mountains. There isn't a distinct path to follow so it's a matter of finding your own way. It's a 5km round trip.

Park at the pier at Derryinver (*53.5722, -9.9811*) and follow the road west for 400m. Walk a short distance up the gravel track on the right, go through the gate and then follow the fence left and through another gate (close the gates behind you). You are now on open hillside and it's just a matter of following the broad ridge to the top which is marked by a cairn (*53.5836, -10.0048*). Return by retracing your steps. The ground can be boggy so wear appropriate footwear.

LETTERGESH BEACH
Public access to this 1.5km long beach is via the small carpark signposted from the Wild Atlantic Way (*53.6021, -9.9083*). At low tide it's possible to walk north along the sand, wading across the Culfin River, to the nicer, northern part of the beach.

GLASSILLAUN BEACH
The horseshoe shaped sandy beach (*53.6148, -9.8749*) just south of the mouth of Killary Harbour is one of the best beaches in Connemara (and therefore the world). See the photo on page 28.

The rocks at either end of the beach are excellent for snorkelling, consult the map in the carpark for details. If it's windy use the more sheltered side of the beach. At low tide you can walk out to the tiny island at the western end of the beach where there is an old lobster holding pool. The water in it is usually a few degrees warmer than the sea.

From the Wild Atlantic Way follow signs for 'Scuba Dive West' down narrow roads to the small carpark.

KILLARY HARBOUR
The dramatic, glacier carved inlet of Killary Harbour marks the border between the counties of Galway and Mayo. And while some geographers may object to it being described as a fjord it's certainly the closest thing to one in Ireland. The Wild Atlantic Way skirts the southern shore, passing through the small village of Leenane before crossing into Mayo at the point where the Erriff River meets the sea (just downstream from Aasleagh Falls, see page 188).

Killary Adventure Centre (killaryadventure.com), offers a wide range of outdoor activities in the area.

Killary Sheep Farm (*53.5956, -9.7932*) is a traditional working mountain farm where you can watch sheepdogs in action, shearing and, in spring, bottle feed a lamb. See killarysheepfarm.com.

There are two kayaking Blueway trails in Killary, see the facing page for details. Alternatively enjoy the Harbour from the comfort of the catamaran

Killary Harbour | RC

Connemara Lady, which departs regularly from Nancy's Point (killaryfjord.com).

FAMINE WALK
This beautiful walk follows a track, known as the Green Road, along the south side of the Harbour. The track, which was built as part of the famine relief program during the 19th century, is rough but fairly level and the views are great.

The route starts at Rosroe Pier (*53.6199, -9.8593*). Park at the pier and walk 200m back up the road. Turn left at the small white cottage and follow the track. After about 5km the track becomes a road and you pass Killary Sheep Farm. The road leads uphill to the busy N59 where you turn right and take the next right. This quieter road leads past Lough Fee. Keep right at the next two junctions and the road will lead you back to your car at Rosroe.

The complete loop is about 16km. If you are short on time you could just walk the length of the Green Road and retrace your steps or else return by speedboat with Killary Adventure Company (killaryadventure.com).

KILLARY KAYAK BLUEWAYS
While the prevailing wind in the Harbour is from the west, these trails shouldn't be used during moderate to high winds from the east. Remember the piers are working harbours, so please park considerately.

NANCY'S POINT TRAIL
This trail travels around the western end of the Harbour. It can be done as an 11km point to point, but probably makes more sense as a 25km loop. From Nancy's Point (*53.5998, -9.7302*) follow the southern shore west to Rosroe Pier before crossing to the other side of the fjord and returning via the more remote north shore.

BUNDORRAGHA TRAIL
This 12km loop starts from Bundorragha Pier (*53.6061, -9.7524*) on the north side of the harbour (you could also start from Nancy's Point). It is best undertaken at mid or high tide. The trail follows the rocky northern coastline east (watch out for strong currents near where the Erriff River meets the sea) before returning along the southern side of the Harbour.

CONNEMARA SEAWEED BATHS
The baths on the outskirts of the small village of Leenane (*53.5951, -9.7058*) are the ideal place to relax after a hard day on the water or in the hills (connemaraseaweedbaths.com). ∎

Oystercatcher Cottage | Aoife Herriott

NORTH CONNEMARA
ACCOMMODATION

CLIFDEN ECO BEACH
53.5239, -10.1345
clifdenecocamping.ie
A gorgeous little campsite that's literally a stone's throw from the water's edge and has a great environmental ethos. An excellent base from which to explore Connemara, with plenty to do within walking distance of the site.

A recent addition is the on-site wood-fired sauna right beside the beach.

OYSTERCATCHER COTTAGE
53.5962, -9.9309
connemara-cottage.com
This cosy white-washed cottage near Renvyle is set in an elevated position with an exceptional view over the sea and the mountains, beaches and islands of Connemara. It sleeps four in two bedrooms and has a compact kitchen and sitting room with great views out the window and from the wooden deck.

THE CONNEMARA HOSTEL
53.5947, -9.7820
sleepzone.ie
This hostel is in a great setting looking across Killary Harbour to the slopes of Mweelrea. It has a dozen rooms with a mix of doubles, larger family rooms that sleep five and dorms.

Next door is Killary Lodge (available for group bookings) and very close by is Killary Adventure Centre (53.5933, -9.7693) which offers accommodation as well as a wide range of land and water-based activities, see killaryadventure.com for details.

INISHBOFIN HOSTEL
53.61593, -10.1983
inishbofin-hostel.ie
Located a ten minute walk from the pier this traditional farmhouse has been converted into a 38-bed hostel with family rooms, private rooms and dorms as well as a full kitchen. Outside there are a number of glamping pods as well as space to pitch a tent.

Misunderstood Heron | MH

NORTH CONNEMARA
FOOD

INISHWALLAH, INISHBOFIN
53.6144, -10.2296
instagram.com/thesaltboxinishbofin
This Asian restaurant serves locally sourced street food with a Keralan twist from a distinctive red and white double-decker bus. Located in the Westquarter of the island, it opens daily during the summer months from 12.30 to 17.00.

THE SALT BOX, INISHBOFIN
53.6135, -10.2126
instagram.com/thesaltboxinishbofin
This family-run food truck serves fresh fish and shellfish caught on their own boat - boat to plate! Located just across from the pier, the menu includes lobster rolls, crab claws, fish and chips, mussels, whatever they catch basically. Open daily from 10.00 to 18.00 during the summer.

LITTLE FISH CAFE, CLEGGAN
53.5563 -10.1114
instagram.com/littlefish_cafe
Seasonal food truck and cafe based in Cleggan, a stones's throw from the pier. Serves fresh shellfish and fish and chips for takeaway or eating in. Vegetarian alternatives are available, but the calamari spice bag sounds like a winner to me!

CONNEMARA WOODFIRE, LETTERFRACK
53.5545, -9.9506
fb.com/connemarawoodfire
Quirky pizzeria with a very interesting indoor/outdoor eating area outside Letterfrack village. Serves burger, pizzas, fish and chips.

MISUNDERSTOOD HERON, KILLARY
53.5931, -9.7694
misunderstoodheron.com
This incredibly popular roadside food truck has a reputation for excellent coffee, local produce and a spectacular setting on the shore of Killary Harbour. The menu changes with the seasons but expect a focus on Irish seafood and meat as well as homemade bakes. There is plenty of outdoor seating and they usually open from Easter until November and are closed Mondays and Tuesdays.

Ceathrú Thaidhg sea cliffs (see page 212) | RC

MAYO

The huge county of Mayo, which has the second longest coastline in Ireland, is home to a number of world renowned sights such as the holy mountain of Croagh Patrick and the beautiful Achill Island, but it also has many less well known, but no less interesting, attractions. Mayo is the third largest county in Ireland but also the second least densely populated, so it's the ideal place for those seeking a bit of space and quiet.

The stretch of the Wild Atlantic Way between the town of Westport and Achill Island is exceptionally well equipped with over a dozen signposted walking and cycling trails including the very popular Great Western Greenway. See mayowalks.ie and irishtrails.ie for more information.

The spectacular scenery of Achill Island has always attracted artists, but nowadays it's also a Mecca for walkers and surfers.

The region of Erris could definitely be considered a hidden gem. It's only in recent years that it has started to be marketed as a destination and it's still very much unspoilt.

North Mayo is home to some of Ireland's wildest and most rugged coastline. The cliffs at Benwee Head are taller than the Cliffs of Moher and steeper than Sliabh Liag, yet they are virtually unknown.

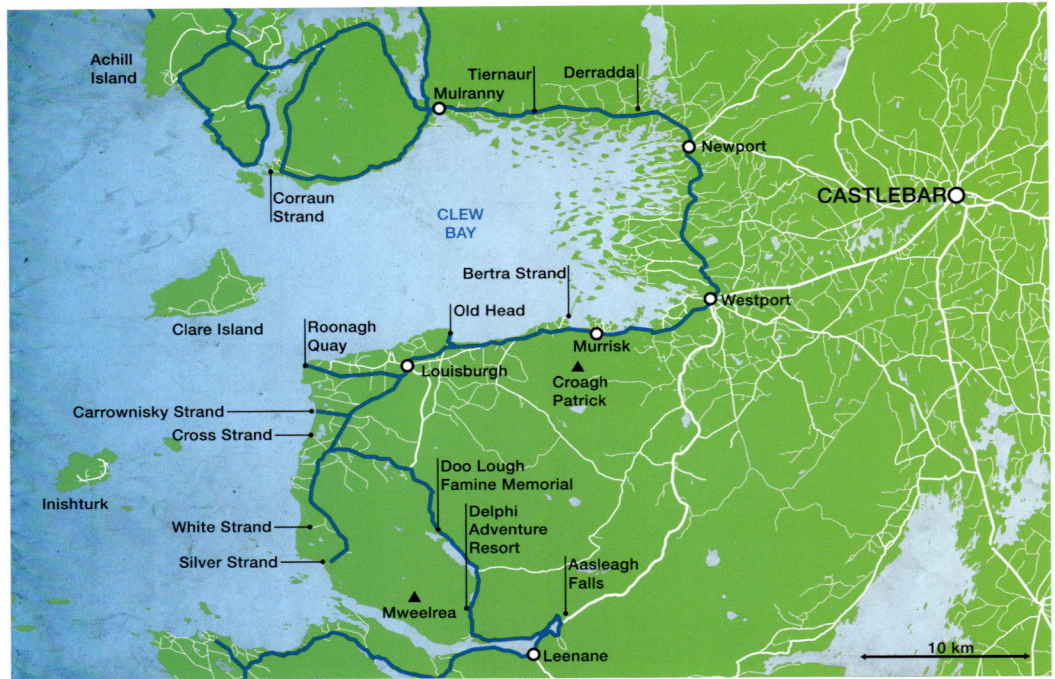

KILLARY AND CLEW BAY

The southern half of Mayo has a huge amount to offer including remote beaches, offshore islands, the iconic Croagh Patrick and the Great Western Greenway.

Just north of Killary Harbour a quiet, but very worthwhile, spur of the Wild Atlantic Way visits two beautiful beaches.

Offshore, the neighbouring islands of Inishturk and Clare Island offer contrasting experiences. Those looking for solitude and peace should make for Inishturk, while those in search of adventure and craic will find it on Clare Island.

The Clew Bay skyline is dominated by the conical profile of Ireland's holy mountain, Croagh Patrick. To climb the mountain on Reek Sunday alongside thousands of pilgrims is a surreal and uniquely Irish experience.

The thriving town of Westport is linked to Achill Island by the walking and cycling route known as the Great Western Greenway, a real success story that has inspired many other cycling routes around the country. This area is also well served with twelve signposted walking trails.

AASLEAGH FALLS

Just north of Leenane, the Erriff River tumbles over a picturesque waterfall shortly before it reaches the sea at the head of Killary Harbour. The waterfall, while not particularly tall, is beautifully situated and is an ideal place for a quick stop to stretch the legs or a leisurely picnic beside the river.

There is plenty of parking just north of the bridge (53.6180, -9.6726) where a short path follows the north bank of the river upstream to the falls.

The Erriff is one of the best salmon fishing rivers in Ireland and if you are very lucky you might see salmon attempting to make their way up the waterfall after heavy rain.

MWEELREA

The massive bulk of Mweelrea dominates the north shore of Killary Harbour. Rising to 814m straight from sea level it's the highest point in Mayo and the province of Connacht. If you are fortunate enough to reach the summit on a clear day you will enjoy magnificent views over the Atlantic, Ben Gorm, the Twelve Bens, the Maumturks and the Sheeffry Hills.

Mweelrea is a serious mountain, with many narrow ridges and steep cliffs, and it's frequently

Aasleagh Falls | Tony Brierton

shrouded in heavy mist. It should only be attempted by experienced hikers who are capable of navigating across complex ground in low visibility. If you are unsure about your ability Walk Connemara (walkconnemara.com) offer guided hikes up the mountain.

DELPHI ADVENTURE RESORT

Set on a 120 hectare site on the eastern slopes of Mweelrea, the resort comprises of a luxury hotel and spa, budget dorm accommodation and an adventure centre (53.6220, -9.7543).

Catering for families, couples and groups, the centre offers a huge range of activities including kayaking, canoeing, stand up paddleboarding, surfing, coasteering, raft building, high ropes, bog challenge, mountain biking, climbing, abseiling, archery, and bushcraft. See delphiadventureresort.com for more information.

DOO LOUGH FAMINE MEMORIAL

Just north of Doo Lough, where the Wild Atlantic Way squeezes between Mweelrea and the Sheeffry Hills, is a small roadside memorial to those who died in the Doo Lough Tragedy during the Famine. It's a beautiful place to stop and admire the view down the valley (53.6662, -9.7813).

WHITE STRAND

On the drive south towards Silver Strand there are plenty of side roads, many of which lead down to small deserted coves. Look out for signs for White Strand. This long sandy beach is worth a visit (53.6683, -9.8989).

SILVER STRAND

Finally the road ends at Silver Strand (53.6499, -9.8804). It's the perfect place to wander, exploring the beach, rocky headlands and sand dunes while enjoying the views across the sea to Inishbofin, Inishturk and Clare Island. Thanks to its remoteness this beautiful beach is rarely busy.

It's possible to walk north from Silver Strand around the headland to White Strand and then follow the road back south to the carpark (about 10km in total). This walk takes you through a quiet and unspoilt area, with beautiful sand dunes, rare machair and interesting archaeology, including a very significant dog whelk midden left by early Irish settlers who extracted a rare pigment from the shells that was highly valued by North African traders. The walk is best at low tide.

LOST VALLEY

Public access to the beach just south of Silver Strand, the wonderfully named Uggool, has been prevented for many years. However, a local farming family

The Tale of the Tongs, Inishturk | Michael McLaughlin

offer tours of the beach and surrounding lands. See thelostvalley.ie for details.

CARROWNISKY STRAND
The 4km Green Coast beach at Carrownisky is a busy spot during the summer (53.7353, -9.8933). Popular with surfers, it's one of the few consistent breaks in the area. Surf Mayo (surfmayo.com) is based at the beach and offers board rental and lessons. There are lifeguards on duty every day during July and August and at weekends during June. You are advised to wear foot protection in the water due to the presence of weever fish.

CROSS STRAND
It's also possible to access the beach at Cross (53.7219, -9.8998). Drive further south along the Wild Atlantic Way towards Silver Strand and look out for the signposted turn right for Cross Beach. As you follow the road down to the beach you will see signs for Bunlahinch Clapper Bridge to the right. It's worth the short diversion to check out this unusual foot bridge (53.7182, -9.8886).

INISHTURK
The peaceful island of Inishturk lies just over 10km off the coast of Mayo. Much quieter than its neighbour Clare Island, this is a place for those looking to get away from it all. What it lacks in tourist amenities it more than makes up for in rugged beauty. The majority of the island's six square kilometres are rough and rocky hillside, perfect for exploring on foot.

Clare Island Ferry Company (clareislandferry.com) and O'Malley Ferries (omalleyferries.com) regularly make the 50 minute crossing from Roonagh Quay (53.7619, -9.9030) to the island.

There are a small number of B&Bs as well as a basic campsite. The Community Centre, which houses a pub and restaurant, is the island's social hub (53.7010, -10.0933). For more information about the island see inishturkisland.com.

BEACHES
There are two sandy beaches on the eastern end of the island, Tránaun, which has a Green Coast award (53.7005, -10.0891) and Corraun (53.7040, -10.0920), both of which have crystal clear water and are well sheltered. On the southern side of the island is Portdoon Harbour (53.6955, -10.1090), this small cove with a pebble beach is very sheltered thanks to the cliffs that only allow access for the narrowest of boats.

WALKS
The island's two signposted walks serve as excellent starting points for getting to know the place. The 4.9km Lough Coolaknick Loop (green arrows) is a short ramble along narrow roads and tracks.

Clare Island Lighthouse | DF

Grace O'Malley's castle | DF

The harbour on Clare Island | DF

Creggan Lough, Clare Island | RC

The 6.6km Mountain Common Loop (purple arrows) is an extension of the Lough Coolaknick Loop. It crosses open ground to a viewing point overlooking the spectacular cliffs on the western side of the island. It's possible to extend this walk to include the highest point of the island, Mountain Common, which, although only 189m high, offers amazing views back to the mainland.

THE TALE OF THE TONGS
Set above the cliffs on the north shore is an installation known as The Tale of the Tongs, which was built in 2013 to commemorate those who have emigrated from the island. The glass-walled structure is an ideal place to take shelter and soak up the view (*53.7087, -10.1066*).

CLARE ISLAND
This vibrant island is only a few kilometres off the coast of Mayo in the mouth of Clew Bay. The gentle east side contrasts with the impressive sea cliffs on the west coast, which is dominated by Knockmore, the highest point on the island.

The island is popular with visitors, particularly hikers and groups who are there to enjoy the nightlife.

The dramatic cliffs and inland habitats support a wide variety of flora and fauna and it is one of the most studied islands in Europe. In 1909 Belfast naturalist Robert Lloyd Praeger led an exhaustive biological survey of the island and since then it has been a focus of interest for botanists, geologists, ornithologists, marine biologists and nature lovers.

With its rich history there is much to see, including the ruined castle at the harbour (famous as the stronghold of the legendary Pirate Queen Grace O'Malley), the 12th century abbey, the Napoleonic signal tower and the Church of the Sacred Heart, as well as many ancient archaeological sites.

Two companies, Clare Island Ferry Company (clareislandferry.com) and O'Malley Ferries (omalleyferries.com), make the short crossing from Roonagh Quay (*53.7619, -9.9030*) a couple of times a day. A ferry crosses over to Cloughmore Pier on Achill Island a few days a week also.

The Community Centre bar (clareislandcommunitycentre.com) holds regular traditional music sessions, set dancing and concerts.

There is plenty of accommodation including a hostel, B&Bs, self-catering cottages and the very luxurious lighthouse (clareislandlighthouse.com). Note that the shop is a long walk from the main village.

There is a basic campsite just above the beach beside the Community Centre with (coin-operated) showers, a tap and toilets. Wild camping is not encouraged. Bay View House (clareislandrentals.com) is a self-catering house ideal for large groups. It sleeps 24 guests and even has its own bar.

Paddleboarding, Carrownisky | RC

Bunlahinch Clapper Bridge | DF

Old Head | DF

Clare Island Adventures (clareislandadventures.ie) offer coasteering, snorkelling, rock climbing, abseiling and raft building.

For general information and details of upcoming events and festivals check out clareisland.ie.

CYCLING
The island is too large to cover on foot in a day so hiring a bike is a good option if you are short on time. Bicycles are available for rent at the harbour and it's also possible to take your own on the ferry. Bear in mind that many of the narrow roads and tracks that crisscross the island are quite rough and aren't really suitable for the narrow tyres of a road bike.

MACALLA FARM
Macalla Farm is a small, family-run retreat centre and working organic farm (*53.8162, -9.9754*). They offer a wide range of residential courses on yoga, mindfulness and cooking. See macallafarm.ie for more information.

A short distance from the farm is the Stone Barn Cafe (*53.8141, -9.975*). This carefully renovated cottage serves vegetarian lunches using homegrown, organic ingredients. It also occasionally hosts a six-course tasting-menu dinner, see fb.com/stonebarncafe for details.

BEACHES
The sheltered, sandy beach in the harbour has a Blue Flag and is ideal for families (*53.8010, -9.9526*). There is a small fishing harbour, known as the Cove, on the northeast side of the island. It's a picturesque spot, ideal for a quiet swim (*53.8210, -9.9707*).

WALKING
The roads and tracks offer lots of possibilities for short and medium length walks and there are two signposted walking routes on the island.

The 2.8km Fawnglass Loop, marked by the green arrows, is a short stroll across the hillside above the village.

The 6.9km Knocknaveen Loop, which is marked by purple arrows, follows the road west before heading north across the centre of the island and rejoining the Fawnglass Loop via the Green Road.

The 462m high Knockmore is the obvious challenge for the experienced hiker. Probably the best approach is to follow the road that runs west across the island to the signal tower (*53.8004, -10.0463*) before climbing steeply up the shoulder to the summit, which is marked by a large cairn and a trig point (*53.8075, -10.0212*). Descend in an easterly direction, keeping well away from the cliff edge, and follow the zigzag track down to the road where you rejoin the Knocknaveen Loop. This is a tough 13km walk with a significant amount of height gain.

Bertra Strand | DF

LOUISBURGH

This small quiet town on the edge of Clew Bay is a good place to stock up on provisions, particularly if you are heading south, as there isn't another town until Leenane in Connemara.

A short distance northwest of the village is Carrowmore Strand (*53.7689, -9.8241*), a small, pleasant beach overlooking Clew Bay. There are lifeguards in summer.

LOUISBURGH CYCLE HUB

Three signposted cycle routes tour the countryside surrounding the town (*53.7621, -9.8100*).

- Route 1 is a 19km loop across flat bog roads and over a few hills that overlook Clare Island, Inishturk, Achill and Inishbofin.
- Route 2 is a 7km loop around the quiet minor roads of Louisburgh, passing close by Turlin Strand.
- Route 3 is a challenging 26km trip through the Sheeffry Hills. Plenty of wonderful scenery and quiet roads, there are even two streams to ford!

OLD HEAD

The sheltered Blue Flag beach overlooking Croagh Patrick is very popular with families (*53.7764, -9.7715*). There is a lifeguard during the summer, plenty of parking, toilets and a cafe (Old Head Café and Ice Cream Parlour) nearby.

The Wild Atlantic Sauna can be found beside the pier on weekends, see thewildatlanticsauna.ie for details.

There is plenty to be done apart from lazing on the sand. Just behind the beach is the Old Head Wood Nature Reserve, a small oak forest. Summer SUP (summersup.ie) offer paddleboarding summer camps, lessons and rentals during June, July and August. There is also a snorkel trail and two kayak trails here.

SNORKEL TRAIL

The snorkel trail starts at the beach just north of the pier and continues north for about 400m. Best at high tide, keep an eye out for anemones, shoals of fish and shore crab.

KAYAK TRAILS

Two kayak trails start from the beach or the slipway beside the pier.

The 5.5km (each way) trail follows the shore east between Old Head and Leckanvy Pier (*53.7832, -9.6900*), passing a number of coves and some short sections of cliff. Only the start of this trail in the vicinity of Old Head is suitable for beginners.

A more exposed 5km (each way) trail extends west from the harbour to the beach at Calla (*53.7712,*

Croagh Patrick | RC

-9.8219), passing some interesting caves along the way. There are no easy exit points along this route so it should only be undertaken by experienced kayakers in good conditions.

BERTRA STRAND
The long, thin neck of sand that stretches out from the foot of Croagh Patrick for 4km into Clew Bay is a 'tombolo', a landform where sand is deposited to create a narrow connection between the mainland and an island (*53.7884, -9.6610*). It is a very popular beach for swimming, walking, birdwatching, kite surfing and windsurfing. It has a Blue Flag and there is a lifeguard in the summer months as well as toilets and plenty of parking.

CROAGH PATRICK
Croagh Patrick is considered the holiest mountain in Ireland. The tradition of pilgrimage to its 764m summit stretches back over five thousand years from the Stone Age to the present day without interruption. Its religious significance dates back to the time of the pagans, when people are thought to have gathered there to celebrate the beginning of harvest season.

The mountain is named after Saint Patrick, Ireland's patron saint, who is said to have fasted on the summit for forty days in 441 AD.

Known locally as the Reek, the mountain attracts the devout and the curious throughout the year but on Reek Sunday, the last Sunday in July, over 25,000 pilgrims climb the mountain, some doing so barefoot. At the summit is a chapel where mass is celebrated through the day. The chapel is open daily between 10.00 and 15.00 during July and August.

The view from the summit gives an almost bird's-eye perspective over the islands of Clew Bay.

The pilgrim path starts from the large carpark in Murrisk (*53.7884, -9.6610*) and follows the steep, rocky track to the summit (*53.7595, -9.6583*). It's a tough 7km climb but, after years of hard work, there is a now a good stone path all the way to the summit.

It's also possible to traverse the east-west ridge of the mountain, starting from the laneway taken by the Western Way near Belclare (*53.7713, -9.5799*) and finishing at the small road southwest of Leckanvy (*53.7681, -9.7190*). This is a longer, less travelled route, but requires either a long road walk back to the car or a shuttle.

MURRISK WALKS
If the weather is bad or you aren't feeling able for the tough hike up Croagh Patrick then the three short signposted walks that start and finish at the carpark in Murrisk (*53.7884, -9.6610*) might be of interest:

- Mountain Loop 3.3km (blue arrows)
- Murrisk Pier 3.1km (green arrows)
- Murrisk Loop 4.4km (red arrows)

Rockfleet Castle | DF

Great Western Greenway | DF

Newport | DF

Mulranny beach | DF

CLEW BAY AND ISLANDS
The unique landscape of Clew Bay is a legacy of the last ice age when the retreating glaciers left behind hundreds of low, elongated hills known as drumlins. These were then submerged by the rising sea levels caused by the melting of the ice caps.

Kayaking is the perfect way to explore the sheltered bay and its many islands. The Adventure Islands (theadventureislands.com), who have a base on Collanmore Island, offer full and half day sea kayak tours of the bay. Alternatively give the arms a rest and take a trip with Clew Bay Cruises (clewbaycruises.com).

WESTPORT
The bustling town of Westport is full of shops, pubs and restaurants. See destinationwestport.com for plenty of information about the town.

On the edge of the town is Westport House (westporthouse.ie) which has a campsite and an adventure centre offering a high ropes course, zip wire, archery and zorbing (*53.8006, -9.5354*).

CYCLE HUB
The Westport cycle hub offers three routes varying in distance from 8km to 24km, but the Greenway (see page 196) will probably be of more interest to most cyclists.

BURRISHOOLE LOOP WALKS
From Westport the Wild Atlantic Way follows the coast north and then west along Clew Bay. This area has 12 signposted loop walks following quiet roads and gravel tracks. Some could also be cycled on a mountain bike.

NEWPORT
There are four loops that start from the village and explore the surrounding countryside (*53.8834, -9.5461*).

- Derryhillagh Loop 7km (purple arrows)
- Doogary Loop 10.7km (red arrows)
- Lecarrow Loop 6.8km (purple arrows)
- Loch Morchan Loop 6.3km (blue arrows)

There are also three very short walks around the village itself.

DERRADDA
Two routes explore Lough Furnace and the foothills of the Nephin Mountains starting from the Derradda Community Centre (*53.9038, -9.5866*).

- Furnace Loop 9.5km (blue arrows)
- Oghillies Loop 10.4km (purple arrows)

Corraun Strand | RC

TIERNAUR
The following walks start and finish at the Newfield Inn (*53.9036, -9.6895*).

- Glenthomas 8.7km (blue arrows).
- Knockbrega 10.6km (purple arrows).
- Tiernaur 13.3km (red arrows).

MULRANNY
Two walks start from the Blue Flag beach just outside Mulranny (*53.8976, -9.7846*). The 4.7km Causeway Loop (blue arrows) crosses the salt marsh and returns via a road. The 5.9km Lookout Hill Loop (red arrows) extends the Causeway Loop by climbing up to the high ground behind the village.

CORRAUN STRAND
This quiet beach is separated from Achill Island by a fast flowing channel (*53.8734, -9.9362*). A nice quiet place to wander but swimming isn't recommended due to the strong currents.

GREAT WESTERN GREENWAY
This 49km off-road walking and cycling trail follows the route of the Westport to Achill railway which closed in 1937. Since it opened in 2011 it has been very popular, bringing an influx of visitors, with 300 people walking or cycling the scenic route daily in the summer. The route is very well signposted and traffic free so it's very safe for children. It is divided into four sections:

- Westport to Newport (11km)
- Newport to Mulranny (18km)
- Mulranny to Achill (15km)
- Achill Sound to Cashel South (5km)

A large number of businesses have sprung up since the Greenway opened, including bike hire, guiding, shuttle services and bike-friendly accommodation. See greenwaysireland.org for route maps and the latest information on bike hire.

THE ROCKY MOUNTAIN WAY
This 19km trail offers a tougher alternative to the Greenway between Newport and Mulranny. It follows old bog roads and tracks across the southern slopes of the Nephin Beg mountains and is suitable for mountain or gravel bikes.

THE BANGOR TRAIL
The Nephin Beg Range is the closest thing to wilderness that we have in Ireland. A vast expanse of hills, lakes and blanket bog, it is relatively untouched by man, however there is an ancient path that has

The Bangor Trail | DF

The Rocky Mountain Way | DF

The Mountain Meitheal hut | DF

been used for over a thousand years to travel through these mountains.

The path, known as the Bangor Trail, starts in the village of Bangor (*54.1405, -9.7363*) and makes its way south through the mountains before joining the road near Newport.

The trail takes the path of least resistance so there aren't many long climbs, but the terrain is difficult, wet and boggy and each step needs to be chosen with care. The route is marked by posts at regular intervals, however in many places the path isn't obvious and it would be impossible to follow in thick mist without a map and compass.

It's possible to complete the 25km walk in a long day. The alternative is to do it over two days staying at either of the huts at the southern end of the trail. The Brogan Carroll Bothy (*53.9893, -9.5728*) in Letterkeen Woods is accessible from the road north of Newport, while the wooden hut (*54.0042, -9.6203*) built by Mountain Meitheal is further north along the trail near Lough Aroher. See page 218 for more information about these shelters and other in the park.

The Bangor Trail and the Nephin Beg mountains are covered by Wild Nephin, East West Mapping's excellent map (eastwestmapping.ie).∎

Big Style Lodge | Big Style Lodge

KILLARY AND CLEW BAY
ACCOMMODATION

BIG STYLE ATLANTIC LODGE
53.7054, -9.9020
bigstyle.ie
This very stylish lodge southwest of Louisburgh is only a few minutes walk from the sea. There are 14 en-suite bedrooms as well as a yoga room and plenty of outside areas to enjoy the views. There is also a pub and restaurant as well as surfing and paddle-boarding lessons.

Just across the road from the lodge is the Big Dipper. The spa, which is also open to non-guests, has a wood-fired sauna, plunge pool and outdoor hot tub with wonderful views across the sea to Inishturk and Clare Island.

COLLANMORE LODGE
53.8279, -9.6304
collanmoreislandlodge.com
Collanmore is one of Clew Bay's many islands, and is home to Collanmore Lodge, which is available for rent with four family rooms, a hot tub and a bar (BYOB). The island has its own beach and the lodge can arrange activities such as kayaking and sumo wrestling. Access is by a short boat trip from Rosmoney pier (*53.8257, -9.6203*).

WESTPORT GLAMPING
53.8053, -9.4428
westportglamping.ie
Stay in a camping pod or a shepherd's hut on this working farm outside of Westport. Get a tour of the farm and enjoy some of its produce, such as fresh eggs for breakfast or beef for the barbecue.

CUCKOO WOOD HEXAGON
53.7725, -9.5500
airbnb.ie/rooms/2546659
This beautiful hexagonal wooden hut is set amid woodland a short drive south of Westport. It has outside decking to the east and west to soak up sun throughout the day, and if the sun doesn't shine you can always light the stove and enjoy the cosy interior.

SHEPHERD'S HUT, NEWPORT
53.8846, -9.5399
airbnb.ie/rooms/25435652
A unique timber wagon on the banks of the Black Oak River within walking distance of Newport. Cosy and beautifully situated, this is a place worth looking into.

The Clare Island Oven | Niall Mc Cabe

KILLARY AND CLEW BAY
FOOD

DELPHI SILVER FOOD TRUCK
53.6453, -9.7467
instagram.com/delphisilverfoodtruck
Operating out of a very scenic layby beside the shore of Doo Lough. The distinctive polished metal caravan serves coffee, toasted sandwiches and sweet treats. This is the ideal place for a quick pit stop on the way between Westport and Leenane.

THE CLARE ISLAND OVEN
53.7996, -9.9519
clareislandoven.com
Located in a renovated shipping container beside the harbour. They serve freshly-baked bread, sweet treats, pizzas and sandwiches for takeaway or to eat in their outdoor area. Open daily during the busier months of the year.

SEVEN WANDERS CAFE, LOUISBURGH
53.7634, -9.8085
instagram.com/sevenwanderscafe
Serving excellent coffee, brunch and light lunches from the centre of Louisburgh village. The breakfast bap comes highly recommended! They also occasionally run wine bar evenings serving a carefully curated selection of wines with small plates and nibbles as well as a monthly supper club.

CORNRUE, WESTPORT
53.8021, -9.5258
cornrue.com
This cafe on New Road, a short walk from the centre of Westport, serves coffee, scones and sourdough bread. All freshly-baked on site that morning. Look our for the cinnamon buns at weekends. Closed Sunday and Monday.

SERVD, WESTPORT
53.7996, -9.5220
servd.ie
This busy cafe on Bridge Street in Westport serves breakfast, brunch and lunch. The menu is modern and diverse with everything from a classics such as a full Irish breakfast to more exotic options like kebabs (cooked over coals to give a distinct flavour).

ACHILL ISLAND

Ireland's largest island, Achill, is connected to the mainland by a bridge so it doesn't quite have the same remote feel as the offshore islands. However, its position, jutting far out into the Atlantic, gives it a distinctive raw beauty all of its own.

At the northern end of the island rugged mountains rise directly out of the sea, while the southern shore is lined with great sandy beaches. This combination of mountains and coast in such close proximity is what makes Achill so special. It also means that the island, particularly the hills, receives more than its fair share of rain and wind, but this makes for dramatic, ever-changing light that enhances the wonderful scenery.

INISHBIGGLE

The tiny idyllic island of Inishbiggle lies in Blacksod Bay between Achill Island and the mainland. Some of the strongest currents in Europe flow around the island and despite its proximity to the mainland there are times when the small community of native Irish speakers is cut off from the rest of the world.

Access to the island is by boat (inishbiggleferry.com) from Bullsmouth on Achill (*53.9969, -9.9300*). The crossing in a open boat equipped with outboard engines takes about ten minutes.

There are two short signposted walks: the 3.3km Gubnadoogha Loop starts/finishes at the east (mainland) side of the island (*54.0034, -9.8852*) and the 3.8km Bull's Mouth Loop starts and finishes on the west (Achill) side (*53.9961, -9.9230*).

ACHILL HENGE

Constructed in 2011 as a protest against the Irish government's handling of the financial crisis, Achill Henge is a strange, circular concrete structure on the hillside between Keel and Dooagh (*53.9786, -10.0995*). Opinion on the piece is divided, with many considering it a blemish on the landscape, and others enjoying the unexpectedness of it in such a place.

The road and track that lead up to it are very rough so the best approach is to park in Pollagh on the R319 (*53.9724, -10.1074*) and make the 2.5km round trip on foot.

THE DESERTED VILLAGE

A short walk from the road near Doogort lie nearly a hundred empty stone cottages (*53.9961, -10.0758*). A fascinating, if a little eerie, spot with great views. Not so long ago they were used as summer dwellings, when cattle were brought to graze the higher ground, a practise known as booleying.

Keem beach | Imagea

BEACHES

Achill has a great variety of beaches, from remote hidden coves to vast expanses of sand. Five have been awarded the Blue Flag, which is very impressive for one island. Keem and Keel are probably the best known but there are plenty of other excellent beaches.

ANNAGH STRAND

The most remote beach on Achill, Annagh Strand, is about an hour's walk from the road on the lonely north coast of the island (*53.9993, -10.1335*). The beach is accessed via a steep descent through a band of cliffs that almost completely seals it off from the outside world. Thanks to its inaccessibility you are likely to have to it all to yourself.

KEEM

The small curved strand at Keem lies at the very end of the road that traverses the island and is worth visiting for the spectacular drive from Dooagh alone (*53.9673, -10.1955*). The Blue Flag beach is surrounded by steep slopes so it can be quite sheltered from the wind. It can get very busy in the summer months.

During the spring and early summer you may spot a basking shark. These filter-feeders are the world's second largest fish and can weigh up to three tonnes.

Up until the sixties Achill Basking Shark Fishery operated in Keem Bay. The sharks, which were valued for their oil, were entangled in nets attached to the cliffs and killed by harpoons from currachs. They were then towed by larger boats to Purteen Harbour where the oil was extracted.

The southern end of the beach is a Blueway, a designated snorkelling spot that is suitable for beginners and it can be used at any tide. Look out for basking sharks, spider crabs and trigger fish. For further information consult the board in the carpark. There is a lifeguard on duty every day during July and August.

KEEL

The 3km Blue Flag beach at Keel (also known as Trawmore Strand) takes the full force of the Atlantic, creating ideal conditions for windsurfing, kiteboarding and surfing. Conveniently there is also more sheltered water suitable for beginners on the lake behind the beach (*53.97360, -10.0734*). The beach is also the perfect place for a bracing walk on a wild winter's day.

Sabhna Saunas (sabhna.ie) operate overlooking the beach (and at Doogort beach as well). They are open daily during the summer and at weekends the rest of the year.

Blackfield Surf School (blackfield.com) offer surfing lessons and rentals. Look out for their double-decker bus that serves as a surf shop and coffee bar.

Keel | Eric Verleene

Keem Blueway | Roland Martins

Annagh Strand | Will Greene

Cycling Loop 1 | DF

There are dangerous rip tides on certain sections of the beach so consult the lifeguards and signs before getting into the water.

DOOEGA
The fishing village of Dooega on the southern side of the island has a small, sheltered Blue Flag beach that is ideal for swimming (53.9212, -10.0184). As it's located away from the island's most popular tourist areas it's rarely busy.

DOOGORT
There are two Blue Flag beaches close to each other, Silver Strand (54.0133, -10.0183) and Golden Strand (54.0122, -9.9949), on the north side of the island near Doogort. Both are close to the road, with plenty of parking and lifeguards during the summer.

The two beaches are linked by a 2.4km kayak trail. It's only suitable for proficient paddlers with sea kayaking experience. Less experienced kayakers should contact one of the providers listed on page 205.

The Blueway should be avoided when the wind is offshore. Start at either strand and follow the rocky coastline. If you are lucky you may spot bottlenose dolphins and seals along the way. Watch out for tidal flows at the eastern headland near Silver Strand.

CYCLING
Cycling is an excellent way to get around the island and it's very popular as Achill lies at the western end of the Greenway (see page 196). There are three signposted loops, all of which start and finish in Keel. Traffic is generally light, but can get busy during the summer, especially on the main road across the island.

The 44km Loop 1 travels around the coastline on the southern end of the island. The route is generally flat but there are a few short steep sections. It's possible to take a shortcut at Ashleam.

The 28km Loop 2 follows quiet back roads north to Doogort, passing the beaches of Silver Strand and Golden Strand, the ideal place to stop for a swim, before returning along the main road.

Loop 3 is a pleasant 12km route with just a few gentle hills. It's worth making a short detour to visit the deserted village (see page 200).

WALKING
Achill offers a wide range of walking, from gentle sunset strolls along the beach to gruelling days in the mountains. As much of the higher ground on the island is in common ownership it is freely accessible.

If you do venture onto the mountains you should be equipped for wet, windy weather and heavy cloud which can arrive without notice. You should carry a map (OSI sheet 30) and compass and be capable of navigating in low visibility.

The view from Minaun | RC

CROAGHAUN

Croaghaun (688m) dominates the western end of the island. Its northern slopes are the highest sea cliffs in Ireland (53.9840, -10.1964).

There are a few possible routes to the top. The most direct is from the carpark at Keem beach (53.9673, -10.1955) but no matter which route you choose it's a hard slog, but more than justified by the sensational views.

It's possible for strong hikers to do both Croaghaun and Slievemore in a day but you will need to arrange a lift back to your car.

ACHILL HEAD

This 7km loop starts and finishes at Keem beach (53.9673, -10.1955). It's a great way to take in the fantastic cliff and coastal scenery of this, the wildest part of the island, while avoiding the hard climb up Croaghaun. See the photo on page 204.

From the beach, head in a southwesterly direction up the steep grassy slopes. Once you reach the cliffs follow them northwest (keeping a safe distance from the edge). At the point where the slender ridge of Achill Head juts into the sea turn east and follow the small stream down the valley back to the beach.

It's possible to extend the walk by following the narrow ridge to the end of Achill Head. The ridge is narrow and steep in places, and not advisable on a windy day, but experienced walkers with a head for heights will savour the sense of isolation at this lonely outpost.

DOOAGH LOOP

This gentle 4.4km signposted walk follows narrow bog roads in a loop above the village of Dooagh (53.9750, -10.1281). It's ideal for stretching the legs on a day when the mountains are covered in cloud. Follow the purple arrows.

MINAUN

Minaun lies above the southeast end of Keel beach. The views from its summit are excellent and it's a great place to watch the sunset. It's possible to drive (signposted as 'Barr an Mhionnáin') to within a kilometre of the top, leaving only a short walk west to the summit, which is marked by a cairn topped with a statue (53.9497, -10.0396).

GRANUAILE LOOP

This 6.2km signposted trail (green arrows) is named after the pirate queen, Grace O'Malley, also known as Granuaile. The walk is mainly on bog roads and some open ground (can be wet underfoot), in a loop around Derreen Hill. Part of the route follows the old funeral path to Kildownet Cemetery. Look out for the piles of rocks where the coffin was placed while the bearers took a rest.

Achill Head | RC

Golden Strand | RC

The walk starts from Johnny Patten's pub (*53.9030, -9.9413*). No dogs are allowed as the walk crosses open farmland.

SLIEVEMORE
The elegant triangular profile of Slievemore rises straight from the sea to 671m, making the climb to its summit a formidable challenge (*54.0098, -10.0588*).

The most interesting route up the mountain starts in Doogort and follows the prominent curved ridge to the summit. The view from the top, if you are lucky enough to reach it on a clear day, is one of the best along the Wild Atlantic Way.

From the beach (*54.0113, -10.0272*) follow the road west along the shore until there is open hillside to your left. Leave the road and head for the ridge. Follow an intermittent path up the left-hand side of the ridge keeping well back from the steep cliffs. The summit is marked by a trig pillar and a small stone shelter.

Return either by retracing your steps or by descending the west ridge to the deserted village (*53.9961, -10.0758*), leaving a 4km road walk back to Doogort. ∎

Surfing at Keel | Ian Boyle

ACTIVITY PROVIDERS ON ACHILL

PURE MAGIC
Kite surfing, stand up paddleboarding
puremagic.ie

ACHILL ISLAND SCUBA DIVE CENTRE
Scuba diving
achilldivecentre.com

CALVEY'S EQUESTRIAN
Horse riding
calveysofachill.ie

ACHILL SURF AND KAYAK
Surfing, kayaking, rock climbing, coasteering,
achillsurf.com

ACHILL OUTDOOR EDUCATION CENTRE
Canoeing, kayaking, sailing, windsurfing, surfing, rock climbing, archery
achilloutdoor.com

TOMÁS MAC LOCHLÁINN
Walking guide
siul@eircom.net

ACHILL BIKES
Dooagh and Achill Sound during the summer
achillbikes.com

CLEW BAY BIKE HIRE
Westport, Newport, Mulranny, and Achill Sound
clewbayoutdoors.ie

WEST COAST CLIMBING AND ADVENTURE
Kayaking, rock climbing, hiking
fb.com/WestClimbAdventure

Nanny Goose's | Rick Strooper

ACHILL ISLAND
ACCOMMODATION

CAMPSITES
There are a number of campsites on the island including Keel Sandybanks beside Keel beach (achillcamping.com), Keel Camping (keelcamping.ie) and Seal Caves (achillsealcaves.com) near Doogort.

NANNY GOOSE'S
53.9786, -10.0497
nannygooses.com
This collection of four wooden pods is located on a hillside a short walk from Keel Beach. Each pod sleeps four with a double bed and a sofa-bed and they are fitted with a kitchenette and bathroom.

THE OLD BEACH COTTAGE, DOOGORT
54.0104, -10.0228
theoldbeachcottage.com
This small stone cottage overlooks Silver Strand in Doogort. It has a cosy, bright interior thanks to the whitewashed walls and sleep four in two singles and a double.

   A short distance east, just past the beach is another property, the Old Fisherman's Cottage (*54.0135, -10.0169*). This recently modernised two-storey house sleeps six in three bedrooms, two doubles and a twin with bunks. See theoldfishermanscottage.com for more information.

THE VALLEY HOUSE HOSTEL
54.0126, -9.9697
valley-house.com
Tucked away down a lane a short distance from the Golden Strand at Doogort this large hostel has double, family rooms and dorms. There is also a cosy bar and a restaurant that opens during the busier months of the year.

WATER'S EDGE
53.8943, -9.9385
airbnb.ie/rooms/733930488380603042
A simple cottage with a corrugated roof and a bright interior. Sleeps two. Right on the water with views across Achill Sound to the mainland.

The Salt Dock | Achill Island Sea Salf

ACHILL ISLAND
FOOD

THE AMETHYST BAR
53.9744, -10.0855
theamethystbar.com
This popular restaurant, in the village of Keel, a short distance from the beach, serves a varied menu of Irish pub classics.

The former hotel was once the home of Paul Henry, the landscape painter whose work is so strongly associated with the island.

ÁR BIA MARA
53.9753, -10.0821
instagram.com/ar_bia_mara
This food truck in Keel specialises in fresh seafood. They serve a varied and ever-changing menu featuring fish tacos, satay prawns, scampi, calamari and fish and chips.

THE SALT DOCK
53.9781, -9.9826
achillislandseasalt.ie
Seasonal coffee shop in Bunacurry serving takeaway coffee, toasties and ice cream. Located right beside the Achill Island Sea Salt factory which has a visitor centre that offers free self-guided tours.

TED'S BAR
53.9520, -9.9721
facebook.com/tedsachill
This pub in Cashel on the main road across the island offers great value daily lunch specials. It also hosts regular events such as cards, bingo and quizzes.

There is a food truck, Blásta, that operates outside the pub. They serves burgers, fish tacos and spice boxes, see instagram.com/blastaatteds for opening hours.

You can also hire a electric or mountain bike here.

NORTH MAYO

The northwest corner of Mayo is the emptiest, wildest part of Ireland. The landscape is characterised by vast swathes of blanket bog and some of the most spectacular cliff and rock architecture in the country.

It's also one of the most overlooked stretches of the west coast, and is much quieter than the better known tourist areas like Dingle or Connemara. However that's not to say it's any less spectacular. Its beaches and coastal walks easily rival those of the more famous regions. It's the ideal destination for those looking to experience the wild landscape of the Atlantic coast in a quiet setting.

The sculpture trails that run along the coast of Erris and North Mayo are the most extensive of their kind in the country. They offer a unique and really interesting way to get to know the landscape. See page 215.

For more information about this region see northmayo.ie.

WILD NEPHIN NATIONAL PARK

One of Ireland's most remote and wild landscapes, the National Park covers 15,000 hectares of blanket bog and mountain. The park is dominated by the Nephin Beg Range and Owenduff Bog, one of the last intact active blanket bog systems in Western Europe.

The Park's visitor centre (54.0245, -9.8235) in Ballycroy village houses an exhibition of the landscape, habitats and species found in the park and the surrounding area. It's a good place to escape the weather on a rainy day.

Beside the centre is a 2km accessible trail that offers panoramic views of Achill Island to the west and the Nephin Beg mountains to the east. The trail, known as Tóchar Daithí Bán, is named after the mythical giant Daithí Bán who built a fortress on the park's tallest mountain, Slieve Carr.

Further south along the Wild Atlantic Way between Mulranny and Ballycroy (53.9573, -9.7926) is the 2km Claggan Mountain Coastal Trail. Further inland, the Letterkeen Bothy car park (53.9891, -9.5728) is the start/finish point for four more trails ranging from 2.5km to 12km.

The park is traversed by the Bangor Trail, a challenging 25km walk that follows an old droving route between Bangor-Erris and Newport that was used for over a thousand years before the advent of more modern roads. See page 196 for more information.

See page 218 for information about the huts, bothies and wild camping in the park.

Ballycroy National Park | RC

The park is a designated Dark Sky Park making it one of the best places to stargaze in the country, see mayodarkskypark.ie for more information.

A free shuttle bus runs between Westport and Bangor-Erris, stopping along the way during June, July and August, See nationalparks.ie/wild-nephin for details.

DOOHOOMA
A quiet peninsula well off the beaten track. The long, sandy, sheltered beach has stunning views of Achill and Blacksod Bay (54.0715, -9.9630). If you pass through the pretty fishing village of Doohooma check out the charming Sea Rod Inn (thesearodinn.ie) which has rooms, a restaurant and pub.

DOOLOUGH
Every August this long stretch of sand hosts horse and greyhound racing, part of the colourful Geesala Festival (54.1413, -9.9525). The rest of the year it's much quieter.

CLAGGAN ISLAND
Claggan Island is Mayo's newest island - it was only officially declared an island in 1991 after storms flooded the narrow sandy causeway (not driveable) that links it to the mainland (54.1779, -9.9669).

The former coastguard station on the island is available for rent, as are two wooden pods. See belmulletcgs.com for details.

Srah Beach connects Claggan with the mainland. The 4km curved strand has a Green Coast award and is perfect for both swimming and strolling (54.1725, -9.9550).

BELMULLET
The town of Belmullet occupies the thin strip of land that joins the Mullet Peninsula with the rest of the world. To the north is Broadhaven Bay and to the south is Blacksod Bay.

BELMULLET TIDAL POOL
A saltwater swimming pool is located a short walk from the town centre, in Blacksod Bay (54.2173, -9.9902). It has a toddler's area and a deeper section for experienced swimmers. During July and August there is a lifeguard as well as swimming and safety lessons for children. Follow the coast south from the western end of the Main Street.

BELMULLET CYCLE HUB
Belmullet serves as a hub for two linear and two looped signposted cycle routes ranging in distance from 37km to 72km. Each route offers breathtaking views of the Mayo coast. Sections of all these routes are on busy roads so take care.

Portglash | DF

Two linear routes join Belmullet and Ballycastle. The more direct option is the 49km North Mayo Linear Route which follows the busy R314. The quieter option is the 72km Rossport and Glinsk Linear Route which includes a short loop around Rossport and follows some very quiet scenic roads between Rossport and Belderg.

There are also two loops around the surrounding area. The Carrowmore Lake Loop is a gentle 37km circuit on good surfaces. There are good views from the R313 out of Belmullet, then a quiet road follows the western shore to Carrowmore Lake before returning along the R314. The Pullathomas Loop is a 50km route that keeps close to the coast and is fairly flat, following good roads with views over Broadhaven and Sruwaddacon Bay.

You can hire bikes from Léim Siar Bed and Breakfast (leimsiar.com).

BEACHES

The coastline on the southern half of the Mullet Peninsula has no shortage of beautiful sandy beaches. As a rule those facing the Atlantic are wild and windswept, while those on the Blacksod Bay side are calmer.

- The Blue Flag beach at Elly Bay is clean, sheltered and ideal for swimming, sailing and other watersports (*54.1623, -10.0865*). On the opposite side of the peninsula is another beach that is popular with surfers. Avoid swimming here when there is a swell as there can be strong currents (*54.1593, -10.0972*).
- Mullaghroe, a quiet Blue Flag beach a short drive from the main road (*54.1386, -10.0768*).
- Termon beach, on the east side of the peninsula, has a Green Coast award (*54.1126, -10.0924*).
- Fallmore is a beautiful south-facing beach, with magnificent views of Achill Island. It's sheltered from a northerly wind (*54.0959, -10.1110*).
- Portglash is a very quiet beach that looks across the water to the Inishkea Islands (*54.1119, -10.1211*).
- Cross Beach (*54.2085, -10.0828*) is a long strand with a Green Coast award.
- Belderra Strand, which is just north of the much larger Cross Beach, is well sheltered and quiet. Watch out for strong currents (*54.2086, -10.0636*).
- Scotch Port is a beautiful bay with a stony beach. The water is crystal clear and there is plenty of colourful marine life so it's an ideal snorkelling spot (*54.2551, -10.0732*).

THE INISHKEA ISLANDS

Inishkea North and Inishkea South lie four kilometres west of the Mullet Peninsula. They are low-lying, with no trees, and are covered in short grass and beautiful fine white sand. The sand lies everywhere and it's

Claggan Island | DF

Cross Beach | DF

Blacksod Lighthouse | DF

The village on Inishkea South | Frank Fullard

slowly filling the abandoned houses that face the beach at the harbour.

In 1927 the island's men went out fishing and were caught in a violent storm in which ten fishermen lost their lives. After this the inhabitants of the island, devastated by their loss, left to live on the mainland.

Now the islands lie uninhabited and are slowly returning to a wild state, home to a thriving population of seals and sea birds. Contact Blacksod Sea Safari (blacksodseasafari.ie) or Belmullet Boat Charters (belmulletboatcharters.com) to arrange a visit.

SOLAS
This new visitor centre on the Belmullet Peninsula (*54.1207, -10.1008*) is designed to highlight the history, heritage and language of the region. See visitsolas.ie for opening hours and booking information.

BLACKSOD LIGHTHOUSE
At the southern tip of the peninsula is Blacksod Lighthouse (*54.0985, -10.0604*), which is famous for the important role it played in the D-Day landings. A report issued from the lighthouse warning of bad weather convinced the Allies to delay the invasion for 24 hours, a decision which averted a military catastrophe. Guided tours are available see visitblacksodlighthouse.ie for details.

CROSS LOOP WALKS
The Cross Loop is a beautiful coastal trail that starts at the ruins of Cross Abbey (*54.2085, -10.0828*). From the walk there is a great view across the water to the islands of Inishkea and Inishglora, the burial place of the mythical Children of Lir. It's best done in a clockwise direction at low tide. There are two options, a 5.7km circuit (green arrows) and a 6km variation (blue arrows).

Both routes follow the beach south around Corraun Point before turning inland and along the track on the shore of Cross Lough. The longer variation loops around the far side of the lake.

To reach the trailhead follow the R313 south from Belmullet town (signposted 'An Fód Dubh'), after 5km turn right at the church in Binghamstown. Continue past Belderra Strand until you see the signpost directing you to turn right.

DOONAMOE POINT
With uninterrupted views of the Atlantic, this is one of the best viewpoints in Erris and is the ideal spot to watch the sun set (*54.2645, -10.0753*). A large sculpture has been built around the impressive blowhole (see page 215) and on rough days sea spray and foam explode up from it.

ERRIS HEAD
Erris Head, the northernmost point of the Mullet Peninsula, is a remote spot with wonderful scenery

Benwee Head | RC

The Sralagagh Loop | DF

The cliffs beside Céide Fields | RC

and a wild feel. It juts out into the sea and takes everything the Atlantic can throw at it. The headland is home to a wide variety of wildlife. Look out for choughs nesting on the cliffs, hares on the cliff tops and seals, porpoises and bottlenose dolphins in the water below.

ERRIS HEAD LOOP
The trailhead for this 3.9km signposted walk is the small carpark at the end of the road (*54.2886, -9.9886*). It is signposted (as 'Ceann Iorrais') from Belmullet. The walk takes a clockwise loop around the headland and the ground can be boggy in places. Keep well back from the cliff edges. This walk should be avoided in very windy weather.

At the northernmost point of the walk there is a railed viewing point where you can enjoy the spectacular views of the surrounding cliffs and the Stags of Broadhaven in the distance.

As you continue along the trail watch out for the World War Two lookout post and the faint outline of 'EIRE 62' which identified the land as neutral Ireland to pilots during the war.

CEATHRÚ THAIDHG
The cliffs near the small Irish-speaking village of Ceathrú Thaidhg (Carrowteige) are some of the most spectacular along the Wild Atlantic Way. The

Dún Briste | RC

village is the trailhead for four signposted walks (*54.3131, -9.8128*). Download maps of the walks from irishtrails.ie.

There are two nice Green Coast beaches in the area, at Portacloy (*54.3312, -9.7835*) and the more sheltered Rinroe Strand (*54.3022, -9.8411*).

CHILDREN OF LIR WALK
This is a beautiful 10.7km coastal walk through a wild landscape of bog and windswept mountainside. It follows surfaced roads, grassy tracks and paths and brings you past the Children of Lir sculpture, which overlooks the most impressive cliffs of Benwee Head. It is signposted with blue arrows.

This walk is named after the famous legend, 'The Children of Lir', which tells of four children who were turned into swans and condemned to wander the countryside for 900 years, with 300 of these being spent on the island of Inishglora, off the coast of Mullet. If you are short of time it's possible to start from the carpark (*54.3236, -9.8404*) beside the Children of Lir sculpture.

There are two variations of this walk. The 6km Beach Loop (green arrows) follows the road down to Rinroe Strand (*54.3021, -9.8411*) and is ideal when it's too windy for the other, more exposed, walks. The other is the 10.9km Black Ditch loop (red arrows) which is a slightly longer version of the original loop.

If you are looking for a more challenging route then you could combine the Children of Lir and Benwee Head walks to create a 16km route along the cliffs from Rinroe to Portacloy.

BENWEE HEAD WALK
This remote 11.3km loop (purple arrows) follows the dramatic coast north of Ceathrú Thaidhg with some excellent views of the huge cliffs. The ground can be boggy in places. The trailhead is in Carrowteige opposite the post office (*54.3131, -9.8128*).

BELDERG POOL
The tiny fishing port of Belderg is home to a natural swimming pool, known as Pol A Sean tSáile, that is popular with locals (*54.3119, -9.5529*). It's a good spot for a swim when the sea is rough. Turn off the Wild Atlantic Way at Belderg (*54.2935, -9.5508*) and follow the small road down to the sea. The pool is behind the harbour wall.

CÉIDE FIELDS
This ancient network of stone walls was discovered in the 1930s by a local schoolteacher when he was cutting turf. It's the most extensive Stone Age monument in the world, consisting of field systems, dwelling areas and megalithic tombs. The stone walled fields, extending over thousands of hectares, are almost 6,000 years old, the oldest in the world.

Lacken Strand | RC

The visitor centre at the Céide Fields explores the archaeology of the site and the botany and geology of the area (*54.3082, -9.4565*). See ceidefields.com.

The remains may be a little underwhelming, but it's worth a stop to admire the view from the platform on the edge of the 100m tall cliffs.

BALLYCASTLE WALK

The Sralagagh Loop is a pleasant signposted loop with great views of Downpatrick Head. The 8.2km route follows narrow roads and tracks and is suitable for both walking and mountain biking. It starts and finishes in Ballycastle village (*54.2798, -9.3734*).

DOWNPATRICK HEAD

Just a few kilometres north of Ballycastle is Downpatrick Head. The spectacular sea stack, Dún Briste (The Broken Fort), which lies just off the headland, is one of the iconic images of Ireland (*54.3228, -9.3458*).

The cliff scenery is spectacular, but the headland is very exposed to the elements so take care near the cliff edge, especially on windy days. There are two blowholes close to the Head. The larger one has a sculpture/viewing platform which is part of the North Mayo Sculpture Trail (see opposite).

LACKEN STRAND

This vast sandy beach is formed in the bay where the Cloonalaghan River joins the sea (*54.2741, -9.2574*). The beach is completely covered by water twice a day so make sure that you don't get cut off by the rising tide. If swimming, be alert for dangerous currents and heed the warning signs.

On the east side of the estuary is Kilcummin beach (*54.2789, -9.2318*). Sheltered and remote, it's backed by towering sand dunes. It is accessible at low tide by walking across the sand from Lacken (watch the tide) and via the back roads from Kilcummin.

The picnic area beside Lacken Church (*54.2741, -9.2574*) is the trailhead for two trails that explore some very quiet lanes and tracks. The Blue Loop is 10.6km (blue arrows) and the Green Loop is 8km (green arrows).

ROSS STRAND

Ross Strand lies on the westerly side of Killala where the River Moy meets the sea (*54.2327, -9.1980*). The most northerly of Mayo's Blue Flag beaches, it has great views across the bay to the coast of Sligo. The flat sand is a great place for a long walk at low tide.

Lifeguards are on duty during July and August. Beware of the strong currents and keep inside the designated swimming areas. The best time to swim is at high tide, but at low tide there are lots of interesting rock pools just north of the carpark.

Sea kayaking near Benwee Head | Gareth McCormack

BELLEEK WOODS
Just north of the town of Ballina, on the banks of the River Moy, is Belleek Woods (*54.1301, -9.1428*). A 4km signposted trail follows a series of paths through the peaceful 400 hectare forest. See coillte.ie/site/belleek for details.

Look our for the *SS Creteboom* sitting on a mud bank in the river (*54.1349, -9.1397*). It's the haunting remains of a failed World War 1 experiment to build ships out of concrete.

NORTH MAYO ART TRAILS
North Mayo is home to two outdoor sculpture trails, Tír Sáile and Spirit of Place. Between the two trails there are over 20 sculptures scattered along the coast, many in scenic, remote locations. Seeking out the sculptures, visiting a place you otherwise mightn't have gone, adds an extra dimension to a visit to this part of the country. See northmayoarttrail.com for a maps and the latest information.

TÍR SÁILE
Tír Sáile, the North Mayo Sculpture Trail, is the largest public arts project in Ireland. It consists of eleven sculptures celebrating the wild beauty of the area and its long history of human habitation.

Most of the sculptures are well signposted (by brown signs marked 'Tír Sáile'), some of the original

ACTIVITY PROVIDERS IN NORTH MAYO

WAVESWEEPER SEA ADVENTURES
thewesternstrands.com

BELLACRAGHER BAY BOAT CLUB
bellacragherboatclub.ie

UISCE
uisce.ie

BANGOR ERRIS ANGLING
bangorerrisangling.com

DUVILLAUN RIDING CENTRE
duvillaunridingcentre@gmail.com

BARRY'S GUIDED TOURS
barrysguidedtours.com

PADDLE AND PEDAL
paddleandpedal.ie

The Thin Places, Sea Eating the Land, Doonamoe | DF

The Crossing, Downpatrick Head | Michael McLaughlin

Deirbhle's Twist, Fallmore | DF

The Thin Places, Land Eating the Sea, Annagh Head | DF

pieces have deteriorated but seven remain in good condition.

SPIRIT OF PLACE

Spirit of Place was conceived by Travis Price of the Catholic University of America. The program designs and builds structures that reflect upon ancient folklore. Spirit of Place has built seven large pieces along the Mayo coast in collaboration with Mayo County Council.

- A Home for the Children of Lir, Ceathrú Thaidhg (see page 212) (54.3244, -9.8401).
- Temple of the Tides of Time, Belmullet (54.2256, -9.9921).
- The Thin Places, Land Eating the Sea, Annagh Head (54.2417, -10.1045).
- The Thin Places, Sea Eating the Land, Doonamoe (54.2644, -10.0758).
- The Vault of Heaven, Annagh Head (54.2426, -10.0894).
- Tale of the Tongs, Inishturk (see page 191) (53.7079, -10.1067).
- The Crossing, Downpatrick Head, (see page 214) (54.3254, -9.3467).

The Brogan Carroll Bothy | RC

NORTH MAYO
ACCOMMODATION

BELMULLET COASTGUARD STATION
54.1803, -9.9723
belmulletcgs.com
This accommodation consists of two camping pods (each sleeps four) and a three-bedroom self-catering option in the old Coastguard Station. Tents can also be pitched near the pods. The location, on Claggan Island, which is cut off during spring tides, is idyllic.

BELMULLET GLAMPING
54.2548, -10.0421
belmulletglamping.com
Set in a rural location on the northern half of the Mullet Peninsula there are four pods available to rent. The luxurious pods sleep four in a double and bunk bed. Conveniently there is a nice pub just across the road.

GERAGHTY'S FARMYARD PODS
54.2180, -9.9799
geraghtysfarmyardpods.ie
Four pods laid out around a farmyard on the outskirts of Belmullet town. The pods sleep four with a double and sofa bed and have a kitchenette and bathroom. There is also a small cottage and mobile home for rent. Guests have the use of a communal kitchen.

WILD NEPHIN SHELTERS
Wild Nephin National Park (page 208) is home to a number of basic free-to-use shelters. The Brogan Carroll Bothy (*53.9892, -9.5728*) is a basic stone cottage.

There are also a pair of open-front wooden huts at Lough Aroher (*54.0036, -9.6200*), which is about 4km from Letterkeen along the Bangor Trail, and Altnabrocky (*54.0498, -9.6085*).

Work is ongoing on converting a number of deserted cottages into bothies, so far four have been completed - Tarsaghaun Cottage (*54.0818, -9.7312*), McCann's House (*53.9952, -9.5360*), Blue Lodge (*54.0013, -9.7264*) and Ailtahuney River (*53.9853, -9.5753*).

CEIDE GLAMPING
54.3050, -9.3919
ceideglamping.com
This family-run business is a short distance from Ballycastle, close to the water and with views across Bunatrahir Bay to Downpatrick Head. There are six wooden pods, each sleeps two, as well as a large hut with a BBQ fireplace to hang out and cook in.

Ginger & Wild | DF

NORTH MAYO
FOOD

GINGER & WILD
54.0245 -9.8234
gingerandwild.com
This cafe in the Wild Nephin Visitor Centre in Ballycroy serves excellent cakes and coffee as well as hearty lunches. The bright modern space offers outstanding views over the National Park and towards Achill Island. There is also a gallery that displays and sells Irish artwork, textiles and jewellery.

BIKE CAFE MAYO, BELMULLET
54.2244, -9.9877
fb.com/bcireland
A small coffee shop for people who take their coffee seriously. The coffee is made on a mobile tricycle coffee machine that sometimes pops up near the coast in the area! Closed Wednesdays.

MARY'S COTTAGE KITCHEN, BALLYCASTLE
54.2798, -9.3728
This cafe is housed in a traditional cottage on the main street of Ballycastle. It serves hearty, traditional lunches, ideal for warming up after being out in the wilds of North Mayo and a range of freshly baked sweet treats as well as homemade chutneys, jams and marmalades.

BRIDGE COFFEE, BALLINA
54.1125, -9.1535
instagram.com/bridgecoffeeballina
Set right on the bank of the River Moy in the centre of Ballina. They serve coffee and sweet treats which you can enjoy in the outdoor seating area overlooking the river.

THE POST HOUSE, BALLINA
54.1125, -9.1559
facebook.com/posthouseballina
Having once served as the town's post office it now serves breakfast, lunch and fresh bakes. With everything from healthy smoothie bowls and sandwiches to full Irish breakfasts. Closed Sundays.

Dunmoran Strand (see page 223) with Knocknarea in the distance | RC

SLIGO AND LEITRIM

The Sligo coast (and the short strip of Leitrim that meets the sea) is one of the gentler sections of the Wild Atlantic Way. Here the green fields run straight down to the shore and cattle graze on the sweet and salty grass.

Looming over the coastline are some impressive mountains that are very different in character to those to the north and south. The geological foundation is limestone that has been eroded to leave vertical cliffs with flat summits, a form that is exemplified in the iconic profile of Benbulbin.

A short distance inland are a number of worthwhile diversions, including the wooded shores of Lough Gill near Sligo Town and the beautiful valley of Glencar in Leitrim, with its spectacular waterfalls.

Sligo is world famous for its surfing, with spots like Strandhill, Mullaghmore Beach, Easky and Enniscrone recognised internationally as having some of the best waves in Europe.

Sligo's gentle terrain is ideally suited to easier walking routes and over sixty coastal, woodland and waterside walks are documented on the excellent Sligo Walks website (sligowalks.ie).

ENNISCRONE
This lively seaside town backs onto a vast, sandy Blue Flag beach that stretches for almost 5km (*54.2122, -9.0972*). There is a lifeguard on duty on weekends during June and September and daily in July and August.

The beach break is an ideal place to learn to surf. Two surf schools offer board hire and lessons: North West Surf School (nwsurfschool.com) and 7th Wave Surf School (surfsligo.com).

Harbour SUP n Sail (harboursupsail.com) run paddleboarding and dinghy sailing lessons in the sheltered waters of the harbour (*54.2199, -9.0953*).

Overlooking the beach is Kilcullen Seaweed Baths (kilcullenseaweedbaths.net).

EASKY
This small village is famous among surfers for the waves that break near the mouth of the river (*54.2859, -8.9607*). There are always a few dilapidated vans and caravans on the commonage beside the castle where camping seems to be tolerated (*54.2912, -8.9573*).

If you follow the track that runs eastwards along the shore for 1.1km you come to a semi-natural swimming hole called Poll Gorm (*54.2932, -8.9420*). Best at low tide.

LOUGH EASKY
Upriver from the village, nestled in the Ox Mountains, is Lough Easky (*54.1594, -8.8436*). A 6km signposted trail (purple arrows) loops around the lake. The trail is pretty flat but, as much of the ground is blanket bog, a good pair of boots is essential if you want to keep your feet dry.

TRÁ BHUÍ
A quiet sandy beach (*54.2607 -8.7933*). Can get busy with camper vans and surfers when the surf is good. Note swimming isn't advised due to dangerous currents.

AUGHRIS HEAD
Near the tip of this rocky headland is The Beach Bar (*54.2690, -8.7570*), a well-known thatched pub that serves food and has a small campsite for campervans and caravans only, no tents. See page 232 for details.

There is a 4km signposted loop that takes in the clifftop path on the east side of Aughris Head. From The Beach Bar walk back up the road and turn right. Just before the pier a small grassy track makes its way west along the coast. Look out for the distinctive curved banks of an Iron Age promontory fort that is slowly being consumed by the sea (*54.2781, -8.7557*). After 3km the path turns away from the

Easky surfing | RC

Coolaney Mountain Bike Trails | DF

Carrowmore | DF

coast and follows quiet roads back to the pier. See sligowalks.ie for more information.

DUNMORAN STRAND
East of Aughris Head is Dunmoran Strand, a sheltered bay with a nice sandy Green Coast beach. The beach can be accessed from the carpark at its eastern end (*54.2626, -8.7242*), or from The Beach Bar (*54.2690, -8.7570*). There is a lifeguard on duty at weekends in July and August.

COOLANEY MOUNTAIN BIKE TRAILS
A network of purpose-built mountain bike trails wind across the southern slopes of the Ox Mountains just outside the village of Coolaney (*54.1790, -8.6129*). There is a Blue Trail (graded moderate), a more challenging Red Trail (graded difficult), which has a number of variations, and a Black Trail (graded Severe). See coolaneymtb.com for details.

PORTAVADE BEACH
A secluded beach with an excellent view across the water to Knocknarea (*54.2552, -8.6415*). Limited roadside parking.

UNION WOOD
Just east of the village of Ballysadare, a few minutes from the busy N4, is Union Wood (*54.2135, -8.4710*). The forest is a mix of broadleaf and coniferous trees

The Glen | DF

and there are great views of Knocknarea and the Ox Mountains from the top of Union Rock.

There are two signposted walks in the forest. The 4km Union Rock Trail (red arrows) has a few steep climbs. It loops around the craggy summit, Union Rock, but it's worth making a diversion to visit the top. The second route is the 5.5km Oakwood Trail (green arrows) which takes a low-level route around the hill, passing through some beautiful oak forest.

CARROWMORE

A short drive from Strandhill in the townland of Carrowmore is one of Ireland's most extensive prehistoric cemeteries (*54.2135, -8.4710*). It is the largest group of megaliths in the country and the second largest in Europe. The monuments are between five and a half thousand and six thousand years old.

The dolmens, which consist of a number of standing stones supporting a large flat horizontal capstone, are the only remnant of the burial chambers which were originally covered with earth and stones. Archaeologists have recorded over sixty tombs, of which thirty are visible today.

The visitor centre is open daily between March and November and offers guided tours and multilingual self-guide options (admission €5). See heritageireland.ie for details.

THE GLEN

Truly a hidden gem, the Glen is a narrow canyon that runs for just under a kilometre (*54.2482, -8.5764*). Almost completely hidden from view and difficult to find, it's a peaceful, still place with a lush, rainforest feel. The vertical limestone walls and the thick vegetation nearly completely obscure the sky.

To find it, follow the Wild Atlantic Way south out of Strandhill. After 3km take the left turn signposted for Knocknarea. Drive 600m up the hill and park in the scenic layby on the right (*54.2481, -8.5733*). Walk back down the hill. After 200m look out for a small well on the right, the often overgrown entrance is directly opposite this. The ground in the Glen is always very wet and muddy so wear wellies or hiking boots.

STRANDHILL

This small seaside village has a real surfer vibe (*54.2694, -8.6102*). The seafront, which has some very nice cafes and coffee shops, is a great spot to watch the surfers in action.

Be warned that swimming is strictly prohibited at the beach due to the very dangerous currents and rip tides. If you want to get into the water then go for a soak at Voya Seaweed Baths (voyaseaweedbaths.com) on the seafront.

Coney Island causeway | DF

SURFING
Strandhill has become a Mecca for surfers from far and wide. It is considered one of the best beach breaks in the country. County regulations prohibit surfboard rental in Strandhill due to the dangerous currents. But if you want to give it a go then you can take a lesson with one of the surf schools who provide all the required equipment.

The beach at Strandhill faces northwest and picks up any swell from southwest to north, making it one of the most consistent breaks in Ireland. The beach is sand-bottomed and is surrounded by many other reef and point breaks.

CULLEENAMORE BEACH
This sandy beach lies south of the village in the sheltered waters of Ballysadare Bay (*54.2593, -8.6006*). It's well protected from the big waves so is a safe place to swim (though there is no lifeguard). On warm summer days look out for seals soaking up the sun on the sandbanks.

There is a nice 7km walk that follows the coast south from Strandhill around the sandy headland to Culleenamore. To return either retrace your steps or take the path through the dunes as a shortcut.

KILLASPUGBRONE LOOP
This 7km signposted walk explores the coast north of Strandhill. From the seafront head north along the dunes or through the campsite (note there is no swimming on this beach due to dangerous currents) following the purple arrows. The trail passes Sligo Airport and then swings east past Killaspugbrone Church, an early Christian site, and along the Nun's Beach before returning along the road to the village.

KNOCKNAREA
The distinctive steep profile of Knocknarea rises up behind Strandhill (*54.2585, -8.5741*). At the summit is a huge pile of stones, known as Meabh's Cairn, that is believed to contain a neolithic passage tomb. Please don't climb the cairn or remove any stones from it.

The reward for the short, steep climb is the spectacular view in all directions, taking in the Ox Mountains, Lough Gill, Benbulbin, Sliabh Liag in Donegal, and on a clear day, Croagh Patrick to the southwest.

Queen Maeve's Trail is a 6.5km loop that takes in the summit of Knocknarea and passes through the forest on its eastern slopes.

The trail offers three direct routes to the summit, the most popular starts from the carpark opposite the Sligo Rugby Club which is just east of Strandhill along the northbound Wild Atlantic Way (*54.27051, -8.5848*). A gravel path and wooden boardwalk lead through the trees to the summit. Decent footwear is recommended as the trail, particularly the wooden boardwalk, can be slippery.

Slishwood | DF

The second approach starts from Grange carpark (*54.2532, -8.5575*) on the south side of the mountain. It's a similar length but usually less busy. The third option starts to the east from Rathcarrick Forest (*54.2597, -8.5492*).

CONEY ISLAND
The 160 hectare Coney Island is the largest and the best known of the three islands off the north coast of the Coolera Peninsula. It is very popular with holidaymakers during the summer.

The only facility on the island is Michael J. Ward's pub (*54.3003, -8.5797*), which opens from Thursday to Sundays during the summer. There are two nice beaches, a small one by the pier (*54.3020, -8.5801*) and Carty's Strand, on the west side (*54.2995, -8.5936*). Caution is required if you are going to swim as there can be dangerous currents. Enquire locally.

Coney Island, which translates as 'The Island of Rabbits', gave its name to Coney Island in Brooklyn. In the 18th century the captain of a merchant ship, a Sligo man, noting lots of rabbits on the New York island, named it after his own Coney Island back in Sligo.

Access to the island is by boat from Rosses Point, or by driving/walking/cycling at low tide over the 2.5km causeway across Cummeen Strand (*54.2795, -8.5522*). Be warned the crossing is rough on cars, with many deep saltwater puddles and hard, rutted sand.

It's vital to check the tide before crossing. The RNLI offer daily tide times via SMS, text Coney to 51155.

LOUGH GILL
A short distance inland from Sligo Town is Lough Gill. Its beautiful, serene waters lie in sharp contrast with the more turbulent Atlantic. The 8km long lake contains about twenty small islands, including the Isle of Inishfree, made famous by the W.B. Yeats poem of the same name.

The lake is surrounded by woodland, mostly of oak, rowan and willow, but also a number of other species such as yew, strawberry tree, and the rare bird cherry and rock whitebeam. The water supports a number of protected species of lamprey, as well as salmon and otter. Plenty of animals also live in the woods, of particular note is the community of pine martens.

The Rose of Inishfree (roseofinnisfree.com) offers boat tours of the lake departing from the quay east of Sligo Town.

CYCLE LOOP
A 40km cycle route circumnavigates Lough Gill in a clockwise direction. While the route is well signposted, some of the roads can be quite busy. En route you will pass many wonderful forests and viewing points so it's a great way to see the lake.

Paddleboarding on Lough Gill | SUP For All

Deerpark Court Tomb | DF

Lough Gill | DF

DOONEY ROCK FOREST PARK
A 1.2km trail follows a path through this mainly coniferous forest on the south side of the lake to the viewing point on top of Dooney Rock (54.2384, -8.4279).

SLISHWOOD
This is a stunning location between the southern shore of the lake and the Ox Mountains (54.2307, -8.4013). A delightful 3km signposted loop passes through the remains of an ancient oak woodland. The wood is home to plenty of native wildlife including mute swans, ducks and herons, while badger, fox and fallow deer may also be seen.

HAZELWOOD DEMENSE
This beautiful lakeside forest is just 3km east of Sligo Town at Half Moon Bay (54.2580, -8.4264). The Wynne family, who built Hazelwood House, planted most of the mature trees in this area, including many species that are not native to Ireland, such as beech, hornbeam, lime, rhododendron and cherry laurel.
    As well as a quiet picnic area there is a 3km nature trail and a sculpture trail. Unfortunately, many of the wood carvings are in a bad state of repair.

DEERPARK COURT TOMB TRAIL
This 2.5km trail follows forest tracks over a series of hills and hollows (54.2820, -8.3756). The court tomb, which dates back to the third millennium BC, is considered one of the finest of its type in the country. From the tomb there are expansive views over Lough Gill and the Glencar Valley.

KAYAKING
Gliding quietly across the water in a kayak is a great way to experience Lough Gill. Sligo Kayak Tours (sligokayaktours.com) run guided tours of the lake and some of the more sheltered coastal estuaries.
    Stand Up Paddleboarding, also known as SUP, is another excellent way of exploring the lake. Sligo Bay SUP offers tours of the lake (sligobaysup.ie).

ROSSES POINT
The jutting peninsula north of Sligo Town is very popular with holidaymakers and gets very busy on nice summer days (54.3088, -8.5707).
    The beach, which has a Blue Flag and a Green Coast award, is divided in two by a small rocky headland. There is a lifeguard on duty at weekends during June and September, and daily in July and August.
    The smaller, southern beach is more accessible and busier. The northern beach, which backs the golf course, is longer and quieter. Look out for the caves, known as the Cellars, at its southern end.
    There is a mobile sauna beside Sligo Yacht Club (54.3067, -8.5763), see thehotboxsauna.ie for details.

Glencar Waterfall | DF

The Devil's Chimney | RC

ROSSES WALK
A very pleasant 7km stroll starts from the main beach carpark (*54.3088, -8.5707*). Follow the beach north skirting the golf course to the end of the long, sandy spit before retracing your steps.

GLENCAR
It's well worth diverting the short distance from the coast to visit the valley of Glencar. Its steep limestone walls give it an almost alpine appearance, hence its alternative name - Swiss Valley. The famous waterfall is very pretty and only a short walk through lush woodland from the carpark (*54.3386, -8.3692*). The great thing about the waterfall is that it's much more impressive on a rainy day, of which we have no shortage!

TORMORE TRAIL
A pleasant but steep 2.3km trail leads through native woodland to the base of Sruth In Aghaidh An Aird, also known as The Devil's Chimney. Roughly 100m tall, the waterfall is one of the highest in Ireland. The Irish name translates as 'stream against the height' which refers to the fact that when the wind blows from the west the water rises back up the cliff. Be warned that the waterfall doesn't flow during dry weather, however it is particularly spectacular after heavy rain.

The walk starts from the north shore of Glencar Lough, 1.5km west of the Glencar waterfall carpark (*54.3405, -8.3930*).

DOONEENS WALK
This steep walk climbs high above the valley floor to gain spectacular views of Glencar Lough, Swiss Valley, and Sligo Bay. The 7km round trip is well signposted (yellow arrows) and on good roads and tracks.

Park at the small lakeside carpark (*54.3408, -8.3748*) west of the waterfall carpark. Just opposite this is a steep, winding road. Follow it up to the plateau. Pass through a set of gates and follow the old bog road right to the end and enjoy the view.

BENBULBIN
The flat summit, steep ribbed sides and angular corners of Benbulbin give it an unmistakable profile. Its spectacular appearance owes more to the South American tepui than the rounded hills more common in this part of the world. The distinctive peak was formed during the last ice age when massive retreating glaciers carved the landscape. Its steeper sides are limestone, while the smoother slopes are shale.

The summit plateau's unusual landscape is home to a wide variety of flora and fauna, including Arctic alpine plants, foxes, wild hares and choughs.

Benbulbin | RC

As there are some access issues with walking to the summit, which is not particularly memorable anyway, this incredible mountain is best appreciated from below.

GORTAROWEY WALK
This 4km walk is a pretty straightforward out and back along forest tracks, but the views of the north slopes of Benbulbin make it very worthwhile. Driving north along the Wild Atlantic Way look out for a right turn (signposted 'Ben Bulben Forest Walk') 3.5km past the village of Drumcliffe (where Yeats is buried). Follow the road to the carpark in the forest (54.3616, -8.5021).

LISSADELL HOUSE
The beautiful house (54.3492, -8.5850) is famous as the childhood home of Constance Markievicz, one of the leaders of the 1916 Rising and the first woman elected to the British House of Commons. For a fee (€16) you get a guided tour of the house, entry to the current exhibitions as well as the beautiful alpine and kitchen gardens. The cafe is open daily in the summer. See lissadellhouse.com for details.

RAGHLY WALK
Raghly is a tiny headland that juts out into Sligo Bay. Apparently the easy 3km loop around its narrow roads was one of Yeats' favourite walks. The views across Sligo Bay to Benbulbin and Knocknarea are excellent.

To get to the start, continue along the road past Lissadell House, following signs for 'Raghley' until you reach the narrow neck of land. Park here on the right (54.3311, -8.6472) and head south along the road following the red arrows in either direction.

YELLOW STRAND
Just north of Raghly is this long, very secluded beach that is a great spot for a walk, but not a swim as there are dangerous currents. The roadside parking is limited (54.3471, -8.667).

STREEDAGH BEACH
This long sandy beach, known as the Back Strand (54.4042, -8.5598), forms a narrow tombolo which connects Streedagh Point to Conor's Island. The Green Coast beach has some good surf suitable for intermediate surfers and there is a lifeguard on duty on weekends during July and August.

This is a great spot for an invigorating walk on a winter's day, with excellent views of Benbulbin, Mullaghmore Head and across Donegal Bay to Sliabh Liag. The beach is very exposed to the elements so it can get wild on stormy days.

The beach was the final resting place of three ships and up to 1,800 men of the Spanish Armada, and the remains of one of its smaller landing boats can still be seen at low tide.

Mullaghmore Head | Gareth Wray

BEACH WALK
Either park in the small parking area beside Trawgar (*54.3974, -8.5668*), the smaller beach west of Streedagh, or on the sand at the end of the road beside the Back Strand (*54.4042, -8.5598*). From Trawgar follow the coastline north around Streedagh Point looking out for fossils in the limestone cliffs. Once on the Back Strand it's just a matter of walking along the beach to Conor's Island. The walk out and back along the beach is 6km and is best at low tide.

INISHMURRAY ISLAND
Lying 5km northwest of Streedagh, the tiny island of Inishmurray, which is just under a square kilometre, is known for its monastic settlement, wild scenery and as a wildlife sanctuary (*54.4319, -8.6481*).

The island served as a secluded retreat for Saint Molaise who founded a Christian monastery there in the 6th century, the remains of which are still remarkably intact. The settlement, known as a cashel, is surrounded by the remains of a 3m thick wall which houses a stone-roofed oratory, two churches, a clochán, a beehive hut and round rocks known as the 'cursing stones' (*54.4315, -8.6570*). After being attacked numerous times by the Vikings in the 8th and 9th centuries, the monks were forced to return to the mainland.

Inishmurray, which had a population of 100 people in 1880, was finally abandoned in 1948. The ruined homes and schoolhouse are the only reminders of the small, thriving community.

Nowadays the island is a wildlife sanctuary of national importance for breeding and wintering birds including shags, kittiwakes, terns, petrels, eider duck and brent geese. It also holds one of the largest colonies of barnacle geese in Europe.

Three companies regularly make the crossing to the island from Mullaghmore Harbour (*54.4666, -8.4477*), Sligo Boat Charters (sligoboatcharters.com), Offshore Watersports (offshore.ie) and Inishmurray Island Tours (inishmurrayislandtrips.com).

For more information about the island see inishmurray.com.

CLIFFONY BAY BEACH
Also known as Trawalua Strand, this long, quiet sandy beach has great views of Classiebawn Castle on Mullaghmore Head. There is room for about a dozen cars to park on the R279 between Cliffony and Mullaghmore (*54.4343, -8.4575*). A 1km walk leads to the beach. Unsafe for swimming due to strong currents.

MULLAGHMORE
The small seaside village of Mullaghmore is popular with both tourists from abroad and Irish holidaymakers (*54.4668, -8.4481*). Near the village is the harbour and a fine, sheltered beach (*54.4614, -8.4527*). There is

Clochán, Inishmurray | Val Robus

Diarmuid and Gráinne's Cave | DF

The view from Baryte's Mill | DF

a small grassy carpark in front of the beach but more parking is available near the harbour.

Mullaghmore has an international reputation among surfers for producing some of the biggest waves on the planet. During winter storms these waves can reach up to 15m in height.

The Wild Atlantic Way does a circuit around the headland and the 4km loop is a popular walk with locals. From the coast road there are great views of the very pretty Classiebawn Castle, with its distinctive conical roofed turret.

BISHOP'S POOL
Just off the coast road is a sheltered rock inlet that is a popular swimming spot on warm summer days *(54.4728, -8.4557)*. You will find it 1.2km north of the village, look out for the narrow inlet shaped like a bishop's crozier, hence the name.

CREEVYKEEL COURT TOMB
54.4390, -8.4337
This tomb, which lies just a stone's throw from the busy N15, was built in the 3rd millennium BC and is part of a large network of similar graves.

THE GLENIFF HORSESHOE
This 10km cycling, walking and driving route in the Dartry Mountains has some of the most spectacular scenery that Sligo has to offer. As you emerge through the trees at the highest point of the loop the legendary Diarmuid and Gráinne's Cave comes into view high up on the steep slopes. It is reputed to be the last hiding place of the ill-fated lovers.

Heading north from Sligo Town on the Wild Atlantic Way, take a right turn 1.5km past Cliffony (look out for the signpost for the Benwiskin Centre). Continue up the road, straight through a number of crossroads. Follow the signs for the Horseshoe. At the T-junction at the end of the loop *(54.4458, -8.3841)* turn right and retrace your steps back to the Wild Atlantic Way.

BARYTE'S MILL
The site of the 19th century Baryte's Mill has been carefully re-invented as a beautiful recreational area by Ballaghnatrillick Environmental Group *(54.3979, -8.4000)*. There are a number of short trails through the woodland and plenty of picnic tables and seats. If you are following the Gleniff Horseshoe in a clockwise direction then the Mill is on the left after a short distance.

COUNTY LEITRIM
As the Wild Atlantic Way heads north on the N15, just before Bundoran in Donegal, it passes along County Leitrim's 5km stretch of coastline, don't blink or you will miss it. The small village of Tullaghan has a pebble beach overlooked by a rather ornamental folly tower *(54.4702, -8.3297)*. ∎

Teapot Lane | Kevin Haughey

SLIGO AND LEITRIM
ACCOMMODATION

THE BEACH BAR, AUGHRIS
54.2693, -8.7569
thebeachbarsligo.com
Campervans and caravans as well as B&B are welcome to pitch up at this well-known thatched cottage pub, right on the beach at Aughris Head. Toilets, showers and power points available.

THE WOODCUTTER'S CABIN, COLLOONEY
54.1940, -8.4881
airbnb.ie/rooms/7728520
This cosy wooden cabin, hidden away on the edge of Union Wood near Collooney, enjoys an elevated setting with plenty of windows to let the light in. Sleeps two.

OX MOUNTAIN GLAMPING
54.1067, -8.8569
oxmountainglamping.ie
Self-catering accommodation for the adventurous, including a tree-house, a cruiser boat, a shepherd's hut, a double-decker bus, a charming one bed cottage and a more conventional guest-house. Also takes campers and runs activities.

GLÓR NA D'TONNTA, EASKEY
54.2849, -9.0491
glampinginsligo.ie
This small site has two bell tents. A short distance west of the village of Easkey they overlook Killala Bay and have direct access to the sea. Pet friendly. Right beside the tents is a refurbished stone shed which contains cooking facilities and has an outdoor seating area.

EASKEY GLAMPING VILLAGE
54.2859, -8.9521
easkeyglampingvillage.ie
A short walk from the village this site has six large wooden pods each with their own wooden decking.

TEAPOT LANE GLAMPING, LEITRIM
54.4460, -8.3822
glampingireland.ie
A beautiful place to camp in style, in one of the three geodesic domes (each sleeps four) or the tree-house (sleeps two). If you want a little more comfort there is also a three-bedroom cottage available for rent, and spa treatments, BBQs and summer campfires available, all in a woodland setting.

Honestly Kitchen | Phil Doyle

SLIGO AND LEITRIM
FOOD

FISH AND BEAN, STRANDHILL
54.3067, -8.5757
fishandbean.ie
Set overlooking the water adjacent to Sligo Yacht Club in Rosses Point, this family-run restaurant serves high quality, locally sourced seafood. There are great views over Sligo Bay from the dinning room and the outdoor decking. Open Thursday to Sundays, booking is advisable.

HONESTLY KITCHEN, STRANDHILL
54.2704, -8.6075
honestlykitchen.ie
This award-winning farm kitchen on Shore Road focuses on simple food made with sustainable, local ingredients, much of which comes from their organic farm in Drumanilra on the shores of Lough Key, just outside Boyle. They serve breakfast, lunch and dinner and there is also a farm shop which sells a selection of products from their farm as well as other local produce such as fruit and vegetables, eggs, beef and baked goods.

They also have another shop in Carrick-on-Shannon (53.9459, -8.0785).

SHELL'S CAFE, STRANDHILL
54.2701, -8.6095
shellscafe.com
Popular, and justifiably so. Gorgeous gourmet food, great coffee and fresh baking throughout the day, a stone's throw from the beach. Avoid peak times if you can.

There is also a shop that sells a carefully curated selection of gifts, homeware, clothes and books.

STRANDHILL PEOPLE'S MARKET
54.2775, -8.5984
fb.com/strandhillmarket
This market offers the best of local food and drink as well as art and crafts from the local community. With the exception of the winter months, it runs every Sunday from 11.00 to 16.00 in Hangar 1 of Sligo Airport. Consult the website for details.

Silver Strand, Glencolmcille (see page 240) | RC

DONEGAL

The huge sprawling county of Donegal fills the northwest corner of the country. And even though it's only a few hundred miles north of the bottom tip of Cork, the change in latitude is apparent in a number of ways. For example the Northern Lights are seen relatively frequently, and the weather is a little cooler, as it's further from the benign influence of the Gulf Stream.

From a tourism point of view Donegal is probably the most overlooked of the counties along the west coast. As it is somewhat of a cul-de-sac and doesn't have quite the same reputation as other more famous regions, it doesn't get the attention it deserves from visitors. Those who do visit will be rewarded with spectacular scenery and a very friendly welcome.

The peninsulas at the top (Inishowen) and bottom (Glencolmcille) of the county offer wild coastline and rugged mountainside. In some areas the terrain has forced the roads inland, away from the sea, leaving some of the most beautiful and remote coast in the country, only accessible by foot and all the better for it.

In contrast, the granite coast in the northwest is a little more serene. It is still rugged, but on a smaller scale. It's a landscape littered with idyllic rocky coves and grassy clifftops.

DONEGAL BAY

North Sligo and south Donegal have much in common, with low-lying coastline, lots of long sandy beaches and excellent surfing. However, as the coastline swings west there is a distinct change, and the vast beaches and green fields give way to rocky hills and jagged coastline.

The peninsula of Glencolmcille is one of the remotest and wildest parts of the Wild Atlantic Way. It's also home to the very impressive Sliabh Liag cliffs, some of the highest in Europe.

BUNDORAN

For many generations Bundoran was a traditional seaside holiday destination, but recently it has reinvented itself as a surf town (*54.4776, -8.2808*). With plenty of beach, reef and point breaks in close proximity, not to mention pubs, cafes, surf shops and schools, it has a decent claim on the title of Surf Capital of Ireland. For more information about the town see discoverbundoran.com.

Surf lessons and hire are available from Surf World (surfworld.ie), Donegal Adventure Centre (donegaladventurecentre.net) and Bundoran Surf Company (bundoransurfco.com).

MAIN BEACH

The sandy beach right in the centre of town has a Blue Flag and is patrolled by lifeguards during the summer (*54.4776, -8.2808*). The narrow inlet at the east end of the beach, known as Rougey Rock, is a popular spot for diving and jumping (*54.4848, -8.2805*). The jump from the highest ledge is something of a rite of passage for the local kids.

Tullan Strand | Kent Wang

TULLAN STRAND
A short walk northeast of the town is Tullan Strand (54.4903, -8.2675). The 2.5km beach is backed by a vast network of sand dunes. One of Donegal's renowned surf beaches, the consistent beach break is open to almost any swell going, with a wave for every level of surfer. High tide is best for beginners.

The water can get very busy in the summer and there is no lifeguard. Jellyfish and weever fish can be a stinging hazard in the warmer months so wear something on your feet when you are in the water.

OUTDOOR SWIMMING POOLS
There are two outdoor pools along the rocky coast beside the town. West End Pool, a large man-made seawater pool, is a few hundred metres west of the Lifeboat Station and can be accessed from the cliff path via a set of steps (54.4779, -8.2926). The other pool, known as the Thrupenny Pool, lies just west of the Main Beach (54.4806, -8.2810).

ROUGEY WALK
This path links the Main Beach with Tullan Strand and offers fabulous views across Donegal Bay. Look out for the Fairy Bridges, a number of precarious sea arches, and the Wishing Chair, both of which are signposted from the path. Keep a close eye on small children as there are many steep drops in this area.

From Tullan either retrace your steps or follow Tullan Strand Road to the junction with the main road where you turn right to return to the Main Beach.

ROSSNOWLAGH BEACH
This Blue Flag beach is very popular and can get extremely busy on good days in the summer (54.5529, -8.2101). There is good surfing, particularly for beginners. Fin McCool Surf School (finmccoolsurfschool.com) offer lessons and you can hire boards from Finnegan's Surf Shop (finnegansshop.com).

It's possible to drive onto some areas of the beach, however you must be on the lookout for soft sand and the people using the beach. Drive slowly and remember the tide.

CREEVY SHORE WALK
A 10km coastal footpath links Rossnowlagh (54.5474, -8.2133) and the mouth of the Erne Estuary just west of Ballyshannon (54.5077, -8.2252). A shorter linear route visits Creevy Head, starting from Creevy Pier (54.5299, -8.2554).

MURVAGH BEACH
This Blue Flag beach is a few kilometres south of Donegal Town (54.6042, -8.1612). The long, wide stretch of sand has a massive tidal range so if you are planning to swim it's best to visit at high tide.

Fintragh Beach | DF

Muckros Head | DF

Rougey Rock | Brendan MacEvilly

Glencolmcille Folk Village | DF

Lifeguards are on duty during the summer months. While the beach itself is quite exposed, it is backed by extensive dunes and forest where there is plenty of shelter.

SAINT JOHN'S POINT
This narrow headland stretches almost 10km into Donegal Bay (*54.5693, -8.4573*). Near the tip of the headland is a lighthouse, a nice sandy beach and excellent views west to the Sliabh Liag cliffs and south across to the Sligo and Mayo coastline.

The sea around the lighthouse is popular with divers due to the very clear water.

FINTRAGH BEACH
Just west of Killybegs is a small sheltered Blue Flag beach (*54.6352, -8.4886*). It was the site of a dramatic crash landing during World War 2, when an American Flying Fortress bomber was forced to ditch due to mechanical problems. Amazingly the crew of ten escaped unscathed.

To find it, follow the Wild Atlantic Way west out of Killybegs. After 4km, shortly after the football pitch in Fintragh, look out for a left turn (signposted 'Trá'). Take this turn and drive down the very steep road to the carpark.

THE 'SECRET' WATERFALL
Tucked away along the coast about 2km west of Fintra is an impressive waterfall that runs down the back wall of a narrow cave. Far from a secret, it's a popular spot. Access is tricky as you need to scramble across slippery rocks and there is a danger of being cut off by the tide.

Park at the Largy Viewpoint (*54.6297, -8.51191*) and walk east along the road for 250m to a gate. Go through this and follow the track down to the shore. You then head west along the coast, across a pebble beach and over a series of rock steps before you reach the waterfall (*54.6262, -8.5134*). A round trip of about 1.5km, visit at low tide.

MUCKROS HEAD
Muckros Head lies between Killybegs and Kilcar (*54.6095, -8.5905*). The small headland, which juts out into the Atlantic, has a beach on either side and some impressive cliffs.

The beach on the western side, Trá na nGlór (Beach of the Noise), has a rip tide so isn't suitable for swimming but sometimes holds some surf. The eastern beach, Trá Bán (White Beach), is a popular family beach and safe for swimming (*54.6145, -8.5771*).

The steep sandstone cliffs at the end of the headland are of great interest to rock climbers and offer good views across the water to the considerably larger cliffs of Sliabh Liag.

Looking towards Bunglass, Sliabh Liag | Gareth McCormack

SLIABH LIAG

The spectacular cliffs of Sliabh Liag are one of the Wild Atlantic Way's must-sees. The summit of Sliabh Liag mountain stands 595m above sea level and its slopes rise directly from the Atlantic. While the cliffs lack the sheer verticality of the Cliffs of Moher they are almost three times as tall.

One interesting way to view the cliffs is from the water. The Nuala Star (sliabhleagueboattrips.com) operates daily boat tours from the pier at Teelin (54.6235, -8.6327) and if conditions are right it's even possible to swim beneath the cliffs.

The viewing point at Bunglass offers one of the best views of the cliffs, but on busy days the small carpark (54.6270, -8.6846) fills up quickly so you may have to park at the lower carpark (54.6265, -8.6639) and walk the 1.5km to the viewing point. The best time to view the cliffs is early afternoon or evening. This gives any cloud or fog a chance to burn off.

There are two walking routes to the summit of Sliabh Liag, both of which should only be attempted by well equipped, sure-footed walkers with a head for heights. Needless to say the cliffs are dangerous, always stay away from the edge. If you plan to attempt either of these walks, carry a map (OSI sheet 10) and pick a clear, calm day as the ridge is no place to be in a strong wind.

CLIFFTOP PATH

From the Bunglass viewing point (54.6270, -8.6846) a good gravel path runs along the ridge to the summit of Sliabh Liag. This route is very popular and it is definitely the more spectacular of the two trails.

It crosses a number of intermediate peaks including one very narrow, rocky rib at Keeringear (sometimes incorrectly called the One Man's Pass), and while it's an easy scramble it's very dangerous and is easily avoided by a path inland. The true One Man's Pass is the narrow ridge that forms the final section to the summit (54.6512, -8.7067).

From the summit of Sliabh Liag it's possible to continue west along the coastline to Malin Beg. You will however need to arrange a lift back to the car but this amazing walk is well worth the effort.

PILGRIM PATH

This route is less exposed, at least until you reach the ridge, and is a better option in bad weather. A good wide track leads from the carpark to the waterfall viewing point. After this point the path deteriorates and the going becomes a lot tougher, only experienced walkers should continue. The steep, rocky path leads to the top of the cliffs and is marked with yellow painted rocks. Once you meet the cliffs it's possible to continue along the One Man's Pass to the summit of Sliabh Liag (54.6512, -8.7067).

The cliffs at Port | DF

To get to the start take the Teelin road south from Carrick. Look out for a signposted right turn after 2.5km. Take this turn and follow the steep, narrow, winding road to the carpark, closing all gates behind you (54.6416, -8.6604).

MALIN BEG

The tiny village of Malin Beg lies at the very tip of the Glencolmcille Peninsula. It's unusual in that it's one of the few villages in Ireland that doesn't have a pub, but there is a hostel (malinbeghostel.com) and another down the road in Malin More, Áras Ghleann Cholm Cille (arasgcc.com).

If you turn right at the crossroads in the village the road leads down to a sheltered harbour (54.6653, -8.7860). You can park here and follow the track to the watchtower where there are great views of Rathlin O'Birne Island and down the coast to Sliabh Liag.

SILVER STRAND

This beautiful beach lies at the far end of Malin Beg (54.6653, -8.7771). Drive through the village to the carpark at the end of the road. The beach is accessed by a steep series of steps and is well sheltered by the surrounding cliffs. See the photo on page 234.

GLENCOLMCILLE

The small village of Glencolmcille is a great base for exploring this remote area, which is surrounded by some of the most spectacular coastal scenery in the county (54.6652, -8.7770).

On the edge of the village is Glencolmcille Folk Village (glenfolkvillage.com). The small cluster of pretty cottages offer an excellent insight into how life used to be in times gone by (54.7070, -8.7410).

GLENCOLMCILLE TO MAGHERA WALK

The 20km walk along the coast between Glencolmcille and Maghera passes through some of the most remote and beautiful coastline in the country. As it covers some very isolated, trackless ground good navigation skills and a map (OSI sheet 10) and compass are essential.

From Glencolmcille follow the Slí Cholmcille (see box opposite) north to the tiny cove at Port (54.7475, -8.7023). Continue east along the clifftops and descend into Glenlough. This wonderfully secluded valley can only be accessed on foot and is probably the most remote spot along the Wild Atlantic Way.

After leaving Glenlough it's a matter of either sticking to the coast or taking in Slievetooey mountain before descending to Maghera (54.7624, -8.5273).

The walk could be extended by starting at Teelin and following the Sliabh Liag ridge west to Malin Beg. This would be an exceptional two day trip with plenty of accommodation available in Malin Beg and Glencolmcille.

Donegal Cycle Route | DF

SLÍ CHOLMCILLE
The Slí Cholmcille is a 65km signposted walking route that travels around the Glencolmcille Peninsula, starting and finishing in Ardara. The route is best tackled in a clockwise direction as this means the best views can be enjoyed on the descents. Highlights include the lonely deserted village of Port and the steep valley of Glengesh.

Most of the route follows narrow roads, some of which can be busy, so take care. There are also sections of bog road and open moorland that can be damp underfoot.

The walk could be done as a continuous hike over a few days either camping or staying overnight in the villages en route, or alternatively a shorter section could be done as a point-to-point day hike. See irishtrails.ie for detailed maps.

INTERNATIONAL APPALACHIAN TRAIL
This extension of the world famous Appalachian Trail, which travels along the spine of the east coast of the United States, links geologically similar terrain in America and Europe. The Irish section of the trail starts at Sliabh Liag and makes its way east across Donegal and through Northern Ireland, combining existing walking trails for a total length of 485km. See walkni.com/iat for more information.

DONEGAL CYCLE ROUTE
This 200km tour starts in Donegal Town and travels north, keeping close to the coastline before finishing near Letterkenny. The route is well signposted and has a couple of spurs and loops which offer short scenic diversions. See donegalcycleroute.ie for more information.

BALLYSHANNON CYCLE HUB
The town of Ballyshannon is the start/finish point for two signposted cycle loops that explore the countryside of south Donegal.

The 39km Route 1 heads east along the shore of Assaroe Lake before turning north and then west to Rossnowlagh. After a short stretch along the beach the route follows the coast south to Ballyshannon.

Loop 2 (36km) heads south to Bundoran and passes Lough Melvin and the village of Belleek before joining Loop 1 on the final stretch into Ballyshannon.

Glengesh | DF

Maghera cave | Tobias Senger

Assarnacally Waterfall | DF

TOWER LOOP
This signposted 10km loop (marked by the blue arrows) starts from the village of Glencolmcille (54.7086, -8.7311) and follows lanes and mountain paths to the watchtower high on the ridge. The Drum Loop (red arrows) is a slightly (3km) longer variation.

PORT
The remote townland of Port was once home to a small fishing village, but it has been deserted since the Famine (54.7475, -8.7023). The beautiful cove is the only breach in the long line of huge cliffs that stretch for many miles. It's possible to walk the grassy clifftops in either direction and admire the amazing rock architecture beneath.

Head east out of Glencolmcille village on the R230 and after 2km turn left (signposted 'Port'). Follow the narrow road for 7km to a junction where you turn left and descend down the narrow road to the sea.

MAGHERA BEACH
A vast sweep of pristine white sand on the north side of the peninsula. At low tide it's possible to explore the caves at the west end of the beach, but be very careful that you don't get cut off by the rising tide. Swimming isn't wise as there are sudden changes in depth and very strong currents.

The steep, narrow road that climbs southwest out of Maghera is known as Granny Pass and it's a very interesting 'shortcut' to or from Glencolmcille. It's not suitable for nervous drivers or large vehicles.

Travelling south from Ardara on the Wild Atlantic Way turn right (well signposted) after 1.5km. Follow the road past the waterfall to the beach carpark (small fee) on the right (54.7624, -8.5273).

ASSARNACALLY WATERFALL
This picturesque waterfall is just off the road between Maghera Beach and Ardara and is well worth a quick stop (54.7587, -8.5140).

GLENGESH
From Glencolmcille the Wild Atlantic Way heads northeast, crossing windswept bog before arriving at the head of Glengesh. From the top of the pass (54.7206, -8.4848) there are great views to the mountains before the road drops steeply, winding its way down to the valley floor.

BALLINREAVY STRAND
This very quiet beach is part of Sheskinmore Nature Reserve. The easiest access is from the east. Follow the Wild Atlantic Way north of Ardara for 5km, turn left onto the L7763 and follow the narrow road to a small carpark (54.7976, -8.4478). Walk west for about 500m and wade the river to access the beach.

Sea stack climbing | Iain Miller

TRAMORE BEACH
This quiet beach is a short distance off the Wild Atlantic Way. There is limited parking along the grass at the end of the road (54.8099, -8.4972) and a path leads through the dunes for 500m to the beach.

NARAN STRAND
With its elegant curve, pale sand and clear azure water Naran (aka Tramore Strand) has a tropical flavour (on a sunny day at least) as well as a Blue Flag (54.8386, -8.4469). During July and August there is a lifeguard in attendance.

Just to the west of the beach is the small village of Portnoo (54.8423, -8.4658).

INISHKEEL
Spring tides (which occur twice a month, around the new moon and full moon) expose a sandbar making it possible to walk across to the island of Inishkeel from Naran Strand (54.8449, -8.4513). Be very careful, it would be very easy to get cut off. The small island was home to a monastery founded in the 6th century and there are a few beautifully decorated stone pillars that are worth seeking out.

BONNY GLEN WOOD
A small, peaceful forest with two short signposted trails (54.8317, -8.4033). From Naran follow the Wild Atlantic Way to the R261 and continue east for 1.5km before turning right. Follow the road for 1km to the entrance to the forest. The shorter walk is a 1km loop around Bonnyglen Lough and the longer trail (5km round trip) follows forest roads and paths to Lough Namanlagh.

SEA STACK CLIMBING
The coastline north of Glencolmcille is extremely rugged and home to dozens of sea stacks. These massive rock towers are formed when sections of softer rock are eroded into headlands and then arches, which ultimately collapse to leave an isolated pinnacle of rock.

Sea stack climbing is quite different from conventional rock climbing. It's much more committing and often getting to the start of the route is harder than the actual climbing.

Iain Miller has done the first ascents of over sixty sea stacks in this area, standing where no one has ever stood before. Iain is a climbing guide and his company Unique Ascent (uniqueascent.ie) takes people out climbing on the cliffs and sea stacks of Donegal. If you are very lucky you may even end up doing a first ascent on a day out with him!

Lough Mardal Glamping | DF

DONEGAL BAY
ACCOMMODATION

THE BEE PODS
54.5529 -8.2054
thebeepods.com
A few minutes walk from the beach at Rossnowlagh. Has five pods, each of which is decorated to a different theme and they are all fitted out with a kitchenette and a wood-burning stove. Each pod sleeps two. On site there are a pair of seaweed baths and facilities to cook your own pizzas.

LOUGH MARDAL GLAMPING
54.5563, -8.0685
loughmardalglamping.ie
A bit inland from the Wild Atlantic Way but well worth the short detour. Set on the shore of Lough Mardal, about 20 minutes drive south of Donegal Town. There are five yurts (sleeping up to two adults plus two kids) and a shepherd's hut (sleeps two) spread across the 36 hectare site, but the centrepiece is the lodge, which houses the kitchen, toilets and a large space to relax in. The amazing circular building has a round-timber structure topped with a mesmerising reciprocal roof and strawbale walls plastered with lime, showcasing a number of fascinating eco-building techniques.

AN PORT COTTAGES
54.7477, -8.6990
airbnb.ie/rooms/2269632
There are few places in Ireland that can rival An Port for that back of beyond feeling. This simple off-the-grid cottage allows you to spend time exploring this special place. Sleeps six.

About 2km up the valley (*54.7459, -8.6676*) is another off-grid cottage (airbnb.ie/rooms/31406487) that also sleeps six.

CON'S COTTAGE
54.6775, -8.4531
conscottage.ie
In spite of the fact that this cottage is only a 15 minute drive from the busy fishing town of Killybegs it has a very remote feel. It is accessed via a very quiet boreen and is surrounded by forestry. The thatched roof and white-washed walls give it a very traditional look, the ideal place to escape to. Sleeps four.

Foam | Conor Conlon

DONEGAL BAY
FOOD

THE SALTY FOX, BUNDORAN
54.4870, -8.2678
thesaltyfoxbundoran.com
On the northern edge of Bundoran and only a few hundred meters from Tullan Strand this popular, family-run cafe serves cooked breakfasts and light lunches including sandwiches and salads. They are also renowned for their cakes and desserts which are baked daily on-site. They close on Mondays and Tuesdays during the off-season.

FOAM, BUNDORAN
54.4810, -8.2723
foambundoran.com
This stylish cafe on the Main Street in Bundoran has a strong focus on coffee (which is roasted just down the road in Sligo) and seasonal food. The simple menu includes staples like burritos and their renowned sausage rolls. Open daily from 09.00 until 16.00. In the evenings they regularly host events, gigs and films.

THE OLDE CASTLE SEAFOOD BAR
54.6544, -8.1105
oldecastlebar.com
Sitting directly opposite Donegal Castle in Donegal Town this bar and restaurant serves classic pub fare with a strong focus on seafood.

SALTHILL CABIN
54.6305, -8.2061
salthillcabin.com
This family-run coffee shop directly opposite Mountcharles Pier has great views across Donegal Bay to the mountains of Sligo. Uniquely it also has a petting zoo where you can meet some very cute animals including a donkey, pygmy goats, an emu, a peacock and llamas.

KILLYBEGS SEAFOOD SHACK
54.6363, -8.4419
fb.com/killybegsseafoodshack
This food truck is based on the pier in the fishing town of Killybegs. Naturally, it serves amazing fresh fish, chips, seafood and award-winning chowder. Open during the warmer months of the year.

NORTH WEST DONEGAL

While the northwestern coastline of Donegal has its share of expansive sandy beaches it also has hundreds of beautiful rocky coves, hidden away, waiting to be discovered and enjoyed in solitude.

A large part of this area is Gaeltacht, which means that Irish is the spoken language.

This part of Donegal is overlooked by many visitors from overseas, possibly because it lacks a world renowned attraction like its neighbours to the north (Malin Head) and south (Sliabh Liag). It's a great place to seek out a quieter, more authentic experience and there is nowhere quieter or more authentic than the numerous remote offshore islands, particularly Tory Island.

The area around the village of Dunfanaghy has plenty of excellent beaches and is very popular with Irish families, particularly with visitors from Northern Ireland.

Inland the ground is barren, consisting of little more than heather, rocky outcrops and peaty lakes. Two distinctive peaks lie a short distance from the coast, the sharply pointed Errigal (Donegal's highest mountain) and the flat topped Muckish. Also a short drive inland, hidden deep in the mountains, is the beautiful Glenveagh National Park.

DOOEY BEACH

This quiet Green Coast beach lies on the opposite side of Gweebarra Bay to Naran (*54.8734, -8.3819*). The carpark is at the northern end of the 3km stretch of sand.

There is a mobile sauna that operates in the dunes overlooking the beach, check

Crohy Head | Gareth Wray

fb.com/Wildatlanticseasaunadooeybeach for opening hours.

CROHY HEAD
Just offshore of Crohy Head is a much photographed sea arch (*54.9146, -8.4563*). There is also a nice beach to the north, on the edge of Maghery village (*54.9282, -8.4437*). In the village is a community centre, Ionad An Mhachaire, which has a cafe and information on many of the walks in the area.

INISHFREE UPPER ISLAND
A square mile of meadows ringed by rocky coves. The beautiful, serene island has recently been re-inhabited after lying empty for many years (*54.9552, -8.4463*). There is no ferry to the island so you will either have to paddle over in a kayak or find a local fisherman who will bring you.

DUNGLOE RIVER WALK
A gentle 2km loop follows the wooded banks of the Dungloe River and lake. The main loop is marked with red arrows, an optional 1.6km extension is marked with green ones. The trailhead is accessed from the N56, just past the bridge (*54.9531, -8.3593*).

BURTONPORT
The small town of Burtonport (or as it's signposted 'Ailt an Chorráin') is a good base for exploring the myriad islands and beaches in this area (*54.9848, -8.4383*). There are three signposted walks based around the disused Letterkenny and Burtonport railway near the town.

- The Old Railway (red arrows) 5.5km each way.
- The 7km Lúb Cheann Bhaile Cruaiche (orange arrows).
- The 5km Lúb Chroicheach Mhór (blue arrows).

For a map of the walks see irishtrails.ie.

BEACHES
The coastline north of Dungloe is a maze of wonderful coves and rocky islands that are well worth exploring at low tide. Look out for a left turn (signposted 'Beach') 1.3km north of Burtonport, and follow the signs to one of the numerous beaches, which include An Chloch Ghlas (*54.9996, -8.4471*) and Portacurry (*55.0062, -8.4281*).

ARRANMORE ISLAND
This large island lies a short distance off the rocky coast of northwest Donegal (arainnmhor.com). It is part of the Gaeltacht and the majority of the island's residents are Irish speakers.

The exposed west coast bristles with high cliffs, sea stacks and caves with names such as Paradise

Arranmore Lighthouse | Ross McDonald

Rock climbing on Gola Island | Michael O'Dwyer

Cavern, the Moon Pool, the Grotto, the Cave of Light, the Sea Eagle's Stack and the Giant's Stack.

The waters surrounding the island are crystal clear with an abundance of sea life. Talk to Arranmore Charters (arranmorecharters.ie) for information about diving and sightseeing charters.

Two ferry companies make the short (15 minute) crossing from Burtonport Pier (*54.9835, -8.4412*) a couple of times daily (see arranmorefastferry.com and arranmoreferry.com).

There are plenty of B&Bs, a hotel, a guesthouse and glamping pods (arranmoreglamping.com) on the island.

SLÍ ÁRAINN MHÓR
The 14km long signposted trail Slí Árainn Mhór takes in most of the island's interesting sights, including the Beaver Island Memorial at Lough Shore (*55.0023, -8.5361*), the island's highest point Cnoc an Iolair (*54.9909, -8.5287*), and the old graveyard (*54.9753, -8.4961*). The walk follows narrow roads and tracks in a loop around the island, starting and finishing at the ferry port (*54.9899, -8.4969*).

The 2km (each way) spur walk to the old coastguard station and lighthouse (*55.0144, -8.5601*) is well worth taking if you have time. The lighthouse complex has two self-catering cottages (each sleeps 6) available to rent, see airbnb.ie/rooms/3146425.

About 150m southwest of the parking (*55.0132, -8.5595*) at the lighthouse is a set of stairs that lead steeply down through the cliffs to the sea (*55.0125, -8.5612*). Originally built to stock the lighthouse by boat, they now offer the sure-footed access to the base of the spectacular cliffs.

BEACHES
There are a number of sandy beaches and coves on the more sheltered southern and eastern shores of the island, notably Leadhb Gharbh (*54.9867, -8.4962*), which is right beside the pier, and the strand at Leadhb Reannach (*54.9719, -8.5228*).

CRUIT ISLAND
This long, narrow island is connected to the mainland by a small bridge (*55.0147, -8.4092*) just north of the tiny village of Kincasslagh. The island is ringed by granite cliffs and is one of the most popular rock climbing areas in Donegal.

There are over a dozen sandy coves hidden along the coast. The most popular beach is found halfway across the island on the western side, just before the thatched cottages (*55.0332, -8.4196*). See the photo on page 10.

The island lies just off the Wild Atlantic Way. Look out for a left turn (signposted 'An Chruit') directly opposite the Viking Bar and Restaurant.

If you want to try some rock climbing, get in touch with Unique Ascent (uniqueascent.ie) who are based nearby.

Owey Island from Cruit | David Ardron

OWEY ISLAND
This small island lies a few hundred metres off the northern end of Cruit (55.0525, -8.4413). During the summer months it's possible to arrange a boat to the island with Dan Gallagher (086 6013893) from the pier near the golf course on Cruit (55.0481, -8.4320). At other times contact Saoire Mara Charters (saoiremara.com).

In the summer many of the cottages are used as holiday homes. The rest of the time the island lies deserted. Even though it's only a ten minute boat ride from the mainland, the island is like another world, with no electricity or services. The islanders get their water from a spring and their houses are heated by turf fires and lit by gas lamps.

The massive granite cliffs, the numerous coves and the deep caverns are of great interest to rock climbers and sea kayakers. In the past the caves were used by poitín (the Irish equivalent to moonshine) makers to hide their illegal wares when the police came to inspect the island.

CARRICKFINN
This small headland is home to Donegal Airport as well as a number of very nice sandy beaches and rocky coves.

The long Blue Flag beach just to the west of the runway is very popular (55.0378, -8.3468). There are lots of small coves south of the beach that are worth seeking out. Follow the signs for the airport, drive past the entrance and park at the end of the road.

There are also plenty of small, sheltered coves at the northern end of the headland. Trá na mBád, Boat Strand, is a charming little cove with a small pier (55.0560, -8.3435). Find it by driving along the road parallel to the runway, turn left at the fork. The next turn left leads to the beach.

GOLA ISLAND
The small island of Gola lies 1.5km offshore. Now uninhabited it was once home to over a hundred people (55.0910, -8.3582). Beautiful and unspoilt, the island is popular with walkers, birdwatchers and climbers. The east side of the island, where the cottages and pier are found, has white sandy beaches, while the western side is more rugged with granite cliffs, narrow bays and sea arches.

A ferry (fb.com/sabba.curran) makes the short crossing from the small pier at Magheragallon (55.0869, -8.3242), just west of Bunbeg, regularly during the summer months. It's possible to camp on the grassy ground between the lake and the beach on the western side of the island (55.0902, -8.3683) and there are two cottages available to rent via airbnb.ie.

SLÍ GABHLA
This 2.7km walk starts at the pier (55.0910, -8.3582) and follows the sandy roads in a loop around the

DONEGAL

Tory Island | RC

eastern part of the island. It's well worth making a diversion to the western coastline. The view from Mweelmore (55.0860, -8.3748), the highest point on the southwestern corner of the island, is wonderful.

BUNBEG BEACHES

A trio of expansive sandy strands just west of the village of Bunbeg. The southern beach (55.0677, -8.3085), Magheraclogher, is home to the iconic shipwreck, Bád Eddie (55.0678, -8.3134). Walk north following the track through the grass to access the larger, quieter beach to the north.

North again is Magheragallon Beach (55.0869, -8.3241), where the ferry departs for Gola Island.

PORT ARTHUR BEACH

This long sandy beach looks out across the water to the island of Inishmeane (55.1016, -8.3156). The commonage near the beach is often used by campers.

BLOODY FORELAND

This broad, rocky headland marks the point where the coast starts to run east rather than north. It gets its name from the red hue that the cliffs take on at sunset. The viewing point on the Wild Atlantic Way is a great place to watch the cliffs change colour as the sun goes down (55.1372, -8.2893).

TORY ISLAND

Lying 11km off the coast, Tory Island is Ireland's most remote inhabited island (55.2649, -8.2273). It is exposed to the full fury of the Atlantic and is often cut off during winter storms. The island is stark and treeless with some very impressive sea cliffs.

There are a number of fascinating historical and mythological sites, including a round tower that once protected monks from Viking raids, the ruins of Saint Colmcille's 6th century monastery and the intriguing Tau Cross which suggests early seafaring links to ancient Egypt.

On the highest point of the island lie the remains of an ancient promontory fort known as Dún Balair (55.2623, -8.1938). A little to the east is the incredibly narrow ridge that terminates in a point known as An Tor Mór. It's possible (with great care) to walk about half way along the ridge but the outer half remains the realm of experienced mountaineers.

As it's a mere 4km long and never more than 1.5km wide Tory is easily explored on foot. The best approach is to follow the 12km signposted trail that loops around the island in a figure of eight. The trail starts and finishes at the ferry port (55.2646, -8.2270).

Catch the ferry (toryferry.com) from Machaire Uí Robhartaigh (55.1467, -8.1743). Be warned the one hour crossing can be rough.

Machaire Uí Robhartaigh | Kent Wang

Bloody Foreland | DF

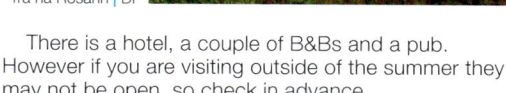
Trá na Rosann | DF

Horn Head | DF

There is a hotel, a couple of B&Bs and a pub. However if you are visiting outside of the summer they may not be open, so check in advance.

INISHBOFIN
Not to be confused with its namesake in Galway, this small island is just 1.5km from the mainland (*55.1772, -8.1764*). With no services and only a handful of year-round occupants this quiet island is a great place to escape the modern world. During the summer season a ferry (boffinferrydonegal.com) serves the island from Machaire Uí Robhartaigh (*55.1467, -8.1743*) to the island.

MACHAIRE UÍ ROBHARTAIGH
This elegant curve of pale sand stretches for almost 5km and shelters the sandy expanse of Ballyness Bay (*55.1458, -8.1733*). Thanks to its exposed position the beach is of great interest to surfers, windsurfers and kitesurfers. It has a Green Coast award and there is plenty of parking at the pier where the Tory Island ferry sails from, as well as toilets and a cafe. Magheroarty is the English spelling of this beach.

DRUMNATINNY BEACH
On the other side of Ballyness Bay lies another fine beach, known as Drumnatinny or the Back Strand (*55.1585, -8.0834*). The 4km Green Coast beach is ideal for a stroll. Swimming is only recommended at the eastern end of the beach.

HORN HEAD
Just north of the town of Dunfanaghy, the Wild Atlantic Way loops around the dramatic coast of Horn Head. The huge cliffs, which rise straight out of the water to a height of 180m, are an internationally important colony for breeding seabirds including the European shag and the razorbill.

Be sure to make the short diversion off the Wild Atlantic Way to visit Coastguard Hill (*55.2229, -7.9790*), the highest point at the tip of the headland. Rather than following the Wild Atlantic Way over the first cattle grid, continue straight on and park at the end of the road (*55.2149, -7.9783*). Walk a short distance up the hill to the watchtower where you can soak up the great views of Tory Island and inland to Muckish and the Derryveagh mountains.

TRAMORE STRAND
A 2km walk through the Lurgabrack dunes will take you to the beautiful remote beach at Tramore. There are dangerous currents so swimming isn't advised.

To get to the start of the walk head towards Horn Head from Dunfanaghy and turn left just after the bridge. The carpark is in the forest on the left after 100m (*55.1854, -7.9870*). Please keep dogs under control.

Ards Forest Park | RC

KILLAHOEY STRAND
Just east of Dunfanaghy is Killahoey Strand (*55.1861, -7.9563*). A quiet Blue Flag beach, it's safe for swimming. During the summer months there are lifeguards on duty.

Access the beach via the road through the golf course, which is on the edge of Dunfanaghy.

PORTNABLAGH BEACH
A small sheltered cove (*55.1816, -7.9274*) 3km east of Dunfanaghy. It's possible to park on the sand, the beach is a popular launching point for kayaks and larger boats.

A mobile sauna operates daily during the summer and at weekends throughout the year from the end of the pier (cocoonsauna.ie).

MARBLE HILL STRAND
This sandy Blue Flag beach in Sheephaven Bay is one of the most popular beaches in Donegal (*55.1762, -7.9018*).

Two watersports providers operate at the beach and elsewhere in the area. Jaws Watersports (jawswatersports.ie) offer surfing, windsurfing, paddleboarding, kayaking and sailing and Narosa School of Surf (narosalife.com) run surf lessons, rental and kids camps.

There is a mobile sauna on Saturdays and Sundays (instagram.com/itsaunatrailer).

HARRY'S HOLE
North of the beach is Harry's Hole (*55.1833, -7.8972*). The small inlet is a popular swimming spot and there are plenty of outcrops of all heights to jump off. Follow the small track north for 500m from the west side of the beach to find them.

ARDS FOREST PARK
On the sheltered western shore of Sheephaven Bay is Ards Forest Park, one of the most beautiful and varied of Ireland's forest parks (*55.1588, -7.8887*). The 480 hectare park contains a large diversity of habitats, with sandy beaches, rivers and forest. Scattered across the park you will find many features of historical and archaeological interest, including the remains of four ring forts and a Mass Rock.

There are eight signposted walks ranging in length from 500m to 13km. See coillte.ie for details.

The entrance to the park is on the Wild Atlantic Way, midway between Creeslough and Dunfanaghy (*55.1500, -7.9283*). There is an automatic pay barrier at the entrance, the fee is €5 per car.

ARDS FRIARY
Adjacent to the forest park is the Capuchin Friary (*55.1583, -7.8642*). A very peaceful place, which is used for retreats, conferences and seminars, it has many paths weaving around its 80 hectares, as well as a cafe and plenty of parking (ardsfriary.ie).

Boyeeghter Bay | Gareth Wray

DOE CASTLE
Sitting on a small peninsula jutting into Sheephaven Bay, this 15th century castle (55.1346, -7.8654) was a stronghold of the MacSweeney clan. To see the inside of the castle you need to take a guided tour, see heritageireland.ie for details.

ROSGUILL PENINSULA
This beautiful peninsula has a number of wonderful beaches and great views.

DOWNINGS BEACH
A popular Blue Flag beach in the village of Downings (55.1943, -7.8366). Lifeguards patrol the beach between June and September.

Just to the south is a quieter beach, Trá Mór, adjacent to Saint Patrick's Golf Links. It can be accessed via a 1km wooden boardwalk that runs from the Donegal Boardwalk Resort (55.1492, -7.8381).

ATLANTIC DRIVE
The Wild Atlantic Way follows a very scenic route, known as Atlantic Drive, around the peninsula. The 12km loop is on narrow roads and could also be walked or cycled. The views are great, particularly those across Sheephaven Bay to Horn Head and over Trá na Rosann Bay.

MELMORE
It's well worth making the short diversion from the Wild Atlantic Way to visit Trá na Rosann, the spectacular beach on the western shore of the low, flat ground that connects Melmore to Rosguill (55.2245, -7.8138). Heed the signs and don't swim near the rocks.

BOYEEGHTER BAY
On the western shore of the headland there is an outstanding beach, one of the best in Ireland. Hidden from the road, it's known as the Murder Hole, however the origins of this sinister name are unclear.

From the carpark (there is a small charge) at the end of the road (55.2428, -7.7942) follow the steep track up and down before crossing some fields to reach the beach. Note dogs aren't allowed and swimming isn't advised due to strong currents. A 2.5km round trip.

TEACH JOHN MICI BÁN
This traditional farmhouse on the eastern outskirts of Carrigart (55.1759, -7.7854) is home to a fascinating and unique private museum of artefacts of rural life. Opening times vary, best phone 087 251 5387 before visiting. If the owners, Hugo and Margaret, are home they will be delighted to give you a guided tour and maybe even a cup of tea!

Glenveagh National Park | Michal Osmenda

Muckish Mountain | Ben Allan

Errigal | Gareth Wray

ERRIGAL
The distinctive conical profile of Errigal, Donegal's highest mountain, is hard to mistake. The most popular route to the summit of the 751m peak is steep and rocky and even though it's only a 4km round trip there is serious height gain (500m). As such it's only suitable for well equipped, fit hikers.

The starting point is the small carpark on the R251 east of Dunlewey (*55.0249, -8.0899*). From the carpark follow the recently built path directly up the hillside. At the large cairn turn left and follow the path towards the ridge. Steep, rocky ground leads past a circular shelter and a number of cairns to the summit (*55.0343, -8.1126*). A narrow ridge separates the two summits, the eastern one is considered the highest point. Take care on the descent, particularly on the loose scree. See errigalmountain.com for more information.

GLENVEAGH NATIONAL PARK
One of seven national parks in Ireland, Glenveagh occupies over 16,000 hectares in the heart of the Derryveagh Mountains. This vast area of mountain and bog is home to many plants and animals including a herd of red deer. At the head of Lough Beagh is a visitor centre and tearooms. The beautiful castle and gardens are a short bus ride or a pleasant 3km walk along the lakeshore.

There are a number of walks in the area and at weekends the shuttle bus will drop walkers to the start of their walk for a small fee.

From Gweedore follow the R251 east. From Termon follow the R255 then R251 to the park (*55.0573, -7.9387*). See glenveaghnationalpark.ie for more information.

MUCKISH MOUNTAIN
The 666m tall mountain derives its name from its distinctive flat top, the Irish being 'An Mhucais' which translates as 'pig's back'. The rocky plateau is a wonderful place but it can be very disorientating in bad conditions so you must be able to navigate using a map and compass.

The easiest route to the summit starts from the shrine at Muckish Gap on the R256 (*55.0886, -8.0023*). A harder alternative is the Miner's Track, which approaches from the north. For details of both routes see mountainviews.ie/summit/163.

If you aren't up for Muckish there are three shorter signposted trails nearby (*55.1257, -7.9866*), see irishtrails.ie for details.

Corcreggan Mill | Donal McCann

NORTH WEST DONEGAL
ACCOMMODATION

MACHAIRE RABHARTAIGH GLAMPING
55.1388, -8.1739
mrglamping.ie
Ten wooden pods overlooking the spectacular beach at Magheroarty and Inis Bó Finne. The pods sleep up to four (two adults and two children) and each is fitted with a kitchenette suitable for preparing light meals. Pet friendly.

CORCREGGAN MILL, DUNFANAGHY
55.1671, -8.0039
corcreggan.com
This former mill just outside Dunfanaghy offers a wide range of accommodation options. As well as en-suite rooms in the main building there are some interesting glamping options including six bell tents (sleep two), five compartments in a 150 year old railway cabin (each sleeps 2-4) and a converted fishing trawler, The Larry McQuaid, which sits in a raised position offering great views over the coast.

Saturday nights are homemade pizza night and they also serve fish and chips from the food truck in the garden.

WILD ATLANTIC CAMP, CRESSLOUGH
55.1198, -7.9047
wildatlanticcamp.ie
This campsite in Creeslough village has modern chalets (sleep four), wooden pods (sleep 2-4) and canvas bell tents (sleep six) as well as bays for camper vans and pitches for tents. The site also has an astroturf pitch, a playground and a 9-hole pitch and putt course.

THE BIRDBOX, GLENVEAGH
54.8891, -8.1512
airbnb.ie/rooms/33555485
This stunning hand-built tree house overlooks Glenveagh National Park (see page 255). The wooden hut sits perched in the trees and is accessed via a bridge. The airy timber-clad interior has tall windows that take in great views of the mountains, a wood-burning stove and a loft double bed.

Also on the same site is a tiny stone cottage, the Cow Shed (airbnb.ie/rooms/3208507) and the Hide (airbnb.ie/rooms/12641718), a compact grass-roofed cabin.

The Shack, Dunfanaghy | DF

NORTH WEST DONEGAL
FOOD

THE WHEELHOUSE CAFE, BURTONPORT
54.9837, -8.4269
thewheelhouse.ie
This local, family-run cafe in Burtonport serves a range of vegetarian, vegan and gluten-free choices as well as more traditional fare. There are nice views to nearby Lackenagh lake and outdoor seating. Pet friendly.

Next door is are nine glamping pods which sleep four. You can even get breakfast delivered!

BATCH. FALCARRAGH
55.1363, -8.1046
batch.ie
This busy restaurant on the main street of Falcarragh serves breakfast, lunch and dinner as well as excellent coffee.

THE RUSTY OVEN, DUNFANAGHY
55.1834, -7.9726
therustyoven.ie
Buzzing restaurant that serves top notch pizza. Their sourdough is left to rise for three days before being handmade into bases and cooked in their wood-fired oven. Find them behind Patsy Dan's Bar on the Main Street, Dunfanaghy. Open weekend evenings.

THE SHACK, DUNFANAGHY
55.1761, -7.9019
shackcoffee.ie
A small wooden hut that overlooks Marble Hill beach in Dunfanaghy. They roast their own coffee beans and offer baked treats and ice-cream.

FISK SEAFOOD BAR, DOWNINGS
55.1943, -7.8405
fiskseafoodbar.com
Mere meters from the sea in Downings village this compact restaurant is all about seafood. Serving Irish classics plus some more modern international dishes from a white-washed outbuilding of the adjacent pub, the Harbour Bar.

FANAD AND INISHOWEN

The peninsulas of Fanad and Inishowen are home to some of the most dramatic coastal scenery in the country as well as many beautiful beaches. The sea to the north has always been an important shipping channel and there are plenty of reminders of this as the coast is littered with forts, shipwrecks and lighthouses.

At the tip of Inishowen is Ireland's most northerly point, the wild and windswept Malin Head. It's a great place to watch the waves surge along the cliffs during a storm.

The scenery at Fanad Head is more gentle, with lots of sandy coves and of course its iconic lighthouse.

The ferries (see page 263) and the Harry Blaney Bridge, which connect Rosguill and Fanad (*55.1895,* *-7.7644*), make it easy to move from headland to headland with minimal driving.

For more information about the area check out govisitinishowen.com.

BALLYHIERNAN BAY BEACH

A long sandy Green Coast beach, backed by low dunes (*55.2469, -7.7274*). To the west of Ballyhiernan, either side of Ballywhorisky Point, are some smaller, even quieter beaches and rocky coves.

FANAD HEAD

For centuries Fanad Head has played an important role in protecting passing ships. There has been a lighthouse here since 1811. The present lighthouse,

258 FANAD AND INISHOWEN

Fanad Lighthouse | RC

which was built in 1886, is picture perfect with its neat whitewashed exterior and elevated position. It's possible to tour the lighthouse during the summer season and there are three self-catering cottages in the lighthouse complex that are available for rent. See fanadlighthouse.com for details.

There is limited parking at the end of the road (*55.2756, -7.6345*) and a larger carpark on the left beside the ticket office (*55.2762, -7.6373*).

GREAT POLLET SEA ARCH
This sea arch is one of the most impressive along the Atlantic coast (*55.2576, -7.6195*). To find it drive south from Fanad Head along the Wild Atlantic Way. After 4km look for a signposted turn left, take this and park in the car park (*55.2551, -7.6307*). Walk down the road and follow the track through the fields down to the pebble beach, the arch is to the left. The round trip is about 2.5km

BALLYMASTOCKER BEACH
This long sandy beach is undoubtedly one of the most spectacular in Ireland, particularly when viewed from the Wild Atlantic Way as it winds its way south over the shoulder of Knockalla Mountain.

The popular beach can be accessed at the northern end via the large carpark (*55.2069, -7.6258*) on the edge of Portsalon village, or at the southern end from a small carpark (*55.1882, -7.6093*). It has a Blue Flag award and is quite sheltered, particularly at the southern end where there are a number of rocky outcrops. There are lifeguards on duty during the summer.

Near the southern end of the beach is Knockalla Caravan and Camping Park (knockallacaravanpark.com).

RATHMULLAN
On the edge of the town is a sheltered, sandy beach overlooking Lough Swilly that runs north for over 2km (*55.0953, -7.5319*). There is a playground beside the carpark. The Swilly Sauna (instagram.com/theswillysauna) is a wood-fired mobile sauna that can be found at the pier on weekends.

Further north is Kinnegar Beach which can be accessed at two points (*55.1070, -7.5286* and *55.1117, -7.5326*).

GRIANAN OF AILEACH RING FORT
This circular stone ring-fort is well over a thousand years old (*55.02468, -7.4268*). Its origins are linked to the mythical Tuatha dé Danann, a race of supernaturally gifted people who invaded Ireland before the Celts. The fort's elevated position makes for dramatic views across north Donegal. It is signposted from the small village of Burt, which lies on the Wild Atlantic Way 30km north of Letterkenny.

Grianan of Aileach | Gareth Wray

Great Pollet Sea Arch | RC

Mute Swans, Inch Wildfowl Reserve | RC

INCH WILDFOWL RESERVE

Inch Island, which is connected to the mainland by two causeways, is a birdwatcher's paradise. It is an internationally significant destination and staging ground for migrating birds from three continents. There are three hides from which to observe the birds connected by a walking trail.

The full loop, crossing to the island on one causeway and returning on the other, is 8km but it's also possible to do a shorter walk by retracing your steps. See inchwildfowlreserve.ie for details.

Travelling north through the village of Burt take a turn left opposite the distinctive church. After a short distance the main road swings to the right but continue straight on for 1km to the carpark (*55.0517, -7.4440*).

BUNCRANA

The largest town on Inishowen, Buncrana is popular with tourists and day trippers. There is plenty to see in the immediate area and it's a good base for exploring the peninsula.

THE WHITE STRAND

The 2km White Strand or Trá Bán lies just south of Buncrana Town (*55.1187, -7.4585*). A short distance further south is Lisfannon Beach (*55.0966, -7.4806*).

Ballymastocker Strand | DF

THE SHORE PATH
A 3km path runs north from Buncrana to Stragill Strand. The route starts at Ladies' Bay, a sheltered cove five minutes walk from the town centre (55.1381, -7.4613). The first point of interest is Ned's Point Fort (55.1407, -7.4739). The Napoleonic battery is reasonably intact but is closed to the public.

Passing by the local landmarks of Father Hegarty's Rock, Highlandman's Rock and Porthaw Beach leads to the end of the path at Stragill Strand.

Stragill is a nice, long sandy beach with great views across Lough Swilly (55.1601, -7.4901). It is accessible from the main road and has plenty of parking.

SWAN PARK
This small but very beautiful park runs alongside the River Crana on the edge of Buncrana. Park either at the southern end of the park (55.1381, -7.4613) as for the Shore Path, or else at the northern entrance at Wilson's Bridge (55.1417, -7.4555) where the Wild Atlantic Way leaves town on the R238.

FORT DUNREE
Originally built as a Royal Navy position during the Napoleonic Wars, Fort Dunree (fortdunree.com) is located on a rocky promontory overlooking Lough Swilly (55.1966, -7.5528). It is now a military museum with detailed exhibitions, many restored guns and an old military camp. There are also displays about the area's birds, marine life and coastal vegetation, as well as a gift shop, auditorium and coffee shop. Three short signposted walks explore the fort complex and the hill above.

AN PORT BÁN
The quiet sandy beach known as An Port Bán, or since Napoleonic times Crummies Bay, is a great place to watch for harbour porpoises. Just north of the point where the road to the fort meets the main road is a small amount of roadside parking. Park here (55.1985, -7.5396) and follow a narrow track down to the beach.

MAMORE GAP
North of Dunree the Wild Atlantic Way cuts steeply through the Urris Hills via Mamore Gap. From the top of the pass there are great views of Dunaff Head.

At the highest point of the road look out for the holy well named after Saint Eigne and a shrine where for centuries local people have made pilgrimages (55.2339, -7.4993).

The gap is home to one of Ireland's 'magic roads', an optical illusion in which a stopped car in neutral appears to roll uphill. The spot is 100m downhill from the carpark. It is marked by a white rock on the left-hand side of the road.

Mamore Gap | DF

Fort Dunree | DF

Urris Hills | Paul O'Connor

BUTLER'S GLEN LOOP
This is a tough 10.5km mountain walk through the Urris Hills. The signposted loop (purple arrows) starts from the carpark (55.2434, -7.5012) on the north slopes of the Gap and follows old bog roads through Butler's Glen.

LENAN STRAND
A short distance north of Mamore Gap is this secluded and unspoilt beach (55.2397, -7.5174). It's well off the beaten track and is an ideal spot for a quiet day by the water.

To get there descend Mamore Gap in a northerly direction, take the left turn at the junction at the bottom of the hill and follow the road until you meet the strand.

URRIS LAKES LOOP
Another tough 6.5km walk through the Urris Hills with great views down into Mamore Gap. The going is steep, with 290m of height gain, but the trail is well marked by purple arrows. There is also a shorter 1.5km version (green arrows). The trailhead is at the southern end of Lenan Strand (55.2391, -7.5165).

LENAN FORT
Just past the northern end of Lenan Strand is Lenan Fort (55.2458, -7.5297). It was one of a number of defensive forts built by the British in 1895 to defend

Carrickabraghy Castle | Grace Smith

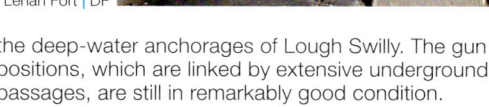
Lenan Fort | DF

Glenevin Waterfall | RC

the deep-water anchorages of Lough Swilly. The gun positions, which are linked by extensive underground passages, are still in remarkably good condition.

It is a fascinating place to explore and has a very empty, eerie feel. If you want to check it out remember to bring a torch and be very careful as there are some uncovered hatches.

From Lenan Strand continue north along the road to a junction. Turn left and after 650m is a right turn. Take this and follow the rough, pot-holed track to the fort.

GLENEVIN WATERFALL

This very picturesque waterfall lies at the head of a beautiful wooden glen (*55.2625, -7.4441*). It is reached by a 1km signposted walking trail that follows the stream gently uphill from the carpark. There are plenty of benches and shelters along the way to stop and enjoy the surroundings.

The carpark (*55.2676, -7.4361*) is right beside the Glen House Tearoom and Guesthouse, 1.2km west of Clonmany village.

POLLAN BAY

A popular location for watersports, particularly surfing and windsurfing. The 3km long sandy beach is just a short distance north of Ballyliffin village (*55.2901, -7.3909*). Be aware that there is no lifeguard on duty

FERRIES

The deeply recessed nature of the bays on both sides of Inishowen mean that it's possible to take a car ferry as a shortcut if you are tight on time or want a break from driving.

FOYLE FERRY

The Foyle Ferry links Greencastle (*55.2035, -6.9835*) and Magilligan Point (*55.1910, -6.9647*) near Limavady, serving as a connection between the Wild Atlantic Way and the Causeway Coast. A continous daily service runs during the summer season and at weekends for a month either side. Consult loughfoyleferry.com for the latest information.

SWILLY FERRY

The Swilly Ferry links Rathmullan (*55.0948, -7.5318*) on the Fanad Peninsula with Buncrana (*55.1277, -7.4632*) on the west coast of Inishowen. The short crossing saves about an hour of driving time. The ferry runs during the summer months. Check the website (swillyferry.com) for the most up to date information.

Doagh Strand | RC

Five Fingers Strand | RC

and there can be strong currents and rips. There is a playground beside the carpark.

A walking trail runs north along the beach between the sand and the dunes. At the far end of the beach are the ruins of the 16th century Carrickabraghy Castle (*55.3158, -7.3742*). On stormy days keep your eyes and ears open for the blowhole near the castle.

DOAGH ISLE

Maybe a few thousand years ago Doagh was an island but nowadays it's connected to the mainland by a wide stretch of low-lying land.

DOAGH FAMINE VILLAGE

The Doagh Famine Village tells the story of life in the Inishowen area from the Famine in the 1840s, through to the present day (*55.3089, -7.3356*). While the museum isn't state of the art it's a good option on a rainy day and is very popular. Guided tours of the village take about an hour. See doaghfaminevillage.com for details.

DOAGH STRAND

The beach directly opposite the Famine Village is great for exploring, with plenty of huge rock pools, caves and cliffs (*55.3093, -7.3350*). Unfortunately it's unsafe for swimming as there is a strong current and the water gets deep very suddenly. Thankfully some of

Malin Head | RC

the rock pools are deep enough to swim in and as a bonus the water in them tends to be warmer than the open sea!

FIVE FINGERS STRAND

One of Donegal's most beautiful beaches, Five Fingers Strand is the ideal spot for an invigorating walk on a wild day (55.3240, -7.3324). The beach, which takes its name from the five sea stacks at its northern end, is backed by massive sand dunes, some of the largest of their type in Europe. The wreck of the Twilight, which sank in 1889 en route from Newfoundland to Derry, is visible at low tide.

Be aware that the beach is unsafe for swimming due to very strong currents.

You will find the beach just off the Wild Atlantic Way (R242) between Malin Village and Malin Head. The road down to the beach is very narrow and there is limited parking so it's best to park at the church (55.3212, -7.3242) and walk the rest of the way down.

MALIN HEAD

Ireland's most northerly point, Malin Head, lies at the very tip of the Inishowen Peninsula. It's a wild and windswept place with dramatic cliffs and crashing waves, but it also has much of historical, scientific and ecological interest.

Birds flock here, blown in by the Atlantic winds. These regular visitors from Iceland, Greenland and North America include gannets, shearwaters, skuas, and auks on their southern migration flights.

The coast around Malin Head is some of the most treacherous water in the world, it's been the site of over four hundred ship wrecks. The insurer Lloyds of London even used the signal tower on Banba's Crown to contact ships offshore, particularly during the World Wars.

The nearest villages are Malin and Culdaff but there are plenty of B&Bs and one hostel, Sandrock Hostel (sandrockhostel.com), in the area.

BANBA'S CROWN

The small hill known as Banba's Crown lies overlooking the cliffs at the end of the headland (55.3810, -7.3738). The signal tower on the top of the hill was built in 1805 by the Admiralty. The carpark at the top offers magnificent panoramic views and between Easter and September there is a small mobile cafe serving good coffee and home-baked treats (caffebanba.com).

Named after Banba, one of the mythical queens of Ireland, this was also the point where people stood to wave goodbye to their loved ones as they set out across the sea to a new life in America.

On the grassy slopes below the tower you can see a series of white stones spelling out 'EIRE'. These stones were placed there during World War 2 to warn pilots they were flying over neutral territory.

DONEGAL

Culdaff Beach | Kent Wang

Malin Head | Paul O'Connor

Portmore Pier | DF

HELL'S HOLE TRAIL
The signal tower is the starting point for a short trail that leads to Hell's Hole (Pólifreann), a long, narrow chasm through which the sea surges on stormy days (55.3806, -7.3823). Also nearby is a picturesque natural arch called the Devil's Bridge.

There are plenty of benches along the way where you can sit and take in the breathtaking views. The official trail ends at Hell's Hole but it's possible to continue further west along the path above the cliffs. Needless to say you should be very careful near the cliff edge.

BALLYHILLIN BEACH
To the east of the signal tower is this unique raised beach system of international scientific importance (55.3795, -7.3647). The beach has four levels that dramatically illustrate the changing relationship between the sea and the land when the glaciers began to melt 15,000 years ago. It is also noted for its semi-precious stones so keep your eyes peeled.

MALIN WELL
East of Portmore Pier is a small road that drops steeply to the coast (55.3682, -7.3174). Here you will find the ruins of Saint Muirdhealach's Church. Beside the church is the Wee House of Malin, a tiny cave carved into the rock. Also close by is a holy well that was a place of pilgrimage until very recently. The

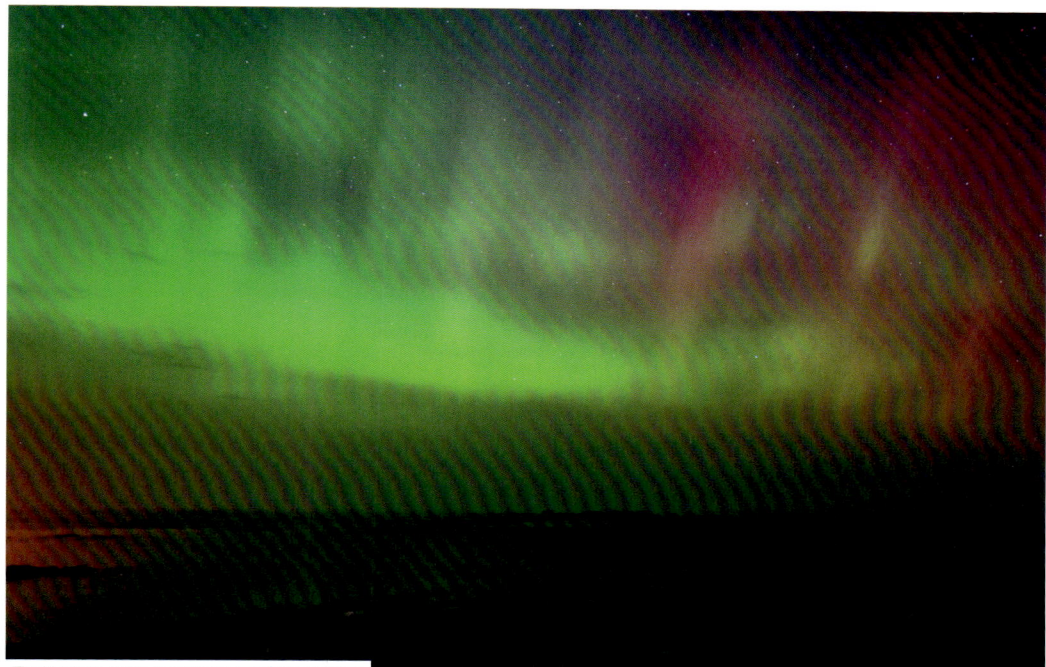
The Northern Lights over Malin Head | Gareth Wray

pebble beach is worth visiting in its own right, with its small sea stacks and an infinity of beautiful smooth pebbles.

CULDAFF BEACH
Culdaff has been popular with Irish holidaymakers for generations. The long sandy Blue Flag beach is 2km outside the village (*55.2917, -7.1450*). There is plenty of parking, toilets, a playground and a lifeguard on duty during the summer months.

Ocean Waves Sauna is based overlooking the beach, see oceanwavessaunas.com for opening hours.

TREMONE BAY BEACH
This small beach lies off the Wild Atlantic Way route so is very quiet (*55.2719, -7.070*).

KINNAGOE BAY
Kinnagoe Bay is a delightful, secluded sandy beach. It's perfect for families and safe for swimming. Facing away from the prevailing wind and backed by forested slopes it's very sheltered. A steep, narrow road leads down to the small carpark (*55.2586, -7.0128*).

The rocky headland at the northern end of the bay marks the point where the Armada vessel La Trinidad Valecera ran aground in 1588.

NORTHERN LIGHTS
The Aurora Borealis, or Northern Lights, are caused by collisions between gaseous particles in the Earth's atmosphere and charged particles released from the sun. Variations in colour are due to the type of gas particles that are colliding. The phenomenon can be seen above the magnetic poles of both the north and south hemispheres.

The lights appear in many forms, ranging from shimmering clouds to streamers, arcs, rippling curtains or shooting rays that light up the sky with a green or pink glow.

Inishowen is the best place in the country to view this amazing spectacle thanks to its northerly latitude and the lack of light pollution. And even though the displays are relatively infrequent and rarely as spectacular as those in the Arctic it's still worth keeping an eye out.

Follow Aurora Alerts Ireland on social media to get a notification of any potential auroras.

Stroove Beach | DF

WILD IRELAND
This 10 hectare wildlife sanctuary, which lies a few kilometres from the end of the Wild Atlantic Way (*55.0525, -7.3390*), is home to bears, wolves, lynx, monkeys, deer and wild boar. With the exception of the monkeys these animals were once native to Ireland. See wildireland.org for more information.

STROOVE BEACH
This small Blue Flag beach is the starting/finishing point for two interesting walks (*55.2269, -6.9291*).

INISHOWEN HEAD WALK
An 8.3km signposted loop follows rough roads and gravel tracks across the hillside above Inishowen Head. There are some wonderful views, and on a clear day it's possible to see Scotland. Follow the purple arrows.

PORT A DORAS
Not far from Stroove is a curious piece of geology that is worth the short walk. From the carpark at Stroove follow the road north. Where the road swings around to the left is a signpost and beside it is a small gate, go through the gate and walk down the field to the sea. Follow the vague path north along the shore. After about 15 minutes you will arrive at a large outcrop that appears to block the way forward. However there is a small, natural doorway in the rock that leads to a hidden pebble cove (*55.2357, -6.9233*). This is the door, or doras in Irish, after which the area is named.

LOUGH FOYLE COAST
There are a number of pleasant seaside villages along the placid shores of Lough Foyle between Inishowen Head and Derry City, before the Wild Atlantic Way starts/finishes rather abruptly at the border between the Republic and Northern Ireland.

MARITIME MUSEUM AND PLANETARIUM
The old coastguard station in Greencastle is home to the Inishowen Maritime Museum and Planetarium which could be worth a visit on a rainy day (*55.2021, -6.9871*). See inishowenmaritime.com for details.

MOVILLE SHORE PATH
This gentle 2km stroll follows the shore north from the attractive Victorian village of Moville (*55.1881, -7.0393*) and has nice views across Lough Foyle to the hills of the Derry and Antrim coast. ■

Paddling past Glengad Head | Loughs Agency

Mamore Gap | DF

KAYAKING

Inishowen is an ideal location for kayaking. The exposed headlands offer the experienced paddler a serious challenge while the sheltered bays are perfect for beginners. Sea Kayaking Donegal (seakayakingdonegal.com), offer guided tours. Inish Adventures (inishadventures.com), who are based in Moville, offer tours, canoeing and river rafting.

EAST INISHOWEN SEA KAYAK TRAIL

This kayaking route travels up the eastern shore of Inishowen from near Derry City to Malin Head. The trail, which is only suitable for experienced sea paddlers or those in the company of a capable guide, offers sea caves, off-shore islands, surf, sheltered harbours and wild camping. The Loughs Agency has produced a free guidebook which is available from loughs-agency.org or by emailing general@loughs-agency.org.

SURFING

Inishowen has some of the most consistent surf in Ireland. Adventure One (adventureone.net) runs a paddleboarding school and surf shop in Rathmullan and a surf school from Ballyhiernan Bay in Fanad. They also offer surf guiding for intermediate surfers. Inishowen Surf School (inishowensurfschool.ie) run surf lessons and summer camps in Ballyliffin, Culdaff and Tullagh Bay.

CYCLING

Grass Routes (grassroutes.ie), who operate out of Termon and Downings, rent both electric and conventional bikes. Far and Wild (farandwild.org) run mountain biking tours as well as a range of other outdoor activities.

INIS EOGHAIN CYCLEWAY

This 55km signposted route loops around the countryside west of Derry City. It follows a mix of traffic-free paths and quiet country roads, passing many interesting spots including Grianan of Aileach, Ballyarnett Country Park and the Foyle Valley Railway Museum. A map and information booklet is available from Cycle N.I. (/outmoreni.com).

ROCK CLIMBING

Instructor Bren Whelan (donegalclimbing.ie) runs rock climbing outings on the steep cliffs and ridges of Malin Head, a mind-blowing setting.

Oul House Thatched Cottage | Lynda Kenny

FANAD AND INISHOWEN
ACCOMMODATION

MAMORE COTTAGES
55.25310, -7.4947
mamorecottages.com
A cluster of five cottages on the northside of Mamore Gap that are finished in the distinctive Inishowen style with rope holding down the thatch and the rounded ridge profile. The interiors are furnished in a very authentic manner and three of the cottages sleep two, one sleeps four and one sleeps six.

HANNAH'S THATCHED COTTAGE
55.2540, -7.4154
airbnb.ie/rooms/982494705073823514
Another beautifully restored traditional thatched cottage. A short distance from the village of Clonmany, this late 1800s cottage has a very stylish interior that blends the modern and the vernacular. Sleeps two.

OUL HOUSE THATCHED COTTAGE
55.2752, -7.3564
irishthatchedcottage.com
This must be one of the most impeccably restored cottages in the country. Only a few minutes east of the village of Ballyliffin it combines the original building with a modern extension giving three bedrooms that sleep six.

PORTSALON LUXURY CAMPING
55.2100, -7.6563
donegalglamping.com
This idyllic hideaway is nestled in the hills overlooking the beach at Portsalon. Their five beautiful yurts (sleeping up to four) are available to rent between April and October. Each is equipped with a wood-burning stove and is fully furnished.

LOUGH FOYLE GLAMPING
55.2187, -6.9609
loughfoyleglamping.ie
This glamping site just outside Greencastle has four timber pods. Each pod has its own private hot tub from which there are great views across the water to Downhill beach and Binevenagh. There is also a communal sauna, plunge pool and a BBQ area.

Tank and Skinny's | Sugar Snap

FANAD AND INISHOWEN
FOOD

TANK AND SKINNY'S, BUNCRANA
55.1283, -7.4633
tankandskinnys.ie
Right on the water's edge in Buncrana this cafe serves breakfast and lunch including some unusual options such as ice cream nachos and chip boxes! They also have branches in Letterkenny (54.9491, -7.7371) and Muff (55.0678, -7.2689) right at the start/finish of the Wild Atlantic Way.

NANCY'S BARN, BALLYLIFFIN
55.2807, -7.3917
nancysbarn.ie
This busy bistro operates from a converted 19th century hay barn in Ballyliffin. Serving breakfast and lunch daily they are well known for their award-winning seafood chowder.

CAFFE BANBA, MALIN
55.3809, -7.3736
caffebanba.com
It's hard to argue with their claim to being the most northerly coffee shop in Ireland given the location right at the end of Malin Head. Serving coffee and freshly baked sweet treats between Easter and September.

They also have a cafe on Malin Street in Carndonagh (55.2516, -7.2611).

SEAVIEW TAVERN, MALIN
55.3674, -7.3311
seaviewtavern.ie
Located on Malin Head with views across the water to Scotland. Much of their menu is sourced from the pier just a stone's throw down the road. They also have a number of en-suite guest rooms. They are happy to allow camper vans stay overnight in the carpark.

CÚL A TÍ, CULDAFF
55.2872, -7.1677
culati.ie
This intimate restaurant on the corner of Culdaff Main Street offers local seasonal vegetarian and seafood options as well as bread and pastries. They serve lunches from Wednesday to Sunday and open on weekend evenings for dinner.

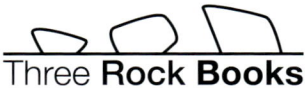

ACKNOWLEDGEMENTS

The authors would like to thank everyone who gave advice, feedback or encouragement or helped in any way. We would especially like to thank the photographers who generously contributed their photos.

PROOFREADERS
Patrick McClean, Inga Bock, Bríd Colhoun, John Creagh, June Creagh, Marius Curtin, Denis Dineen, Lorraine Doyle, Brian Flanagan, Julie Flanagan, Darina Lawlor, Ronan McLoughlin, John Murphy, Kathleen Murphy, Conor Ryan, Diarmuid Smyth.

PHOTOGRAPHERS
All photographs by David Flanagan (DF) and Richard Creagh (RC) unless credited otherwise. We would like to thank the following people and organisations for kindly allowing us to use their photographs (all reproduced with permission or with CC-BY-SA, CC BY-SA 2.0, CC-BY-2.0, CC BY-ND 2.0).

Kris Acton, Ben Allan, David Ardron, Terry Ballard, Richard O'Beirne, Jennifer Boyer, Ian Boyle, Chris Brooks, Terry Casserly, Michele Cati, Greg Clarke, Owen Clarke, Taylor Floyd Mews, Aoife Herriott Paul O'Connor, Gareth McCormack, Allie Couture, Alan Cronin, Denis Dineen, Dingle Horse Riding, Donal McCann, Dromquinna Manor, Shaun Dunphy, Michael O'Dwyer, Brendan MacEvilly, Frank Fullard, Matt Gillman, Will Greene, Paul McGuckin, Valerie Hinojosa, Imagea, Nicole Johnson, Lynda Kenny, Michael McLaughlin, Conor Lawless, Ilaria Leschiutta, The Loughs Agency, Roland Martins, Iain Miller, Marcus Murphy, Seán Murray, Michal Osmenda, Todd Parker, Pure Camping, Nicolas Raymond (freestock.ca), Val Robus, Patricia Ronan, Ross McDonald, Tobias Senger, Dale Simonson, Rick Strooper. SUP for All, Christopher Tierney, Pauric Ward, Becky Williamson, Gareth Wray, Yoko Nekonomania, Féron Benjamin, Conor Ryan, Chris Cant, Dingle Horseriding, Kent Wang, Bernd Thaller, Grace Smith, Allan Henderson, Andy Haslam, Eric Verleene, Tony Brierton, Brendan MacEvilly, Emilija Jefremova.

ABOUT THE AUTHORS

David Flanagan is a writer and publisher from Dublin. This is the sixth book that he has written and published under the Three Rock Books imprint. Three of his previous books - *Bouldering in Ireland*, *Bouldering Essentials* and *Rock Climbing in Ireland* - were finalists in the guidebook category of the Banff Mountain Book Award.

Richard Creagh is a photographer and writer from Cork with a great love of all things outdoors. He has spent most of the past twenty years living in and travelling around the west of Ireland and is now based in West Kerry. His other books include *Ireland's Islands* (The O'Brien Press) and *Exploring Ireland* (Three Rock Books). More of his photography can be seen at richardcreagh.com.